Flipping Houses FOR DUMMIES®

by Ralph R. Roberts with Joe Kraynak

BICENTENNIAL
1807
WILEY
2007
BICENTENNIAL

Wiley Publishing, Inc.

Flipping Houses For Dummies®

Published by
Wiley Publishing, Inc.
111 River St.
Hoboken, NJ 07030-5774
www.wiley.com

WILEY

About the Authors

Ralph R. Roberts's success in real estate sales is legendary. He has been profiled by the Associated Press, CNN, and *Time* magazine and has done hundreds of radio interviews. Ralph is a seasoned professional in all areas of house flipping, including buying homes, rehabbing, and reselling them quickly and at a handsome profit. He has penned several successful titles, including *Sell It Yourself: Sell Your Home Faster and for More Money Without Using a Broker* (Adams Media Corporation), *Walk Like a Giant, Sell Like a Madman: America's #1 Salesman Shows You How To Sell Anything* (Collins), *52 Weeks of Sales Success: America's #1 Salesman Shows You How To Close Every Deal!* (Collins), and *REAL WEALTH by Investing in REAL ESTATE* (Prentice Hall). In *Flipping Houses For Dummies,* Ralph reveals the tips and tricks he has hammered out and nailed in his over-30-year career.

Joe Kraynak is a freelance author who has written and coauthored dozens of books on topics ranging from slam poetry to computer basics. Joe teamed up with Dr. Candida Fink to write his first book in the *For Dummies* series, *Bipolar Disorder For Dummies,* where he showcased his talent for translating the complexities of a topic into plain-spoken, practical advice. In *Flipping Houses For Dummies,* Joe teams up with legendary real estate pro Ralph Roberts to produce the ultimate guide to profitable real estate flipping — flipping the right way.

Dedication

From Ralph: To my father, Ralph E. Roberts (a.k.a. The Boss), who taught me the skills and sticktoitism to pursue my dreams, and to my daughter Kolleen Roberts (a.k.a. KoRo) — the ultimate dream I was blessed with while I pursued those other dreams.

From Joe: To my brother John, who kept asking me when this book would come out, and whose eagerness and enthusiasm inspired me to do my best.

Special thanks to Lois Maljak, a key member of the construction team that built this book. While Ralph provided the vision and building materials and Joe laid the brick and mortar, Lois served as the general contractor and worksite expediter, shuffling e-mails back and forth, attending to the critical details, and keeping the project on track and on schedule. Without Lois, this book would be little more than one of Ralph's wild ideas.

Authors' Acknowledgments

Although we wrote the book, dozens of other talented individuals contributed to its conception, development, and perfection. Special thanks go to acquisitions editor Lindsay Lefevere, who chose us to author this book and guided us through the tough part of getting started. Georgette Beatty, our project editor, deserves a round of applause for acting as a very patient choreographer — shuffling chapters back and forth, shepherding the text and photos through production, making sure any technical issues were properly resolved, and serving as unofficial quality control manager. Thanks also to Sarah Faulkner, our copy editor, who read through everything — forward and backward — to identify and obliterate our many grammatical goofs and typos. We also tip our hats to the production crew for doing such an outstanding job of transforming a loose collection of text and illustrations into such an attractive bound book.

Throughout the writing of this book, we relied heavily on a knowledgeable and dedicated support staff, who provided expert advice, tips, and research, so we could deliver the most comprehensive and useful information. Lois Maljak proved invaluable not only as a resource person but also as the communications hub for the numerous ideas swirling about on a daily basis. Jim Maiorano contributed his expertise to guide the outline of the book and supply priceless insights from real-world experiences. Jenny Kelly and Sarah Hodges toiled for hours tracking down and snapping before-and-after photos and assembling the artwork. Paul Doroh, sheriff-sale and cash buyer for Ralph Roberts Realty, added his experience and expertise to guide the direction and content for the chapter on foreclosures. Char MacCallum assisted on gathering the tips that appear on the Cheat Sheet, and virtual assistant Kandra Hamric helped us tie up the loose ends. Thanks also to Ralph's brother, Jeff Roberts, property manager at Ralph Roberts Realty.

We owe special thanks to our technical editor, accomplished real estate pro Brad Donaldson, for ferreting out technical errors in the manuscript, helping guide its content, and offering his own tips and tricks.

Publisher's Acknowledgments

We're proud of this book; please send us your comments through our Dummies online registration form located at www.dummies.com/register.

Some of the people who helped bring this book to market include the following:

Acquisitions, Editorial, and Media Development

Project Editor: Georgette Beatty

Acquisitions Editor: Lindsay Lefevere

Copy Editor: Sarah Faulkner

Editorial Program Coordinator: Hanna K. Scott

Technical Editor: Brad Donaldson

Editorial Manager: Michelle Hacker

Editorial Assistants: Erin Calligan, Nadine Bell

Cover Photo: © Royalty-Free/Corbis

Cartoons: Rich Tennant
(www.the5thwave.com)

Composition Services

Senior Project Coordinator: Kristie Rees

Layout and Graphics: Claudia Bell, Carl Byers, Lavonne Cook, Denny Hager, Stephanie D. Jumper, Clint Lahnen, Barbara Moore, Barry Offringa, Heather Ryan

Proofreaders: Laura Albert, Jessica Kramer, Susan Moritz, Techbooks

Indexer: Techbooks

Anniversary Logo Design: Richard Pacifico

Special Help
Sarah Westfall

Publishing and Editorial for Consumer Dummies

> **Diane Graves Steele,** Vice President and Publisher, Consumer Dummies

> **Joyce Pepple,** Acquisitions Director, Consumer Dummies

> **Kristin A. Cocks,** Product Development Director, Consumer Dummies

> **Michael Spring,** Vice President and Publisher, Travel

> **Kelly Regan,** Editorial Director, Travel

Publishing for Technology Dummies

> **Andy Cummings,** Vice President and Publisher, Dummies Technology/General User

Composition Services

> **Gerry Fahey,** Vice President of Production Services

> **Debbie Stailey,** Director of Composition Services

Contents at a Glance

Table of Contents

Introduction

Maybe you know somebody who knows somebody who buys and sells houses and makes as much money on a single transaction as you make in a year. Or perhaps you caught an episode of one of those house flipping TV shows that demonstrates just how easy it is to buy a house for $250,000, fix it up for another $75,000, and sell it for a half million bucks in a matter of days. Now, you want in on the action. You want your slice of that capitalistic cannoli.

But where do you start? You can't imagine where you'd be able to get your mitts on the cash you'd need to finance a flip. You have no idea where to start looking for undervalued property, and even if you could find a suitable house to flip, the only experience you have fixing houses is plunging the toilet. Surely you're not qualified to invest in the complicated world of real estate.

Well, it's time to stop all the negative self talk and start reading *Flipping Houses For Dummies.* I started out with $900 that my grandmother gave me in the early 1970s. From the ripe old age of 19 to the present day I've flipped one house after another and earned millions of dollars along the way. It wasn't easy. I made plenty of mistakes, and I didn't profit from all my transactions. I did, however, have a plan in place and the sticktoitism (pronounced stik-*to*-it-izm) to successfully execute it. By following through, I was able to succeed, and so can you. (By the way, "sticktoitism" is a word I've been using since the 1960s to describe the determination and dogged perseverance required to build wealth in real estate. I could use "stick-to-itiveness," which appears in the dictionary, but I like my word better.)

About This Book

This book isn't a manifesto promoting the practice of flipping houses. In fact, if you don't have the determination and the work ethic necessary to become a weekend warrior, I strongly encourage you to reconsider. Keep your day job, buy an affordable house, and spend quality time with your family. Flipping houses is hard, agonizing, and often aggravating work.

Unlike what other books, TV shows, and late-night-TV gurus may tell you, this book takes an honest look at the practice of flipping houses. I lead you through a process of self-evaluation so you can determine whether you have the right mindset and resources to buy, renovate, and sell houses. I show you how to project your profit before you even make an offer on a property. And I reveal how much cash you can expect to keep after paying taxes on your profit.

In this book, I reveal what I've learned in more than 30 years of flipping houses and working with buyers, sellers, and other real estate professionals. I show you how to do everything from securing the cash you need to finance your venture to finding undervalued homes and negotiating the price and terms that improve your chances of selling at a profit. I guide you through making renovation decisions that promise to deliver the most bang for your buck, and I show you how to spruce up a home to draw in more buyers.

I don't want to see you get in over your head or blow your entire life savings on a failed business venture, so throughout this book, I provide plenty of time- and money-saving tips, cautions to help you avoid catastrophe, and sanity checks to keep your projects within budget and on schedule. I steer you clear of any risky, unethical, and illegal ventures and encourage you to wade out slowly and remain well within your comfort zone. After you successfully flip a few easy properties, you quickly become aware of when you're ready to take on bigger projects, and by that time, you no longer need my advice.

My goal is to help you decide whether house flipping is for you, and if it is, I provide you with the tools you need to succeed. Flipping houses is one of the most rewarding and profitable ways to invest your time and money. This book shows you how to do it right.

Conventions Used in This Book

I don't like to think of *my* book as *conventional,* but I do have some standard ways of presenting material. For example:

- ✔ *Italics* highlight new, somewhat technical terms, such as *capital gains,* and emphasize words when I'm driving home a point.
- ✔ **Boldface** text indicates key words in bulleted and numbered lists.
- ✔ Monofont highlights Web addresses.

In addition, even though you see two author names on the cover of this book — Ralph and Joe — you see "I" throughout the book when I, Ralph, am describing my personal experiences with flipping and offering my expert advice. Joe's the word maestro, making sure that I say things right. Who knows, maybe one day I'll convince Joe to flip a house!

What You're Not to Read

This book encourages you to skip in and dip in at any point to find the information you need most right now, but I don't encourage you *skip over* any of my advice. Flipping houses successfully requires you to build a strong investment team and know as much about the process as possible. One false move, and your flip can easily flop. You may get away, however, with skipping Chapter 12 on buying and selling foreclosure properties, if you're not interested in that sort of thing.

You also can safely skip anything you see in a gray shaded box. I stuck it in a box for the same reason that most people stick stuff in boxes — I was tired of looking at it. However, you may find the stories and brief asides uproariously funny and perhaps even mildly informative (or vice versa).

Foolish Assumptions

In some books that cover advanced topics, authors must assume that their readers already understand some basic topics or have acquired beginning-level skills. For example, if this were a book about molecular biology, you'd have to know what a molecule was.

In this book, the main foolish assumption I make is that you're a homeowner. Speaking for the man on the street, I wouldn't buy a car from a car salesman who didn't drive, and I wouldn't buy a house from someone who rented an apartment. When you own your own place, you pick up some street smarts about the value of a home, its emotional effect on people, its value as an investment, and the work required to properly maintain it. If you're not a homeowner, sell this book and put the proceeds toward a down payment on a house. Come back in a couple years. I'll be waiting for you.

Other foolish assumptions I've made include but aren't limited to the following:

- ✔ **You're of sound mind and body.** You can be a little kooky and out of shape, but if you can't make rational decisions or talk coherently on the phone, house flipping may not be for you.

- ✔ **You're interested in residential, not commercial, property.** Assuming you're new to this house flipping thing, focus on the type of property you would buy as a homeowner. Later, when you're more experienced, you can venture into the world of commercial real estate.

- ✔ **You're prepared to learn from your mistakes (and mine).** I can't guarantee that you'll profit on your first flip, but I can guarantee that you'll make mistakes. Consider them an essential part of your education. This book was made possible by all the mistakes I've made. Without those mistakes, I'd have little wisdom to impart. The more you take away from the mistakes I made, the fewer mistakes you have to make yourself.

- ✔ **You want to flip properties legitimately.** Con artists often flip properties to scam buyers and lenders. I'm not a con artist, and I denounce this type of flipping. By flipping legitimately, you stand to earn much more than a low-life con artist, and you get to keep your reputation and integrity intact.

How This Book Is Organized

I took the chapters that make up the book and divvied them up into six parts. Here, I provide a quick overview of what I cover in each part.

Part I: Laying the Foundation for Successful Flipping

Just as a house rests on its foundation, your house flipping venture requires a strong foundation to support it. The chapters in this part introduce you to the concept of flipping houses, lead you through a self-evaluation to determine whether you have the right stuff, guide you through the process of devising a flipping strategy that works for you, and assist you in building a solid team of real estate professionals and others who can help ensure your success.

Part II: Fiddling with the Financials of Property Flipping

When you flip houses, you become a real estate investor, and you need to deal with the money side of flipping in order to finance your flips, profit from them, and pay your taxes. The chapters in this part show you how to project your profit so you know how much to offer for a house in order to make a profitable transaction. I show you how to secure the cash you need to finance your venture. And I provide several tips to show you how to trim your tax bill so you can keep a larger portion of your hard-earned profit.

Part III: House Hunting with an Eye for Flipping

After you find someone willing to loan you some dough to finance your flip, the next big challenge is to find and buy a house that's packed with profit potential. When you're shopping for a home to live in, you look for the prettiest house that you can afford. When you're shopping for a home to flip, you're often hunting for the ugliest house on the block. This part shows you how to hone in on a promising neighborhood, track down undervalued properties, and negotiate to get the house for the price and terms you want.

Part IV: Fixing Up Your Fixer-Upper

Homeowners don't typically like to sell showcase homes for 30 to 40 percent less than their market value, so when you're flipping houses, you usually have to do some repairs and renovations before placing it back on the market. The chapters in this part guide you through the renovations that offer the highest return on investment and increase buyer interest the most. Here you discover information on everything from doing a quick cosmetic job to performing major structural overhauls. I can't always explain specifically how to do the repairs and renovations, because that would require a couple more books, but I do show you how to team up with contractors to get the work done.

Part V: Sold! Selling Your Rehabbed Home

You make money at various stages of the flipping process. By buying a house below market value, you make money going in. By doing some of the renovation work yourself, you save the cost of labor, and when you sell the house, you make money going out. The chapters in this part show you how to market your home to generate as much buyer interest as possible, stage your home to make a great impression when buyers come to see it, and negotiate the sales price and terms to close the deal as quickly as possible, so you can start on your next project.

Part VI: The Part of Tens

No *For Dummies* book is complete without a Part of Tens. Turn to this part for a list of the top ten signs of a great house flipping opportunity, ten renovation cost-cutting strategies, ten common house flipping blunders, and ten strategies for keeping afloat in a slow housing market.

Icons Used in This Book

Throughout this book, I sprinkle icons in the margins to cue you in on different types of information that call out for your attention. Here are the icons you'll see and a brief description of each.

I want you to remember everything you read in this book, but if you can't quite do that, then remember the important points I point out with this icon.

When you're buying and fixing up a house, it's easy to get a little carried away and blow your entire budget on garden gnomes. Before you get too carried away, read the text marked with this icon to rein yourself in.

Tips provide insider insight from behind the scenes. When you're looking for a better, faster way to do something, check out these tips.

"Whoa!" This icon appears when you need to be extra vigilant or seek professional help before moving forward.

Where to Go from Here

Think of this book as an all-you-can-eat buffet. You can grab a plate, start at the beginning and read one chapter right after another, or you can dip into any chapter and pile your plate high with the information it contains.

If you're looking for a quick overview of house flipping, check out Chapter 1. Before you even start house hunting, check out Chapter 4 to discover how to build a strong support network and Chapter 6 to find out how to finance your flip — you need cash and plenty of it to flip a house. Chapter 5 can help you determine how much to offer for the house, so you can profit from the flip. And the chapters in Part III are indispensable in helping you track down potentially profitable properties and negotiating the purchase.

Of course, after reading the book, you're welcome to dip back into it at any time to pick up something you missed or take a brief refresher course.

A handy hint: In a few chapters I include fill-in-the-blank forms and worksheets you can scribble on. Although you can fill out these forms and worksheets in the book, you may want to make copies to write on, especially if you borrowed the book from your library or plan on reselling it on eBay when you're done with it. These forms and worksheets are incredibly valuable at helping you project your profits and plan your renovations, so keep a small stack of them tucked away at the back of your legal pad.

One last thing: Selling a house for top dollar requires a successful marketing campaign. You have to increase the visibility of your house to generate interest and perhaps even spur a bidding war among interested buyers. Selling books requires some savvy marketing, as well. So, I'm going to ask you to do a favor for me. If you like the book, buy stacks of them for holiday and birthday presents and make sure all your friends and relatives have a copy. While you're at the bookstore, pick up several copies of the book and move them to other sections of the store . . . facing out, of course. This is great practice to hone your own marketing skills. Enjoy!

Part I
Laying the Foundation for Successful Flipping

The 5th Wave   By Rich Tennant

In this part . . .

You wouldn't pour a concrete slab on marshland, so don't set out to flip houses until you build a strong foundation. In this part, I introduce you to the concept of flipping properties and reveal the eye-in-the-sky view of the process from start to finish. You discover what it takes to flip properties — time, money, energy, and commitment — so you can see for yourself whether flipping is in your future. I show you how to develop a winning strategy to minimize your risk while maximizing your profit potential and lead you through the process of assembling a team of experienced and talented individuals to complement your skills and advise you along the way.

Chapter 1

Wrapping Your Brain Around the Idea of House Flipping

In This Chapter

▶ Understanding the concept and challenges of flipping

▶ Flipping the right way — legally and ethically

▶ Developing a winning strategy and the right connections

▶ Surveying money matters and savvy renovations

▶ Marketing and staging a house properly to maximize your profit

*F*lipping sounds easy. You can flip a pancake. You can flip a coin. Without too much effort, you can even flip out. Flipping a house, on the other hand, requires a level of knowledge, expertise, and sticktoitism unrivaled by any of these mindless tasks. It requires access to cash, and lots of it. It demands time, energy, vision, attention to detail, and the ability and desire to network with everyone from buyers and sellers to real estate professionals, contractors, and lenders.

In this chapter, I offer a broad overview of what flipping houses is all about. I introduce the overall strategy of flipping houses — buy low, renovate, and sell a property at fair market value to earn a fair market profit. I reveal the difference between flipping the right way — legally and ethically — and flipping the wrong way — ripping off buyers, sellers, and lenders for a quick wad of cash.

Throughout this chapter, I recommend a strategy that's worked for me during my over-30-year stint as a house flipper and real estate professional. I've built my approach on a strong foundation of honesty, integrity, dedication, and hard work, and I recommend that you do the same. With a positive mindset, a strong commitment, and the right approach, you have a much better chance that your first flip won't flop.

Grasping the Concept of Flipping and Its Challenges

In investment circles, the secret to success is cliché — buy low, sell high. This same principle applies to flipping houses. To succeed, you buy a house 25 to 50 percent below market value, repair and renovate the property to make it a more attractive purchase, and then turn around and sell it at market value. That three-step process — buy, fix, and sell — certainly sounds easy enough, but each step carries with it a host of unique challenges, as I point out in the following sections.

To buy low, you have to be in a position to buy quickly. The trick is to have your financial ducks in a row before you go house hunting. Chapter 6 reveals various ways to finance your flips.

Spotting distressed property . . . and property owners

Homeowners don't exactly line up around the block waiting to sell their homes for less than they're worth. As a house flipper, your job is to hunt for the homes in your area that are *don't wanners,* as in "the owners don't want her." These orphan homes usually appear bedraggled. The yard looks like a weedy wasteland, the gutters are hanging off like a pair of old false eyelashes, the paint's peeling, and the interior is completely trashed. These properties are often referred to as *distressed,* and their appearance indicates that the owner is distressed, as well. The home has become an albatross around the owner's neck.

When the homeowners need to shed the burden of home ownership, they're more likely to work out a deal with a serious investor. In Chapter 9, I point out several successful techniques for scoping out distressed properties.

The average house hunter wants a nice house. When you're flipping houses, you want the ugliest house on the block. To succeed in finding potentially profitable homes, you may need to change your perspective, so you can see the beauty in a beast.

Making a few minor (or major) alterations

When you buy a house at a bargain-basement price, it usually requires some tender loving care to make it marketable. In some cases, a thorough cleaning along with a fresh coat of paint (inside and out) and new wall-to-wall carpeting does the trick. In a matter of days or a couple of weeks, and with a small investment, you can often boost the value of a home just by making it *look* brand-new again.

Other houses require more extensive renovations to make them marketable and boost your bottom line. You can transform a two-bedroom house into a three-bedroom house by converting unused attic or porch space into a bedroom; knock out a wall or two to combine the kitchen, dining room, and living room into a great room; install all new replacement windows; or even build a second story. The chapters in Part IV cover everything from quick-flip cosmetic jobs to extensive renovations and provide plenty of tips and cautions to prevent you from sinking money into home improvements that offer little payback.

Avoid the temptation to over-improve a house. You may be able to convert a $100,000 house into a $1 million mansion, but if a buyer wants a $1 million mansion, she buys a house in a neighborhood with $1 million homes. Shoot for making the house you buy competitive with other houses in its price range. Don't go overboard.

Reselling your rehabbed property for big bucks

The old adage of house flipping is that "You make your money buying in." But you realize your profit only after selling the house. Assuming you purchase the property at the right price, you don't overspend on repairs and renovations, and the housing market remains relatively stable, you should have no trouble selling the house at a profit simply by selling it at or near market value.

Holding costs (insurance, property taxes, and utilities) can chip away at your profit. I estimate daily holding costs at $100, so for every month that your house lingers on the market, you're out about $3,000. To sell the house quickly at a fair price, set a price that's competitive with the prices of comparable houses in the same neighborhood. If your asking price is too high, it'll cost you.

The chapters in Part V show you how to set an asking price, market the property, properly stage the home for a successful showing, and ultimately close the deal.

Flipping Ethically: The Good, the Bad, and the Illegal

In real estate circles, the word "flip" is often construed as just another four letter word. Utter the F word at a real estate conference or seminar, and you're liable to be spending your lunch break at a cozy table for one. The reason for this cold shoulder from the real estate community is that back in September of 2001, HUD (the federal department of Housing and Urban Development) released FR (Final Rule)-4615 Prohibition of Property Flipping, which made flipping illegal.

So, why am I writing a book that promotes this illegal activity? Because the word "flip" has a double meaning, a split personality, a sunny side and a sinister side, as the following sections reveal.

Flipping illegally: Real estate fraud and other scams

Criminal minds have invented countless ways of milking the real estate industry, and one way is to flip houses. This sinister type of house flipping typically relies on some form of fraud — lying or misrepresenting information. In some cases, the con artists hook up with crooked appraisers who artificially inflate home values and then sell overpriced homes to ill-informed buyers.

Another way con artists scam the system through flipping is to build a team of buyers, none of whom intends to own the property for any length of time. They buy the home off one another, increasing its price with each sale. False appraisals or crooked appraisers make the price hikes look legitimate, and corrupt loan officers often expedite the loan approval process. As the value of the property increases on paper, the amount of equity in the property increases. The final buyer takes out a whopping loan to pay the previous owner and then defaults on the loan. The team splits the proceeds, sticking the lender with the bill and leaving a legacy of foreclosures and vacancies.

The dark side of flipping destroys credit ratings, raises interest rates, and ruins neighborhoods. Over the long haul, it threatens to squash the American dream of home ownership. It's unethical, immoral, and illegal.

Flipping legally: Buy, fix, and sell

Flipping the right way is a perfectly legitimate strategy for making money in real estate. You buy a property below market value, fix it up, and sell it for more than you invested in it. Do it well, and you can earn a handsome profit. Make a serious blunder, and you suffer a loss. This fix-it-and-flip-it approach has a positive effect on the real estate market. It increases property values, improves neighborhoods, and provides quality housing for those who need it. It's the American way — capitalism at work.

Throughout this book, I encourage you to flip the right way and I caution you to avoid the gray areas that can get you into trouble. Flipping the right way allows you to legitimately profit from the system without having to tiptoe through legal minefields. It ensures that you establish the solid reputation you need to flip profitably for however long you want.

Determining Whether You're Ready for Flipping

Although anyone can profit from flipping houses, it's not quite as easy as it looks on TV. Buying a house that's brimming with potential for 25 to 50 percent less than you know you can sell it for is a huge challenge in itself, but after you take possession of the property, the real fun begins. Your contractor disappears after collecting your deposit. The landscapers hack through a buried cable. You find out that the septic system needs to be replaced. And the neighborhood association rejects every single one of your planned improvements.

To successfully deal with the unexpected twists and turns you're sure to encounter, you need to have the right stuff, as I describe in Chapter 2: time, money, personality, family, and tools.

Novice real estate investors often become unnecessarily overwhelmed by all the work that they think is involved in flipping a house. Flipping requires time and effort and it has its share of aggravation, but it's only overwhelming if you try to take on too much. Start with a relatively easy house at first — a property that requires only cosmetic work. (In Chapter 14, I show you exactly how to give a house a quick makeup job.) Then, slowly move up to more involved projects. Don't be afraid to call for help. You can often save money and aggravation by calling a professional.

Devising Your Own Surefire Flipping Strategy

No two investors follow the same flipping strategy. Some investors choose to live in the house they flip, while others find that too stressful. Some flip a house every two years to maximize their tax savings, while others flip a house once every month or two for quick profits. Some fly solo, while others team up with real estate agents. Many investors focus on a niche market, such as foreclosure properties, HUD (Housing and Urban Development) properties, or FSBO (For Sale By Owner) homes.

The strategy you ultimately settle on is yours to invent. What's important is that you have a strategy and the system and resources in place to execute it. With an effective strategy and the proper advance planning, you have a much better chance of avoiding common snags and hooking a profit. Before you make an offer on your first house, you should already have the essentials in place:

- ✔ Financing not only to purchase the house but also to cover holding costs and the cost of repairs and renovations

- ✔ A plan for repairing and renovating the property (such as buying low, applying makeup, and selling high, or living in your flip while you renovate it)

- ✔ A realistic estimate of the costs of repairs and renovations and the monthly expenses for holding the property

- ✔ A schedule for completing the project

- ✔ Reliable contractors who are available to begin working on the property immediately

- ✔ A date on which you plan to put the house back on the market

Flipping a house is like taking a vacation. You have to know your destination before you book your flight. Before you buy a house, know exactly what you're going to do to improve the property, how much the improvements are going to cost, how much you can sell the house for, and an estimate of your net profit. Chapters 3 and 5 can assist you in developing an effective plan.

Assembling a Team of Advisors and Experts

You probably won't find a course on flipping houses at your community college. The only school that offers such a course is the college of hard knocks. You learn by doing. But when you're gambling with more than $100,000 of your own or someone else's money, learning by trial and error can be catastrophic.

A safer way to develop the skills and foresight needed to reduce costly mistakes is to learn from the mistakes of others. Develop your own house flipping team and rely on the following professionals to guide and educate you:

- ✔ Real estate agent
- ✔ Financier/lender
- ✔ Accountant
- ✔ Title company
- ✔ Appraiser
- ✔ Home inspector
- ✔ Real estate lawyer
- ✔ Contractors

In Chapter 4, I describe the role that each of these valuable individuals plays on your team, and I provide some criteria to show you how to select the best of the bunch.

Time is money, and your time is valuable. If you can make more money doing your day job than you'd pay a contractor, you're usually better off hiring a contractor. In addition, if one contractor charges a little more but can complete the job on schedule, you may save money by hiring a slightly more expensive contractor. When you're flipping houses, overlooking the clock is easy when you're staring at dollar signs, but in flipping, time really is money.

Managing the Moolah

The ultimate goal of house flipping is to make money, and the way to accomplish that is fairly simple — you need to sell the house for more than it cost you to buy it, fix it up, and sell it. The process becomes a little more complicated, however, when you begin attending to the details.

At each stage of the project, you have numerous opportunities to make money, save money, and waste money. By remaining vigilant, you can cut expenses and beef up your bottom line, as I explain in the following sections. I show you how to estimate the profit on a flip, secure funds for your flip, and handle taxes smartly.

Estimating your profit

Never buy a property unless you're sure that you can profit from it . . . at least on paper. By jotting down a few numbers and doing the math, you can project your profit well in advance to determine whether the potential profit is worth the risk, not to mention your time and effort. Your goal is to earn at least a 20 percent profit on your total investment. To ensure a 20 percent profit, you need to adjust your goal based on whether current market conditions are increasing, flat, or decreasing.

In Chapter 5, I give you more information on each of the three main types of market conditions, and I guide you through the process of estimating your profit upfront and provide you with a profit projector to help you determine how much you can afford to offer for a house.

If you get in over your head and stand to lose money when the time comes to sell the house, consider going with plan B. Plan B is to hold onto the property and lease it until the market improves and you can sell the property at a profit. In Chapter 25, I provide ten tips for surviving in a slow market.

Getting your mitts on some ready cash

In the land of house flipping, cash is king. By making a cash offer on a house, you give yourself a strong platform for negotiating a lower purchase price and closing the deal in a matter of days or weeks rather than months. With cash on hand, you can begin renovating the property as soon as you take possession of it. Cash also enables you to hold the property, so you're not forced to accept the first low-ball offer you receive from a buyer.

How do you get your hands on this cash? You can tap into any of several resources:

- ✔ Borrow against the equity in your home. This isn't exactly cash, but it's the next closest thing.
- ✔ Hook up with a private lender.
- ✔ Ask family members or friends.
- ✔ Establish an effective partnership.
- ✔ Secure financing through the seller.
- ✔ Convert your IRA or a portion of it into a self-directed IRA.

In Chapter 6, I reveal the pros and cons of these financing options and show you various ways to gather the cash to finance your flip.

Borrowing money gives your personal investment more leverage. If you put up $20,000 and borrow $180,000, you can take on a $200,000 project. Sell the house for $240,000, and you've just made $40,000 — a 200 percent return on your investment! If you put up $100,000, borrowed $100,000, and sold the house for $240,000, your profit would be the same, but it would represent only a 40 percent return on your investment. Use other people's money to leverage the power of your personal investment, as I discuss in Chapter 6.

Keeping more of your hard-earned cash by handling taxes wisely

Whenever you make money, the government usually demands its cut. If you make a career of flipping houses, the IRS treats your profits as self-employment income and slaps you with an income tax . . . and perhaps even self-employment tax to cover social security and Medicare. Otherwise, your profits are taxed as investment income — short- or long-term capital gains. However, if you choose the slow-flip strategy and live in the house you flip for a couple of years, and depending on the tax rules in place at the time, your entire profit may be entirely tax exempt!

As you can see, this tax stuff can get a bit complicated. In addition, tax laws change from year to year, and taxes vary depending on your unique financial portrait. I offer some tax-saving advice in Chapter 7, but the only way to ensure that you're complying with current law and paying the necessary state and local taxes is to consult a CPA who's accustomed to dealing with real estate investment income in your area.

Paying a boatload of tax is a good thing. It means you're making a boatload of money.

Finding and Buying a Property Ripe for Flipping

The most critical stage of flipping a house is finding and buying the right house to flip. Buy a lousy house in a lousy neighborhood for more than it's worth, and you've already lost the game. Finding a house that's dripping with potential for 25 to 50 percent less than you can sell it for is quite a challenge, but as a flipper, that's the fun part. Flipping is an adventure, a treasure hunt, and a poker game all rolled into one. Finding and buying a property is a four-step process:

1. Scope out a fertile neighborhood — often an area with homes that are at least 20 years old and are ripe for rehabbing and reselling. See Chapter 8 for details.

2. Zoom in on a don't wanner — a distressed property that the owner obviously doesn't want or can't afford to keep. A distressed house usually has a distressed owner. See Chapter 9 for details.

3. Inspect the property closely inside and out and carefully estimate your potential profit. Before you make an offer on a property, you should be fairly certain that you'll earn at least 20 percent for your trouble. In Chapter 10, I provide you with a list of items to pack for your inspection mission along with a list of key features that give a property flip-appeal.

4. Haggle with the seller to purchase the house at a price that virtually ensures that you will profit from the flip, as I explain in Chapter 11.

Rehabbing Your Fixer-Upper to Maximize Your Profit

When you buy a house to flip, it's like buying a beat up antique at a garage sale. You got the house for a bargain because it needs work that the seller isn't motivated to do. By cleaning up the joint, fixing whatever's broken, and perhaps doing a few renovations, you can bring the property up to market standards and sell it for its full market value. In the following sections, I walk you through the types of renovations you can make.

Putting your renovations in order

Repairs and renovations require careful planning and execution to keep them on schedule and within budget. Before you begin, prioritize your renovations, so you know what's most important; I give you all the tools and tips you need in Chapter 13. Invest your time and money in the renovations that promise the most bang for your buck, and then if you need to trim costs, you can skimp on the less important stuff.

Schedule the work so that it proceeds logically. If you install new tile and carpeting before painting the walls and ceiling, you risk ruining the new tile and carpeting. A good rule of thumb is to work on the infrastructure first — the foundation, electricity, plumbing, heating, and air conditioning. Then, work from the top down, finishing with the floors. Don't paint yourself into a corner.

Applying a little makeup

The ideal house for a first-time flipper is one that requires only cosmetic work. Cosmetic work, which I cover in Chapter 14, includes the following low-cost repairs and renovations:

- A fresh coat of paint throughout the house
- New wall-to-wall carpeting in any rooms that need it
- New light fixtures
- New outlet and light switch covers
- A thorough cleaning inside and out
- Window washing
- Storm window and door repair or replacement
- Lawn mowing, weeding, trimming trees and shrubs, and other basic landscaping

Cosmetic repairs don't add as much real value to a house as, say, a new kitchen may add, but they attract buyers. Often a house is undervalued simply because prospective buyers can't stand looking at it.

Tidying up the exterior

Curb appeal is everything when you're trying to sell a house. If prospective buyers pull up in front of a house that doesn't look inviting, they're likely to pull away before you have time to open the front door. To sell your house for top dollar, the house has to make a good first impression. Chapter 15 shows you how to landscape and prepare the exterior of the house to make it draw passersby inside for a closer look.

Focusing on kitchens and bathrooms

Kitchens and bathrooms sell houses or sink deals depending on their condition. A spacious kitchen with plenty of counter space and all the essential amenities — a clean range, refrigerator, microwave oven, and dishwasher — creates an impression that the kitchen is a great place to prepare meals and hang out with friends and family members. A sparkling clean, well-lit bathroom with plenty of storage space creates a sense of comfort and cleanliness that permeates the house.

Although you should never over-improve a property, renovations that bring the kitchen and bath up to market standards in your area always pay for themselves by adding real value to the property and making it more attractive to buyers. See Chapter 16 for the full scoop on renovating kitchens and bathrooms.

Making moderate changes

Somewhere between painting a room and building a room addition are moderate changes that you can make to a house to improve its value and draw more buyers. These improvements include installing replacement windows, replacing the screen doors or entry doors, and refinishing wood floors or installing tile or vinyl flooring. Chapter 17 lays out your options.

Overhauling the structure

Some houses are begging for a few major overhauls. Maybe the house has an unfinished attic that's perfect for an additional bedroom or it has a beautifully landscaped backyard that has no easy access to it and no deck or patio. In some cases, you may discover a dinky house surrounded by mansions. By raising the roof and building a second story, you can double the living space and boost the house into a higher bracket. Chapter 18 takes on some of these major renovations, stimulating your own creative visions.

Selling Your Renovated Pad

As soon as you take possession of the house and begin renovating it, you draw attention to the house and fire up your marketing machine. A brief visit with your closest neighbors ignites the flames of word-of-mouth advertising, and by throwing a few more marketing logs on the fire, you can fuel a successful and fast sale. The following sections highlight the main factors that ensure success.

Every day your house remains on the market costs you about $100 in holding costs. To maximize your profit, you not only want the house to sell for a good price, but you also want it to sell quickly. Holding costs vary, so calculate the actual daily or monthly holding costs for each property individually, as I demonstrate in Chapter 5.

Setting the right price

A key mistake that many homeowners make when they're trying to sell their house is to set the price too high or too low. Set the price too low, and you cheat yourself out of some extra dough. Set it too high, and the property is liable to languish on the market for several months.

To sell a house quickly for the going rate, you need to offer a house that's in as good or better condition than comparable houses in the area at a price that's at or slightly below market value. Don't get greedy. Chapter 19 has tips on setting an appropriate asking price.

Marketing your property

REMEMBER

The more people are aware that you have a house for sale, the better chance you have of selling it quickly at a handsome price. In a strong market with more buyers than sellers, a savvy marketing campaign can even trigger a bidding war that drives the price beyond your expectations. As I point out in Chapter 19, every marketing campaign should include the following:

- ✔ An attractive and informative For Sale sign planted on the front lawn
- ✔ A listing with all the MLS services in the area
- ✔ An online listing
- ✔ Flashy flyers that highlight the most attractive features
- ✔ A classified ad in the local newspaper
- ✔ Word-of-mouth advertising

Sprucing up your house for a showing

For a house to sell, the buyers have to picture themselves living in it. Nobody wants to live in a cluttered pigsty, so remove any clutter, clear off the kitchen and bathroom counters, and make sure the house is impeccably clean. Remove the family photos. Hide any religious icons. Open the windows and set out a beautiful bouquet of fresh-cut flowers. And then clear out, if possible, when prospective buyers show up to tour the property. Chapter 20 features many more tips on properly staging your house for a showing.

Some clever entrepreneurs have created businesses that specialize in staging homes. They actually deliver oriental carpets, furniture, and other décor designed to transform an ordinary house into showpiece. You can even take a course in home staging!

Making the big sale

First time home buyers often are completely unaware of what they want in a house until someone tells them. As you or your agent is showing prospective buyers the house, you may need to prod them a little to convince them that your house has all the features and amenities they're looking for.

In Chapter 21, I offer several suggestions on how to spin your marketing pitch to appeal to a wider range of buyers. Then I go on to show you how to negotiate the sales price and terms and complete the necessary paperwork to seal the deal. Whether you choose to sell the property yourself or with the assistance of a real estate agent, as I recommend, this chapter can help you sell your house quickly for top dollar.

Chapter 2

Do You Have the Right Stuff for Flipping?

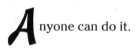nyone can do it.

If I had a nickel for every time I heard someone say that about flipping houses, I could retire on my own private island in the Pacific. When a real estate investment guru says "Anyone can do it," what she really means is "Anyone *like me* can do it."

I prefer presenting house flipping in a more realistic light by saying "Anyone who has sufficient desire, energy, and sticktoitism can do it." By following the advice in this book, you can acquire the necessary knowledge, gather investment capital, and find plenty of properties to flip, but if you don't have sufficient gusto and grit, your flips most assuredly will flop.

This chapter leads you on a journey of self-examination to determine whether you have the right stuff to flip real estate — time, energy, a strong financial position, organizational expertise, people skills, tenacity, decisiveness, imagination, endurance, and a healthy sense of humor.

Tabulating Your Time Budget

Most casual house flippers are weekend warriors. They hold down a day job of 40 or so hours a week and then work nights, weekends, holidays, and vacations on flipping houses. These part-time flippers typically invest anywhere from 20 to 40 hours a week, depending on how dilapidated the houses are, how ambitious they are to turn a profit, and how much of the work they want or need to do themselves.

Full-time flippers have no day job, so they can work 24/7 flipping houses, assuming they have enough cash on hand to finance their flips and cover their living expenses. These full-timers typically invest 40 to 80 hours a week. Again, this amount varies depending on how much money they need or want to make, how hard they're willing to work, and how much of the work they choose to do themselves.

If your spouse works full time and earns enough to cover the bills, and if you have plenty of time on your hands, consider flipping houses full time. Of course, you need to make sure your spouse is 100 percent behind you or the decision could have some negative consequences on your relationship.

Although you may be able to delegate most of the work that goes into flipping a house, several tasks demand your uninterrupted time and focus:

- House hunting
- Negotiating and closing the deal
- Securing financing for purchases and renovations
- Budgeting and other accounting tasks
- Planning, executing, and supervising rehab projects
- Marketing and selling the property

The amount of time required for these tasks varies greatly depending on how you choose to have them done. For example, if you hire an agent to help you find houses to flip, you may spend only a few hours checking out prospects, but if you choose to cruise the neighborhood for "For Sale By Owner" properties, you may spend several days or even weeks finding a good prospect.

In the following sections, we explain the advantages and disadvantages of part-time flipping, tell you when you can safely start flipping full-time, and list the tasks that you should (and shouldn't) delegate to save time.

For the time-strapped: Part-time flipping

When you're just starting to flip properties, keep your day job. Moonlight as a house flipper until you establish yourself. Part-time flipping offers a host of benefits that you shouldn't just toss in the dumpster:

✔ Your day job provides steady income and security.

✔ Steady income enables you to secure traditional financing with attractive interest rates.

✔ Your weekly paycheck helps you cover the mortgage payments, finance renovations, cover your quarterly income tax payments, and stay afloat when the housing market cools.

✔ A full-time job typically provides you with health and dental insurance, retirement funds, and other benefits you don't get from flipping houses.

You never have to become a full-time flipper. Most house flippers, even when they're well-established, continue to flip houses part time.

Although a day job provides part-time flippers with the income and security required to fuel this venture, it has its drawbacks:

✔ Flipping part time dilutes your focus. You may be in the middle of a complex renovation project late Sunday night and then have to show up for work bright and early Monday morning.

✔ Working overtime on flipping projects can sap the time and energy you have for your family and your day job. Keep in mind that part-time flipping is like having a second job.

✔ When you work a full-time job, you're less available for fielding calls and dealing with problems that arise when you're buying, renovating, and selling a property.

To compensate for some of the drawbacks, consider the following solutions for integrating part-time flipping into your life:

✔ Work the second or third shift, so you can focus on flipping during the day.

✔ Schedule vacations around your rehab schedule.

✔ Ask your spouse for help with paperwork and fielding phone calls while you're at work — a perfect job for the work-at-home parent.

✔ Become a weekend warrior, performing cleanup, yard work, and other chores on your days off. If you're married with children, make the project a family affair (see "Ensuring That Your Family Is on Board," later in this chapter, for details on involving your family).

✔ Partner with a trustworthy friend or relative who has more free time or a more flexible schedule.

All the time in the world: Full-time flipping

Full-time flipping requires a big time commitment and a cash reserve to back it up. You need enough cash on hand not only to fuel your flip but also to cover several months of living expenses, including your current house payment, property taxes, utilities, groceries, and car loan. Most flippers choose to become full-time flippers only after they successfully flip several properties, have a proven system in place, and have the financial resources to live without another source of income for at least one full year.

Consider quitting your day job and flipping full time only if you suddenly become independently wealthy or you're absolutely certain you can double your income by flipping houses. You know you're ready to flip full time after you complete all the items on the following checklist:

- ✔ Spend five years successfully buying, fixing, and flipping real estate on a part-time basis.

- ✔ Sock away at least one year's salary in reserves.

- ✔ Secure health, dental, disability, and life insurance and have sufficient funds to cover the premiums.

- ✔ Obtain a blanket insurance policy that covers liability.

- ✔ Set up a line of credit that enables you to carry out two projects at the same time.

- ✔ Develop a solid business plan. For professional guidance with a touch of humor, get *Business Plans For Dummies,* 2nd Edition, by Paul Tiffany and Steven D. Peterson (Wiley).

- ✔ Assemble a team of experienced advisors with varied backgrounds — financial, legal, construction, and so on. (See Chapter 4.)

Without these essentials — a strong work ethic, determination, sufficient cash reserves, a well-defined goal, and a solid plan to achieve that goal — failure is almost guaranteed.

Delegating time-consuming tasks

You can get more done in less time by making use of other people's time — delegating tasks. But be careful when choosing tasks to delegate. You can safely farm out any of the following jobs:

- ✔ Lawn mowing and snow shoveling to any day laborer, even your own or someone else's kid, unless you find these activities therapeutic

- ✔ Heating, plumbing, gas, and electrical repairs to licensed and insured contractors

- ✔ Sale of the home to a qualified and trusted real estate agent, who can list the home, handle the mundane details, and call you when a serious lead develops

- ✔ Setting up appointments to look at houses to your agent, your spouse, or another family member or friend

- ✔ Cosmetic repairs, such as painting and carpeting, to qualified painters and carpet layers

- ✔ Marketing the rehabbed home, including distribution of signs and flyers, to a family member or friend

- ✔ Showing the rehabbed home to prospective buyers to your agent or a family member or friend

Think of tasks in terms of time and money. If you earn $25 an hour, hire someone to do the $10-an-hour jobs, and do the $50-an-hour jobs yourself.

Some tasks are way too important to delegate, unless you trust the person nearly as much as you trust yourself. Avoid outsourcing any of the following jobs:

- ✔ Securing financing for purchases and renovations.

- ✔ Anything that requires the handling of money, including making monthly mortgage payments and paying property tax and quarterly estimated taxes. You can hire an accountant to manage the record-keeping, but handle the money yourself.

- ✔ Meeting city inspectors.

- ✔ Accompanying home inspectors.

- ✔ Managing your files and data systems. (When you hit the big time and can afford it, you can hire a licensed and bonded professional to accomplish these tasks.)

- ✔ Visiting properties prior to purchase.

- ✔ Negotiating and closing the deal. (Your agent can advise you and present your offers for you, but call the shots yourself.)

- ✔ Planning and supervising rehab projects. (You can hire people to do the work, but you need to visit the worksite regularly to ensure quality and control costs.)

Shaking Your Piggy Bank

You don't need a lot of your own money to finance your first flip. You can beg, borrow, or partner up with an investor (see Chapter 6 for details on these options). Before setting out to flip your first property, however, tally the costs and your financial health, have a solid plan for obtaining financing, and know your debt tolerance, as I explain in the following sections.

Figuring out how much you need to get started

When you flip a house, you want your expenses (the cost of the house, repairs, renovations, and expenses to hold and sell the property) to be less than 80 percent of the amount you expect to get out of the house when you sell it. To determine what you need to get started, you should have a good idea of the rehabbed house's potential sales price. From there, you can figure out approximately how much you should expect to spend in buying the house and getting it ready to flip.

How much money you need to finance your first flip depends on the grand total of all the costs for purchasing the property, fixing it up, and selling it. You never know the actual costs until you resell the property, but you can do some ballpark estimates, just to see whether this house flipping thing still appeals to you. The profit projector in Chapter 5 can give you a pretty clear estimate of just how much you can expect to invest in a specific property and profit from it.

The nomadic flipper

I'm currently living in house number 23, where my family has lived since 1990. I moved 19 times before getting married. Marriage kind of slowed me down. Before moving into a house, I'd fix up the bathroom, kitchen, and one bedroom. Then I'd live there for a few months to a year, fixing up the rest of the house. When the house was in pretty good shape, I'd either convert it into a rental or sell it for quick cash. I drew up a mini business plan for each property. Each plan was contingent upon the current economic climate, my cash flow needs, and the estimated long-term appreciation of the property.

Not all my deals were blockbusters, but from the span of 1976 to 1990, I amassed property and cash worth hundreds of thousands of dollars. You can do the same, but don't expect it to happen overnight. I invested 14 years and 19 hectic moves in flipping properties before I had anything significant to show for it. Draw up a successful long-term plan, start slow, and stick to it.

Finding cash to fuel your flip

Coming up with a cool hundred grand, two hundred grand, or three hundred grand to flip a house may seem a little out of reach at first, but several financing options are available, including the following:

- ✔ Flip the house you live in.
- ✔ Borrow against the equity in your current home.
- ✔ Borrow from relatives or friends.
- ✔ Partner with someone who has money to invest.
- ✔ Borrow *hard money* from an investor. (Hard money is a loan from a private lender that typically costs money upfront, requires lump-sum payments on specific dates, and charges a higher than standard interest rate.)

Chapter 6 explores these and other financing options in greater depth.

Many lending institutions refuse to loan money for the purpose of flipping properties, but hard money is usually available through private investors. Expect steep interest rates — double or even triple the current rates for standard loans. The lender may also require as much as 6 percent upfront in discount points and large monthly payments in the form of *cash calls* (lump-sum payments on scheduled dates).

Taking stock of your financial health

To borrow money at a reasonable interest rate, you have a better chance if you can prove that you have money (or at least some valuable stuff), are currently making money, and generally pay your bills on time.

Having a strong financial position is a big plus, because it gives you access to cheaper loans, but it isn't essential. If you have a great plan in place and can convince someone to loan you sufficient funds to fuel a flip, you can succeed.

To take stock of your financial position, formulate a financial statement that includes the following figures:

- ✔ Everything you own — cash, investments, house, car, boats, coins, jewelry, retirement accounts
- ✔ Everything you owe — mortgage, second mortgage, auto loan, credit card balances, back taxes
- ✔ Gross monthly income
- ✔ Total monthly bills

Treat your financial statement like a report card and update it every six months to grade your progress. An A+ financial statement gives you the power to borrow money at lower interest rates. See Chapter 6 for more information about figuring your financial health and using that information to secure funds for flipping.

CYA: Cover Your Assets. In general, the more you risk, the more you stand to gain, but don't overreach and put your current financial health at risk. To protect your assets, don't finance a house flip with your retirement money . . . at least until you've flipped several properties successfully and are confident that you know what you're doing. If you're married, put real estate investments in your name or your spouse's name, not both. Establish a home equity account for financial emergencies and use it only for emergencies.

Honestly evaluating your debt tolerance

Flipping properties requires a moderate tolerance for debt, especially early in your career. You have to owe money for extended periods of time while you earn a profit off the debt. Some people just can't handle debt. What about you? You may be debt intolerant if you

- ✔ Pay cash for a vehicle when you're offered 0 percent financing
- ✔ Pick up the tab every time you eat out, so you won't owe somebody lunch
- ✔ Prepay your utility bills several months in advance
- ✔ Own only one credit card with a high credit limit just for emergencies

Debt can be good or bad. Debt used to finance investments that have a higher rate of return than the interest you pay on the debt is good debt. Bad debt is any debt racked up on spending sprees for stuff that's worth less now than when you bought it. When flipping houses, loans and their costs can be fairly steep, but if you account for those costs in your budget and still turn a profit of 20 percent or more, the loan and related costs are worth it. (See Chapter 6 for the lowdown on good versus bad debt.)

Taking Your Personality Pulse

Not everyone has what it takes to flip houses. Some people are too nice, too nervous, too timid, or too lazy to pull off a successful flip. Others may get so emotionally attached to a house that they pay too much for it. And some people can't handle the math and extra paperwork. Those who excel are thick-skinned, high-energy, multi-tasking, task-delegating dynamos . . . but that's pretty much true for anything in life that's worth pursuing.

The following sections lead you through a self-assessment to determine whether you have the personality traits required for flipping properties.

Would you categorize yourself as a couch potato?

Flipping houses is stimulating, but the work involved can sap your energy faster than an overdue tax notice. To evaluate your energy level, rate the truth of the following statements on a scale of 0 to 5 — 0 being completely false and 5 being so true you can barely admit it:

> I spend more than 8 hours a week watching TV, chatting online, or playing video games.
>
> I sleep more than 10 hours a day.
>
> I go blank when someone asks, "So what are you doing this weekend?"
>
> I quickly change the subject when someone introduces the topic of goal-setting.
>
> I frequently turn down invitations to parties and get-togethers.
>
> I have a permanent impression of my body on the couch.
>
> I have to make a conscious effort to breathe.

If you scored 0–10, consider yourself an active adult; 11–25, you have a glimmer of hope; 26–35, you're a lost cause, don't even consider getting involved in flipping properties — it'll just cut into your downtime.

How do you perform in a crisis?

Nothing is better at inducing insanity than real estate deals gone bad. You can have your life savings on the line and find yourself in a situation that's completely outside your control. What could possibly go wrong? Plenty.

You may first run into problems when dealing with the **purchase** of your property. Consider the following crises:

- The seller agrees to sell you the property, and then, at the closing, has an epiphany that he's selling too cheap and refuses to close.
- On closing day, you do your routine walk-through and notice that the new kitchen that was there when you first saw the house is gone!
- Three days before closing, the house burns down.

> ✔ Your generous uncle who promised to loan you $75,000 marries a woman who thinks that's not such a good idea.
>
> ✔ Expecting your new house to be vacant, you walk through the front door and meet the family of four who's been living there for the past two weeks.

Managing to come through the purchase unscathed doesn't mean you're in the clear. **Renovation** is the next step in house flipping, and it carries the following potential problems:

> ✔ After collecting his $1,000 deposit, your contractor disappears or refuses to complete the job unless you agree to pay him $5,000 more than you originally agreed to pay.
>
> ✔ Materials for the renovation supposedly delivered yesterday are nowhere to be found.
>
> ✔ Three days after you take possession of the house, you receive a water bill for $1,000.
>
> ✔ Someone shows up at the house, introduces himself as the owner, and says, "And you are . . . ?"

Imagine that you found, purchased, and renovated a house — all the hard work is done, right? Maybe not. **Resale** carries its own risks, such as those in the following list:

> ✔ The buyer's financing falls through or she loses her job and can't close.
>
> ✔ The house appraises for $10,000 less than the sales price.
>
> ✔ The lender's appraiser or the buyer's home inspector declares the property uninhabitable.
>
> ✔ You've had the house on the market for 60 days without a single showing, and your agent suddenly decides not to return your phone calls.
>
> ✔ The market tanks just before you're about to stick the For Sale sign on the front lawn.

These three lists show just a few of the unexpected problems that can pop up when you're buying, renovating, and reselling properties. Go back through the lists of surprises and ask yourself how you would react in such situations. How do you react in minor crises? If generally you're calm and cool, take a problem-solving approach, and can be assertive without becoming violently angry, then you probably have the temperament to flip houses. If you break down in tears or flip out over minor problems, then flipping may not be the best way to spend your time.

How bad can a house flip be?

We (Ralph Roberts and company) discovered a fantastic foreclosure property — a $2 million beauty we could get for a cool $900,000! Although the owners, whom we refer to as Mr. & Mrs. Rose, were currently going through a divorce, they seemed willing to work with us at first. They even convinced us to stay in the house and start rehabbing it while they were living there. Mr. Rose lived in one half of the house, and the Missus resided in the other half.

As soon as the contractors showed up, the War of the Roses commenced. Mrs. Rose declared certain areas of the house to be no-work zones, and these zones changed daily. She tried to seduce the contractors, and when real estate agents arrived to show the house, she called the police. During the rehab, the Rose's son was caught doing drugs in the house.

Mrs. Rose moved out only to be replaced by Mr. Rose's girlfriend. When the contractors returned to work, they found the girlfriend at the top of the stairs, dressed only in her nighty, drunk and in a jealous rage. She proceeded to fall down the stairs, shedding her wig along the way. By the time the Roses cleared out, the place was completely trashed.

We finally managed to take possession of the house, complete the rehab, and place the property back on the market. We were willing to sell for $1.8 million, and when we got our first offer for $2.2 million, we were ecstatic, but we weren't out of the rose bushes yet.

During negotiations we found out that the instrument the buyer was using to pay for the property qualified as an illegal use of treasury bonds. The FBI became aware of the deal and set up a sting operation to nab the bad guys. The fraudsters showed up three hours early, discovered the sting, and split town.

We eventually sold the house for $2 million and netted a $250,000 profit for about a year's effort. Not bad for a year's effort, but it wasn't the quick and easy money we had expected.

Do you have organizational expertise?

Flipping requires strong organizational skills, attention to detail, and the ability to schedule work for maximum efficiency. If you have these skills, you have an edge over less-organized flippers, but if these skills are lacking or completely absent, don't give up. You have at least two options:

- **Get organized:** If you're good with a computer, learn how to use a personal organizer and contact manager, such as Microsoft Outlook. This type of software comes complete with a contact manager, calendar, and to-do list, and can even send you reminders several days in advance of important events.

- **Hire an assistant:** Although a part-time flipper can rarely afford a full-time assistant, you may be able to hire an assistant to work part time answering the phone and managing your schedule. A more cost-effective option is to ask your spouse or another family member or friend to handle the scheduling and record-keeping or teach you the skills you need.

More and more people are working out of their homes as *virtual assistants*. A virtual assistant works for you but uses his own equipment and typically charges an hourly rate for only the hours he works. In other words, you don't have to cover the high costs of equipping a full-time employee, paying him for 40 hours a week when you need him to work only 5 hours a week, and paying benefits. As you become more successful and require more help, you simply ask the assistant to work longer hours or you hire another assistant.

Are you good with people?

The most successful property flippers are approachable motivators with good people skills . . . or they partner up with someone who fits the bill. The ideal candidate is someone who can

- Knock on a stranger's door without fear of being shot
- Calmly motivate others involved in the deal to move quickly
- Empathize with the needs of others and meet those needs in a way that boosts their motivations to work for you
- Be flexible enough to deal with ever-changing situations and quickly develop workable alternatives
- Build solid relationships with agents, contractors, financial institutions, and others on whom you rely for help
- Let everyone in the deal know how valuable she is

If you're not a people person, outsource most of the people-management skills to others. Your real estate agent may be willing to take on some additional work, especially when dealing with buyers and sellers. If you're married and your spouse is better than you are at dealing with people, trade your spouse some household chores for his or her management skills.

The value of approachability

I started buying homes in an area in 1975 with no trouble, but in 1989, that started to change. I noticed that somebody was consistently beating me out on deals . . . and offering less money! After digging around a little, I found at that my capable competitor was simply a more approachable person. She spent more time with the sellers and earned their trust.

I realized that I couldn't beat her, so I recruited her to work with me. She's not over-the-top outgoing like I am, but she has great experience and instincts and an approachable personality — a winning combination.

Can you ask for (and get) what you want?

Waffling is the demise of many novice real estate investors. You don't have to be bossy to be assertive. Know what you want, ask for it, and don't settle for anything that's outside your comfort zone. While negotiating the purchase or sale of a property or trying to convince someone to do something for you, remember that "no" can have different meanings:

- ✔ **No.** When some people say "no," like my dad, for instance, they mean "no."

- ✔ **Maybe.** Some parents say "no" when they really mean "maybe." Kids usually figure this out the first day out of the womb.

- ✔ **I'm willing to walk away.** In buying and selling houses, a buyer or seller often says "no" as a way of communicating his unwillingness to agree to the terms of the deal.

- ✔ **Know.** Through the course of my dealings, I've determined that "no" really means "I don't *know* enough to say 'yes.'" This kind of "no" keeps the discussion going so both parties can negotiate a compromise.

Do you like juggling numbers?

Flipping for profit requires rudimentary math skills — addition and subtraction with a little multiplication thrown in for good measure. To keep your bottom line black rather than red, you simply have to make sure that you sell the home for more than you invest in it. The required tools are readily available:

- ✔ A legal pad and a pencil

- ✔ A standard calculator

- ✔ Real estate calculators on the Web, such as the mortgage calculators at www.realestateabc.com and realestate.yahoo.com

Can you handle rejection, failure, and success?

When you flip houses, you encounter a higher than average share of variables outside your control. On your road to success, you experience plenty of triumphs, failures, and rejections, such as the following:

- ✔ Rejected offers

- ✔ Flipping a property for a loss

✔ Overanalyzing a good deal to the point of losing it

✔ Underestimating the time involved

✔ Getting stuck with a money pit

✔ Buyer or seller backing out

✔ Rejection from investors and partners

✔ Inability to find quality contractors

✔ Underestimating the time for selling the house

Don't get discouraged if your first flip flops. Flip at least three properties before you make the decision to skedaddle. Some of the most successful real estate investors have failed their way to fortune.

Success can be just as daunting as rejection and failure. Just look at how many families crumble under the oppressive weight of lottery winnings! You may not know just how you and your loved ones will react if you strike gold, but keep in mind that success can have some life-shaking effects on you and those around you.

Don't let success get you down. If your first flip is a grand slam and you're not careful with the next flip, the loss can soak up the profits you made with your grand slam.

Ensuring That Your Family Is on Board

Unless you're single with no kids, house flipping is a family affair, whether you plan it that way or not. If you and your spouse can't wallpaper a room together without consulting a marriage counselor, you may not make the ideal house flipping team. In the following sections, I show you how to evaluate your readiness as a family before setting out on the journey.

Getting the okay from your spouse

If you're constantly coming up with money-making schemes that flop, pitching your house flipping plan to your spouse may just garner a silent response accompanied by the rolling of eyes. Don't even consider real estate flipping if your spouse isn't 100 percent behind you. Ultimately, the decision affects several areas of your relationship:

- ✔ **Quality time together:** Partnering with your partner can increase the quality time you spend together or drive a wedge between you, depending on how you both handle it.

- ✔ **Finances:** Hefty profits can alleviate financial burdens and significantly enhance your lives, but a loss can test an already strained relationship.

- ✔ **Emotional and psychological health:** Added stress from dealing with the daily headaches of owning and renovating a home, especially if you're flipping the house you live in, can often push a relationship over the edge. You may also grapple over which property to buy, how much to spend, how to manage renovations, and so on.

- ✔ **Energy levels and libido:** Working side-by-side and often around the clock can invigorate or exhaust you. Your love life may become better than ever or completely disappear.

Long-term success requires short-term sacrifice.

Keeping your kids and pets in the loop

A family is like a house of cards; if one person tumbles, the whole house folds. Consider treating house flipping like your family business. Get the kids involved in the weekend cleanups and yard work, and share the profits. House flipping provides the family with an opportunity to work together to achieve a common goal and first-hand experience investing in real estate.

Encourage your kids to have outside activities, as well, so house flipping doesn't consume their lives.

Fido and Morris may be perfectly content to lie around in the backyard all day while you tear out all the cabinets in your kitchen, but some pets suffer psychological strains similar to the ones people do. Unless you have well-trained animals with opposable thumbs, your pets probably can't take on much work to help you out, but you should at least take them along to the worksite. Just keep them out of the paint trays.

Gathering the Essential Tools of the Trade

Every job requires a collection of specialized tools. For flipping houses, make sure you have the following bare essentials:

- ✔ Day planner or tablet for jotting down names, addresses, phone numbers, and appointment times and locations
- ✔ Cell phone
- ✔ Reliable transportation
- ✔ For Sale signs (if you're planning on selling the home yourself)

Chapter 3

Devising an Effective Flipping Strategy

In This Chapter

▶ Exploring a variety of flipping strategies

▶ Plotting your course well in advance

When most people think of flipping houses, they immediately envision a process of buying a ramshackle house on the cheap, fixing it up, and then reselling it for more than they've invested in it. That's certainly the underlying theme, but the actual process of flipping houses spawns a tool shed full of choices and questions, including the following:

- ✔ Are you going to live in the house while fixing it up?
- ✔ How long can you afford to hold the house before selling it?
- ✔ How extensive are the renovations you're willing and able to perform?

Before you even consider making an offer on a house, know how you're going to profit from it. Are you going to buy it at a bargain and resell it immediately at market value, do a quick makeup job and resell it, perform some major renovations, or fix it up and use it as a rental? Each of these strategies has benefits and drawbacks, but each strategy is a perfectly legitimate way to turn a profit flipping property.

This chapter explores several house flipping strategies and then encourages you to develop your own strategy based on your personality, your neighborhood, and the resources you have at your disposal.

Surveying Different Strategies

When developing a game plan, you want to maximize your strengths, minimize your weaknesses, and fully exploit the opportunities that surround you. Many a flipper have already developed their own strategies that achieve those three goals. By becoming more aware of these existing strategies, you can choose the one that fits you best and perhaps even improvise to invent your own strategy.

In the following sections I reveal the top house flipping strategies that many flippers currently practice with varying levels of success.

Always buy low. If you can't get a house for 25 to 30 percent or more below what you estimate to be its market value, keep looking. Chapter 5 shows you how to guesstimate your profit before you make an offer.

Buy into a hot market

In a sizzling real estate market, you can turn a profit fairly quickly by buying a house, moving in, and then sitting back and watching the real estate values soar. This approach works only if you have time on your hands, are speculative by nature, and have a knack for purchasing houses in a hot market at just the right time. This strategy offers several benefits:

- ✔ If the market remains strong, your property value rises without your having to lift a finger.

- ✔ Your equity in the property rises, boosting your borrowing power for other investments.

- ✔ By living in the home for two years or more, up to $250,000 of your profit ($500,000 for a couple), is tax free, at least according to the tax laws that were in place when I was writing this book. See Chapter 7 for more tax-saving tips.

Buying into a hot market also carries some significant risks:

- ✔ In areas where property values are soaring, the housing bubble may burst, leaving you with a home that is worth less than what you paid for it.

- ✔ Stuff happens. You can have a great house at a great price in a hot market with the top agent working to sell it, and the house still may not sell. Prepare yourself for all possibilities.

What goes up sometimes comes down — sometimes very quickly — but all markets can be good for investing as long as you recognize the conditions and opportunities and react appropriately.

Chapter 8 has more details on taking the temperature of the real estate market in any neighborhood you're scoping out.

Buy low, do nothing, and sell quick

Occasionally, you stumble on a house that's priced significantly below market value and requires few or no repairs. The property may be in foreclosure or perhaps is part of an estate that's being liquidated, making the owner very motivated to sell. By being at the right place at the right time with ready cash and a solid plan in place, you can pounce on the deal and then put the house back on the market the very same day!

Sounds great, huh? Well, getting a house that's way below market value is great when it happens, but being in the right place at the right time takes time and effort. You need to build a solid team (see Chapter 4 for details), do plenty of research, secure some solid investment capital (see Chapter 6 for tips on finding money), and be properly equipped to pull this strategy off. If you haven't done your homework and you're ill-prepared, you're more likely to fall prey to unscrupulous schemes. With the proper preparation and persistence, you're more likely to put yourself in the right place at the right time.

Beware of deals that are too sweet. If a stranger approaches you at an investment seminar with a hot tip on a piece of real estate, for example, he may just be looking for a sucker to buy a property he got stuck with. Unless you know the market values in the area, you see the house with your own eyes, and you research the title, as I explain in Chapter 12, don't take the hook.

Buy low, apply makeup, and sell quick

You can learn a lot from used-car salesmen. The first thing they do when they take possession of a vehicle is clean and polish it and vacuum the interior. The car may still be a clunker, but with the right cosmetics and an air-freshener hanging from the rearview mirror, the vehicle becomes an attractive clunker that can sell for hundreds of dollars more.

Even a good home, if not clean and well-maintained, can look disheveled. Many homeowners place their homes on the market without properly *staging* (showcasing) their homes. They don't mow the lawn, trim the bushes, touch up the paint, or even tidy up the house during showings. Unknowingly, they turn away prospective buyers, and the house lingers on the market until even their agents lose interest. The homeowner may then lower the price to generate interest.

This kind of home gives you a perfect opportunity to swoop in and get a great deal. You buy the home for significantly less than market value, add elbow grease, and then resell the home for thousands of dollars more than you invested in it. Chapter 14 shows you how to give a home a quick makeover, and Chapter 20 shows you how to properly stage a home to get top dollar.

This is an excellent strategy for the first-time flipper. By purchasing a property that's an easy rehab job, you can focus on the process of flipping rather than on the complexities of rehabbing. After you master this strategy, you're better prepared to move on to bigger jobs.

Buy low, renovate, and sell high

Some homes are undervalued because they're missing an essential feature — a livable living room, a third bedroom, a deck, or a laundry room on the main floor. Other homes may have major eyesores, such as an outdated kitchen or bathroom. In either case, moderate to major renovations are required to improve the marketability of the house in two ways:

- ✔ **Increase the home's actual value.** Wear and tear depreciate a home over time. Updates restore value, while added living space can boost the house into a higher price bracket.

- ✔ **Expand the pool of interested house hunters.** A two-bedroom house, for example, appeals only to those people who are looking for a one- to two-bedroom house. Adding a third bedroom attracts anyone looking for a one- to three-bedroom house or a house with office space.

Adding to the real value of a home is a great way to maximize your profit, but don't take on more than you can handle. If you're a weekend warrior or you have contractors on your team (see Chapter 4 for details), consider this strategy. If not, you may want to hold off until you have the necessary personnel in place.

Buy low, move in, renovate, and sell high

To maximize your profit, reduce expenses, and take a more hands-on role in rehabbing a home, consider moving in to the home you purchase and renovating it at your own pace. If you and your family don't mind living in the chronic chaos of a construction zone, this approach is appealing for several reasons:

- ✔ By living in the home you're flipping, you avoid a second mortgage payment, tax bill, and utility costs.

- ✔ Because you're living in the home, you get a better feel for the types of renovations that can make the house more attractive to future buyers.

- ✔ If you live in the home for at least two years, up to $250,000 of your profit ($500,000 for a couple) is tax free, at least according to the tax laws that were in place when I was writing this book.

- ✔ You're onsite for any repairs or renovations you have to hire out. And you're around more often to prevent thieves from walking off with your tools and materials.

If you're single or married with no kids, this strategy is an excellent choice. However, if you have children in school, I recommend that you avoid this strategy, unless you intend to remain in the same school system. Your children begin to make relationships, and big moves can put a serious crimp in their social lives.

If you're planning major renovations like gutting the house or completely rehabbing the kitchen, consider performing that renovation before you move in or plan on taking up residence elsewhere during the renovation, especially if you have kids and pets. The persistent noise, dust, and inconvenience can rattle nerves and strain relationships.

Buy, hold, and rent

You don't have to sell a house to profit from it. Many real estate investors opt to buy a house and rent it out for at least enough to cover the monthly expenses of holding it — mortgage, taxes, maintenance, utilities, and so on. Here's a rundown of how this strategy works:

✔ You buy the house at less than market value, so you earn equity at the time of purchase. In other words, if you buy a $100,000 house for $80,000, you immediately earn $20,000 in equity. You don't realize your profit until you sell the house, but you can borrow against the equity.

✔ Assuming the rent you charge covers your mortgage and other expenses, the rent pays down the principal of the loan, so your equity in the home gradually rises. (Your renters are paying off your debt.)

✔ As real estate values rise, your equity in the home rises accordingly, so the house is worth more when you sell it.

In short, you're making money three ways: when you buy the house, when you hold the house, and when you sell the house. If you perform some value-add renovations while you own the property, you may even boost your profit when you sell. Of course, with this strategy you won't see the immediate influx of cash that accompanies a quick flip, but your net worth (the value of your assets minus what you owe on those assets) gradually rises until you cash out your chips at the end of the game.

Leasing your property is an excellent safety net in the event that real estate values plummet. I discuss this strategy in Chapter 25.

Invest in new construction

A home doesn't have to be old and beat up for you to flip it. Many real estate investors profit from flipping new homes or condos, especially when builders are having trouble selling the final few units. Unless you're focusing on a niche market that rules out new construction (see the next section for more about niche markets), don't overlook newly constructed homes.

If you can buy into a division early on that's growing in popularity, you can often score a handsome profit, although I don't recommend speculating on the market as a solid investment strategy. In addition, builders sometimes get stuck with a few homes at the end of the project and offer special deals to unload them so they can move on to their next project.

When purchasing a newly constructed home or condo, read the purchase agreement very carefully and check the following:

- ✔ The purchase agreement should have a clause stating that the purchase is conditional upon the satisfactory completion of the building and on your ability to secure financing for the purchase. If you sign a purchase agreement and then are denied financing, the builder may foreclose on the property and take it back for next to nothing.

- ✔ Watch out for clauses that give the builder a percentage of the profit when you resell the unit. In a strong market, builders often insert wording that if you sell the unit within a specified time period, you must pay the builder all or a significant portion of the profit.

- ✔ Beware of inflated profit estimates. Developers who are trying to get their projects off the ground often make unrealistic estimates, sometimes claiming that their properties will double in value over a short period of time. You've probably heard stories of people who invest in a development and make $100,000 in short order. What you don't hear are the stories of people who lose money, and those stories are much more common.

- ✔ If, after doing your research, you're convinced of the benefits, then at least make sure that you're one of the first 10 percent of buyers. These buyers make the lion's share of the profit. Those buyers who come late to the table get scraps or losses.

Focus on a niche market

When you're looking for homes to flip, the first impulse is to cast a wide net in your search for the best deals, but sometimes you can find better deals by fishing deeper in one spot, such as one of the following:

- ✔ **Foreclosures:** You can find more homes in foreclosure than you could possibly flip, and by focusing your efforts on these properties, you quickly figure out the ins and outs of locating them and effectively negotiating the price and terms you want. See Chapter 12 for details about foreclosures.

✔ **VA Foreclosures:** To narrow your scope even further, consider focusing on VA foreclosures.

✔ **Probate:** You can get leads from probate lawyers and the neighborhood grapevine to locate families who need to unload a house in order to settle an estate.

✔ **Divorces:** When couples divorce, they're often stuck with a home that neither of them can afford. By keeping your ears open and letting people know that you buy houses, you can often get first dibs on these houses.

✔ **HUD homes:** Working with an agent who specializes in HUD homes, you can build a career purchasing these homes at a discount and rehabbing them for quick, profitable sales.

✔ **FSBO (For Sale By Owner):** When everyone else is searching the MLS for great deals, you may prefer driving around the neighborhood looking for homes with a For Sale or For Sale By Owner sign on the front lawn.

✔ **Seized homes:** County law enforcement agents commonly seize property and then have to unload it. By focusing your energy in this area, you can corner the market on seized homes.

✔ **Teardowns:** Homes that are beyond hope may still hold opportunities if the price and location are right. Some investors earn a great return by tearing down old homes and building new ones in their place.

With the other strategies covered in this chapter, you can pick a strategy and run with it. Focusing on a niche market, however, is a strategy that's effective regardless of any other strategy you choose to follow. When you're first starting out, focus on a single niche. As you gain experience and gather more resources and assistance, you can widen your scope to include other niches.

Don't try to be a high roller and master everything all at once. Select a niche (foreclosures, probate, divorce, whatever) and work that until you achieve success. After you establish yourself in that area, you can add another to expand your operation. Chapter 9 provides more guidance on niche markets. Your niche market can also be a specific area that you farm by becoming an expert in the area and establishing a strong network. Chapter 8 offers additional details on how to effectively farm an area.

Flip contracts (or do it all on paper)

Technically, you don't even have to lift a hammer to flip a house. If you can lift a pen and a phone, you have all you need to flip contracts. *Flipping contracts* consists of locating a distressed property and then contracting with the homeowner to sell it to an investor.

Chances are good that you've already heard a little about flipping contracts. Here's how it works: You pay the homeowner a deposit, typically $1,000 or 5 to 10 percent of the purchase price. In return, you get a purchase contract giving you the right to sell the property to an investor. You then find an investor who's willing to purchase the property and pay you a fee in excess of the amount you have tied up in the property.

This strategy may sound rosy, but I strongly discourage you from flipping contracts. I include the strategy here only because you're going to hear about it elsewhere, and you should be aware of the high risk. This is where the unscrupulous lurk in the bushes. I frown on flipping contracts (commonly called *pass-throughs*). I frown on the people who do them and the real estate gurus who teach this practice. Work from A to Z — roll up your sleeves and make something out of your business and the neighborhoods in which you invest. This hard work may seem to be the long way to wealth, but it's the best way.

If someone ties up a $100,000 house and wants to sell you her purchase agreement for $5,000, you're purchasing the house for $100,000 *and* paying a fee of $5,000. You're taking all the risk and giving that person $5,000. If it's such a good deal, you need to analyze it and ask yourself why she's not flipping the house herself.

Cook up your own strategy

Successful investors, whether they invest in real estate or stocks, devise unique strategies based on their personalities, abilities, and the resources they have at their disposal. If you like to help people and you're good at dealing with uncomfortable situations, for example, you may want to focus on foreclosures or divorces. If you're good at primping a house but not so good at rehabbing, consider focusing on homes that require only a little makeup.

You can even mix and match strategies to develop a custom strategy of your very own. You may, for example, choose to buy a quick flip in a hot market or buy only duplexes that need a lot of work, move into one half, and rent out the other half while renovating the half you're living in. The variations are truly limited only by your imagination.

Re-evaluate your situation and be ready to shift your strategy as your skills, knowledge, resources, and market change. At this point, you may not feel confident taking on major renovations, but in a year or two, it could well become your area of expertise.

Drawing Up a Detailed Plan Well in Advance

Every day you own a property, holding costs chip away at your profit, unless of course, the property is a rental. *Holding costs* are the daily expenses — mortgage interest, property taxes, utility bills, and maintenance costs. The trick to reducing these costs is to flip the property as quickly as possible, and that means planning well in advance. Make sure that your plan covers all three stages of the flipping process:

- ✔ **Purchase:** Secure financing before you go house hunting. This tip may seem counterintuitive, but with financing in hand, you can move on the deal much faster than other buyers and negotiate from a position of power. Know how much you can afford to pay and still have sufficient funds for renovations before you make your offer.

  Chapter 5 has details on estimating your profit potential, and Chapter 6 has details on how to secure financing for your flip.

- ✔ **Rehab:** Jot down a list of improvements you want to make to the property when you first see the house, and schedule the work before you close on the purchase. Ideally, you should start renovating the property the same day or the day after closing.

  Chapter 10 walks you through the process of inspecting a property for the first time; Part IV is devoted to fixing up your fixer-upper.

- ✔ **Sale:** As soon as you know your closing date, determine the date on which you want to put the house back on the market (see Chapter 13 for help) and decide whether you want to sell the house yourself or work with an agent. You don't have to wait to sell the house until renovations are complete — the activity that surrounds the house during renovations can be an excellent marketing tool. It gets the neighbors talking. Part V is all about selling your rehabbed home.

Devising a Plan B: Surviving a Flip That Flops

Throughout this book, I provide tips, tricks, and warnings to enable you to maximize your profit and minimize your risks, but that doesn't guarantee a successful flip. Flips sometimes flop, even for experienced investors. You may buy a house that has costly, unforeseen problems; buy into a market that tanks soon after you close on a property; or encounter a host of unexpected problems that can derail your dreams. Know the risks before you roll the dice, and always have a plan B in place. The following tips can help you avoid some of the more serious situations and recover your composure when something goes wrong:

- ✔ If your flip flops due to a dip in the housing market, skip to Chapter 25 for advice on how to cope.

- ✔ As soon as you can see that a property is a money pit, cut your losses. Don't throw good money after bad. You may need to sell the house now at a loss rather than selling later at a bigger loss.

- ✔ Keep in touch with your team, especially your financial backers and agent, when a situation sours. Communication is key, especially when times are bad. Good team members can help you out of a jam and assist you in your recovery.

Don't give up just because one flip doesn't turn out as well as you expected it to. Failure is one of the best educators, and if you can work through it, it can be a real confidence builder. If I gave up every time I failed, I would never have achieved my current level of success. Flip three or four houses before throwing in the towel. I know that the possibility of a flop isn't something you want to hear about. Certainly the late night TV gurus don't teach or talk about this possibility. Your plan, however, must include an exit strategy for all possibilities; otherwise, your flop will take you by total surprise and you won't know what to do.

Chapter 4

Building Your Dream Team

In This Chapter

▶ Picking a real estate agent with flipping know-how

▶ Acquiring some sound financial advice

▶ Covering your back with a title company, appraiser, inspector, and attorney

▶ Hiring contractors and subcontractors to handle the heavy lifting

Most people who talk themselves out of investing in real estate are defeated by a false assumption — that they have to do it alone. The truth is that you don't have to do it alone. In fact, attempting to fly solo is one of the most common and serious blunders you can make when you're first starting out. Investors who excel at flipping houses are team builders, capable of selecting talented players, coordinating their efforts, and maximizing their skills.

By surrounding yourself with a team of experienced and talented people, all you really need to succeed is a big, fat Rolodex (and I don't mean a watch), a phone, a pad of paper, a pencil, and some people skills. You don't know what a house is really worth? Consult a qualified real estate agent. You're not good with money? Hire an accountant. Can't hammer a nail? Call a contractor.

Sure, hiring these additional people costs extra, but as long as you can accurately estimate the total costs, calculate them into your budget, and still profit from the flip, you win. (See Chapter 5 for more details on budgeting and projecting profit.)

I don't have all the essential qualities to successfully flip houses. What I do have is the ability to admit that I lack certain qualities and a knack for finding people who complement my skills. In this chapter, I show you how to build your own house flipping dream team.

A dream team is more than just a skilled workforce. It's a combination of people who have your best interests at heart. They want you to succeed. Money alone can't buy a dream team. You have to do a little nurturing by rewarding the people who reward you through their expertise and hard work. Fair payment on time, sincere compliments and thanks, positive referrals, and free food go a long way.

Hooking Up with a House Hunter — A Quality Real Estate Agent

A real estate agent (or house hunter) who knows the ropes and has the right contacts can assist you in managing the two transactions that are critical to your success — purchasing a house at less than market value and selling the rehabbed house quickly at a profit. In the following sections, I explain the beneficial services that agents can provide and give you guidance on finding the best agent for your flipping needs.

Although you may be able to handle one or both transactions (selling and buying) on your own in an attempt to trim costs and boost your bottom line, I strongly discourage it, especially when you're flipping your first property. You're about to invest tens or perhaps hundreds of thousands of dollars. A qualified agent can help you navigate the process and avoid common pitfalls that can turn a plump profit into a big, fat loss.

Recognizing the value of agents

A good real estate agent is more than just a clerk who pushes paperwork through the system and juggles numbers. He's more like the concierge at an upscale hotel. He's dedicated to serving your real estate needs, whatever they may be. And if he can't personally attend to those needs, he can flip through his big, fat Rolodex or tap away on his computer to find someone who can.

Sure, a qualified real estate agent costs some money, typically a 6 to 8 percent commission, but when you consider the amount of money you're investing, a single mistake can cost you thousands more. A real estate agent who has plenty of experience working with investors can assist you with the following:

- ✔ Determining how much money you can borrow and which type of loans are best and helping you obtain pre-approval for a loan. (See Chapter 6 for more about loans.)

- ✔ Finding houses that meet your search criteria, even when those houses aren't actively advertised as being on the market. (See Chapters 8 and 9 for more about scoping out neighborhoods and houses.)

- ✔ Assisting in evaluating properties that you may want to purchase so you don't pay more for a property than it's worth. (See Chapter 10 for tips on evaluating specific properties for purchase.)

- ✔ Ensuring that your offer has appropriate conditions in place to protect you. For example, you may want to make your offer contingent upon the sale of another property you own, your ability to acquire financing, the property passing inspection, and the title company's assurance that the title work is in order. (See Chapter 11 for details on offers and negotiations for buying a home.)

✔ Negotiating price, financing, terms, date of possession, and other sticky areas of a purchase agreement.

✔ Expediting the closing to ensure that nothing goes wrong at the last minute and offering solutions when everything goes wrong at the last minute.

✔ Assisting you in estimating the cost of repairs and renovations.

✔ Referring you to contractors, subcontractors, and other professionals who have a good track record (see "Contacting Contractors and Subcontractors" later in this chapter).

✔ Broadcasting your rehabbed home to every real estate agent in the neighborhood via the Multiple Listing Service (a listing of homes for sale that goes out to all the real estate agents in your area), and helping you sell it in half the time it would take you to sell it yourself. (See Chapter 19 for more about marketing your rehabbed home.)

✔ Evaluating offers on the rehabbed home in a way that doesn't compromise your position in the market. Some offers, for example, can tie up your home and leave you little compensation if the buyer backs out. (See Chapter 21 for info on negotiating and closing the sale of your rehabbed home.)

✔ Navigating the closing to ensure smooth sailing.

✔ Advising you on how much rent you can charge for a property if you want to hold onto it for awhile and you need some cash flow.

A talented agent can help you locate excellent investment properties in a fraction of the time it would take you to do the same thing, and help you purchase properties for thousands of dollars less than you would pay if you negotiated the purchase yourself. On average, you take twice as long selling a property yourself than you do when you work with a real estate agent, and every day your home sits on the market costs you money.

Picking an agent with the right stuff

Any licensed real estate agent can help you find, purchase, and sell a house, but you want someone whose experience and training are rooted in the business of flipping properties. The qualities to look for include

✔ **Personal experience flipping properties.** Personal experience is a big plus, because the person knows what flippers need to turn a profit and typically has a strong network of affordable contractors for repairs and renovations. Preferably, the person is no longer in the business of flipping properties; otherwise, she may take the best deals for herself.

Don't use experience in flipping houses as your sole criteria for choosing one agent over another. You want a quality agent — experience in flipping is an added bonus.

- ✔ **Internet savvy.** The tools and information available on the Internet can give you a significant edge.

- ✔ **Specialty in your target area.** The agent should know the market in which you want to invest and be well-versed on property values, market conditions, and neighborhood news that may affect future property values.

- ✔ **Access to all MLS listings in your target area.** More than one MLS company may publish listings for your area. If the agent subscribes to only one of these listings, you may receive information on only about 30 percent of the available properties. Find an agent who has access to all MLS listings or use multiple agents.

- ✔ **Experience in other methods for finding homes to purchase.** Shop for a real estate agent who specializes in your area of interest, such as FSBOs (For Sale By Owners), foreclosures, or HUD (Housing and Urban Development) homes. A real estate agent who checks only the MLS listings may overlook the best deals.

- ✔ **Proactive.** The agent shouldn't wait for you to call but should call you with any leads for properties in your target area.

- ✔ **Eager to show houses.** The agent should be willing to show many houses before arriving at the right house.

- ✔ **Available on short notice.** If you see a For Sale sign in someone's yard, and you want to see the house, you should be able to quickly contact your agent to set an appointment for viewing the house at a convenient time for you. The agent should have a cell phone number, home number, and e-mail address; check for messages regularly; and promptly return phone calls. If your agent is going to be out of town, she should notify you of the dates and place someone in charge of handling your affairs.

- ✔ **Unafraid of presenting low-ball offers.** If an agent cringes at offering a price well-below market value, he's not the agent for you. He should be willing and able to pitch one or more low-ball offers with a poker face.

The best way to find an agent is through referrals from other homeowners (buyers and sellers), preferably your friends, relatives, or neighbors. As you search the classifieds and notice For Sale signs and brochures in the neighborhood, you can get a better feel for which companies and agents do a better job of marketing their properties. When you have a list of 10 to 15 names, start calling around and interviewing your candidates to compare their experience, education, and certification as described in the preceding list.

Real estate agent or Realtor: What's the difference?

A real estate agent is anyone who has a state license to negotiate the sale or purchase of a property and works for a real estate broker or brokerage company. A Realtor is a real estate agent who's also a member of The National Association of Realtors. The U.S. has more than 2 million real estate agents, but only 1.2 million are Realtors.

So, what's the difference? Because the qualifications for obtaining a real estate license vary from state to state, the quality of real estate agents varies much more than the quality of Realtors. The National Association of Realtors requires its members to complete additional training and testing to improve their knowledge and abilities and encourages members to follow a strict code of ethics. The association also provides its members with additional resources and tools to assist in finding and marketing properties effectively.

Of course this association membership doesn't mean that a particular Realtor is more qualified than a given real estate agent, but the odds are pretty good that you receive superior advice and service from a Realtor. To find a bona fide Realtor, look for the Realtor logo on business cards and stationery. Almost all Realtors make a point of proudly displaying this logo. You also can find a Realtor in your area by checking out www.realtor.com.

Many books on buying and selling houses recommend that you try to convince the agent to accept a lower percentage in commissions or a flat fee for helping you buy or sell a property, but this tactic can backfire. I suggest that you find the best agent and then pay the agent the going rate or a little more. When you pay less, your agent is going to work harder for the clients who are paying more, and no card carrying capitalist can blame her.

Recruiting Moneymen (and Women)

Flipping properties for a profit is all about money — getting it, spending it, paying taxes on it, and using it for your next flip. To succeed, you need someone who's good at managing the finances while you're busy buying, rehabbing, and selling. Actually, you may need three people who are good with money — one to loan you money, a second to help you manage it, and a third to recommend the best way to invest it. The following sections describe the types of financial assistance you need.

Finding financiers

Unless you're independently wealthy, you need a source of cash to get started. You may be able to tap into your savings account and max out your credit card, but strong financial backing from investors can provide you with the capital you need to leverage your personal investment. The big question is: Who can you ask for investment capital? Here's a list to get you started:

- ✔ Start with friends, family, and your attorney. They already know you, and charity begins at home.

- ✔ Tell everyone you come in contact with that you flip houses. An investor may hear about it and contact you, but be careful — an investor may be looking for a newbie to snooker into a raw deal. Question any deal that requires you to take on an inordinate share of the risk.

- ✔ Contact doctors, lawyers, dentists, and other highly paid professionals you know who may be looking for a better return on their money.

Whomever you borrow money from is going to want a mortgage in the first position that protects their investment. If you're investing in foreclosure properties, make sure that you purchase a first mortgage — not a second mortgage or a junior lien. Chapter 12 discusses mortgages and liens in detail.

If you contact everyone you know and you're still short on cash, consider approaching a *hard money* lender. Hard money is typically a short-term, high-interest loan. In Chapter 6, I discuss various types of loans, including hard money.

Finding investors initially can be a frustrating chore, but your future success will draw investors to you who are willing to share the risk. Chapter 6 has more info on creative ways to finance your flip; you also can find information there on other traditional ways to secure money for your flip, such as unlocking the equity in your current home and refinancing your mortgage.

Hiring an accountant

Most of the accounting that applies to house flipping consists of simple addition and subtraction. Add up the costs of buying, renovating, and selling the house and subtract that from the amount you receive when you sell the house, and if you come up with a positive number, you made money. (Chapter 5 has the lowdown on estimating your profit from a flip.)

Unfortunately, reality is a little more complex, and having a professional accountant on hand can help you avoid unnecessary expenses and legal woes. Your accountant can take all your money and receipts out of your shoe box, sort through them, figure out whether you made any money, and if you did make money, he can calculate the amount of tax you owe. An experienced accountant also delivers the following services:

✔ Saves you money on income tax while remaining in compliance with complex IRS tax laws. (See Chapter 7 for more about tax issues.)

✔ Ensures that you pay your property taxes on time.

✔ Evaluates your house flipping activity to determine whether you're considered an investor or a self-employed dealer.

✔ Makes sure you pay your quarterly estimated taxes if you're considered a self-employed dealer.

✔ Ensures you pay your quarterly estimated taxes on your capital gains if you're considered an investor.

✔ Offers a sanity check to make sure that your grand vision for the house doesn't blow your budget.

Ask your family and friends for referrals to qualified accountants who have experience with real estate. If you already have an accountant who has little experience in real estate, ask her whether she knows of someone. Interview at least three candidates, and make sure that you ask about their experience.

Obtaining sound investment advice

When the money starts rolling in, your first impulse may be to roll your profits into your next flip, but that's not always the most savvy approach. You may want to sock away some money in tax-deferred accounts to save on taxes and protect your gains. A knowledgeable financial advisor can provide the advice you need to make the best use of your profits.

People who flip houses often are short-sighted. They focus three to six months into the future but can't see 20 to 30 years down the road. A financial advisor trains her vision on the long-term financial future and can help you take appropriate action now to build wealth for your retirement years. For details about long-term financial planning, check out *Personal Finance For Dummies,* 4th Edition, by Eric Tyson, MBA (Wiley).

Consulting a Title Company to Cover Your Back

When you sign on the dotted line to purchase a property, you own not only the property but also all the problems associated with it. Buy a property from someone who's facing foreclosure, and you may just own a property that has one or more *liens* against it — legal claims against the property to secure a debt. (See Chapter 12 for more information about foreclosures and liens.)

To avoid unforeseen problems associated with the title of a property you're about to purchase, hire a title company to search the title history. A title search ensures that:

- ✔ The property that you think you're buying is the property you're buying.
- ✔ The person selling the property is the person who owns it.
- ✔ You're aware of any liens against the property or taxes due.
- ✔ Any rights, such as mineral rights, are transferred to you.
- ✔ Your deed or title is in recordable form.
- ✔ You're aware of any restrictions on the property; for example, if you're buying a home in a historical area, the renovations may have restrictions.

Reputation and location are the two main considerations in choosing a title company. Pick a company that's nearby and has the best reputation for smooth closings. Your real estate agent can recommend a title company that has a solid reputation in the area.

At the closing, obtain a copy of the final title insurance policy, which the seller typically pays for. This policy is your guarantee that the title is clear. If any hidden issues arise later, the title insurance company is accountable.

Locating a Valuable Appraiser

When someone buys a home, the person typically borrows money from a lender and uses the property as collateral for the loan. The bank or other lending institution orders an appraisal of the property to make sure it's worth enough to cover the loan in the event that the buyer defaults on the loan. The buyer typically pays for the appraisal as part of the closing costs.

As a flipper, you don't need an appraisal unless you're borrowing money from a lender who requires an appraisal to approve the loan. However, if you're unsure of the value of a particular piece of property, an appraiser can help you confirm the potential profitability of a property or perhaps present you with some figures that make you think twice about making an offer. You can ask the appraiser to provide you with two estimates: property value before repairs and renovations and property value after repairs and renovations. An appraisal may cost a little extra, but the additional information may help you make a better decision, especially when you're first starting out.

If you're in the market for an appraiser, ask your real estate agent, title company, or attorney for a recommendation.

To determine whether a property is worth buying, check out the recent sales prices of comparable properties in the same neighborhood and consult your real estate agent or another experienced investor for a second opinion. An appraisal may do you little good when you're buying distressed properties at a deep discount.

Whether you're buying or selling a home, beware of inflated appraisals. Some real estate scams rely on inflated appraisals to sucker mortgage companies into lending more than the home is actually worth. If the seller is willing to take $185,000 for the house, but it appraises at $225,000, paying the seller $225,000 with the intent of receiving cash back from the seller is fraudulent. Nefarious appraisers may also jack up the value of a home to inflate the homeowner's equity, so the owner can qualify for a loan. Don't rely solely on an appraisal to determine the true value of a property. By specializing in properties in a certain price range, you can become an expert on property values in that range.

Adding a Real Estate Lawyer to the Roster

All lawyers are not created equal. Some specialize in corporate law. Others focus on personal injury lawsuits. You can find attorneys who specialize in divorce or disability or criminal law. When you're flipping properties, you want a real estate lawyer. An experienced real estate lawyer can offer valuable assistance in the following areas:

✔ **Purchase agreement:** Purchase agreements are complex documents that cover not only the sales price but also the terms of sale — tax prorations, occupancy issues, water bills, personal property in the house, and so on. Unless it's in writing, a purchase agreement is subject to dispute. Inexperienced real estate agents often introduce errors, costing their clients hundreds or thousands of dollars.

✔ **Title:** Your lawyer can advise you on the best way to take title in your situation. For example, you may want only your name on the title or your name and your spouse's name if you're married. A lawyer can also inspect the title work to ensure your protection. (See the earlier section "Consulting a Title Company to Cover Your Back" for more details.)

✔ **Complex transactions:** Some transactions may include an assumption of the mortgage or enable the seller to finance the purchase. When complexities arrive, having a lawyer on call is always a plus.

To find a qualified real estate lawyer, ask your real estate agent, friends, and family for referrals or contact your local bar association. Don't resort to flipping through the phone book unless you really have to. The ideal candidate possesses the following qualities:

✔ **Efficient and affordable:** Attorneys often charge by the minute, so beware of long talkers.

✔ **Supportive:** Someone who second-guesses your decision to invest can paralyze you with doubt.

✔ **Unobtrusive:** Your lawyer should protect you from unseen risk without sinking the deal. Some lawyers justify their fee by becoming too technical with the documents, and that's just plain irritating.

✔ **Available:** A good lawyer is available when you need her.

✔ **Experienced:** A real estate attorney who owns real estate and rentals is better than one who doesn't.

✔ **Generous:** A lawyer who shares his leads can help you find properties that you couldn't find on your own.

Lawyer fees can range from a hundred to a couple thousand dollars. Compare rates and services closely, and make sure that you consult a lawyer who specializes in real estate.

Lining Up a Home Inspector

Whenever you make an offer on a house, make the offer contingent upon the house passing inspection. Then, have the home professionally inspected. This contingency ensures that you don't get stuck holding the bag on any of the following big-ticket items:

✔ Damaged foundation or other structural anomalies

✔ Electrical wiring problems

✔ Broken sewer lines, poor plumbing, or aging septic systems, especially if the house has been vacant for some time

- ✔ Leaking, nonfunctioning, or nonexistent gas lines

- ✔ Poorly functioning furnace or central air conditioning units

- ✔ Leaking or ramshackle roof

- ✔ Termite damage

- ✔ Health hazards, such as lead-based paint, toxic mold, radon gas, asbestos, and hazardous insulation

- ✔ Neighboring structures built on your property. Always check the survey to make sure that the homeowner didn't agree to allow the neighbor to build his new garage ten feet over on your property.

Although most buyers hire private home inspectors, I prefer using city inspectors, because they tend to be more thorough and they're well-versed on local building codes. The city inspectors in our area show up as a team that typically includes a plumber, an electrician, a heating and air-conditioning specialist, a builder, and someone who specializes in zoning. You get a thorough inspection and a complete write-up for about the same price you pay a private inspector. If the inspection uncovers problems, you can sign off on the recommendations, agreeing to make the necessary repairs after you take possession. However, not all towns and cities offer inspections, and some offer them only for new homes, so this option may not be available to you.

If you decide to hire an inspector, you can crack open the Yellow Pages and find listings for dozens of home inspectors in just about any area of the country. Finding a qualified home inspector, however, is a challenge. Begin by asking your real estate agent or other real estate professionals you know for references.

NACHI (the National Association of Certified Home Inspectors) is a nonprofit agency that works toward educating and ensuring the quality of home inspectors. Its Web site at www.nachi.org features an online referral service that you can search to find certified home inspectors in your area.

When you have a few leads, contact your candidates and ask them the following questions:

- ✔ **Are you certified, licensed, and insured?** Certification and licensing ensure that the inspector has the basic qualifications for the job. Insurance covers any serious defects he may overlook.

- ✔ **How long have you been a home inspector?** Length of service is often, but not always, a good indication of experience and expertise.

- ✔ **How many homes have you inspected?** "One or two," isn't the answer you're looking for. A busy home inspector is usually busy because she's good.

- ✔ **What did you do before becoming a home inspector?** Someone who's a retired carpenter or home builder is probably a better candidate than, say, a burned out dance instructor.

✔ **Do you have references I can call?** If the inspector has a good track record, people don't hesitate to provide positive references.

✔ **Do you recommend remedies or simply identify problems?** Look for an inspector who's had experience in construction. The builder who constructed my home made an excellent home inspector and actually moved into this field full time. His approach was to not only point out problems but also recommend repairs and renovations.

You don't want a home inspector who makes mountains out of mole hills. He can deflate your balloon of enthusiasm with a thousand pin holes. Don't nitpick a great deal. A homeowner who's selling a property at a clearance price often does so to avoid the costs and headaches of making repairs. Nitpicking can ruin your chances of acquiring a great piece of property. Also, don't hire your inspector as your contractor — such a move only tempts your inspector/contractor to find more problems with the property.

Contacting Contractors and Subcontractors

When flipping a house, you can do as much of the fixing up as you're qualified, comfortable, and willing to do (see Chapter 13 for details on determining do-it-yourself projects). For everything else, hire a professional — contractor or subcontractor:

✔ A *contractor* (or general contractor) is the boss. He or she manages the budget and workflow, hires subcontractors, coordinates the work from start to finish, and hands you the bill.

✔ *Subcontractors* perform specific tasks, such as wiring, plumbing, installing ductwork, and so on.

On isolated jobs — jobs that require only one subcontractor — you can often do the contracting yourself. For more extensive projects that require the coordination of multiple craftsmen, a general contractor may be better suited. To me, a general contractor represents additional overhead I don't need to pay for. By working closely with the subcontractors to coordinate the work, you should be able to handle the general contracting yourself, but if you have any doubts about your own abilities in managing the project, hire a qualified contractor. Chapter 13 can help you plan and manage your renovations so that the subcontractors aren't tripping over each other.

In the following sections, I explain the duties of a general contractor and methods for finding and hiring contractors and subcontractors. I also tell you when a handyman may be better suited for your needs.

Acting as the head honcho

If you're a control freak or you enjoy planning and managing projects, and you have a flexible schedule that enables you to spend time at the worksite, you qualify for the position of general contractor, especially for basic renovations. As general contractor, you assume the following responsibilities:

- ✔ **Budgeting:** Estimate a budget for the project and then ensure that the expenses don't exceed the budget.

- ✔ **Hiring:** Gather bids for various aspects of the project, such as laying new flooring or carpet, installing drywall, and updating the plumbing, and then choose the subcontractors to complete the work.

- ✔ **Scheduling:** Coordinate each phase of the project to avoid conflicts between subcontractors. In a bathroom renovation, for example, you have to make sure that the rough plumbing and rough electrical work are complete before the drywallers show up.

- ✔ **Overseeing:** Your presence at the worksite ensures that the slackers don't slack and that tools and materials don't mysteriously disappear. If you're absent, you don't really know what's going on.

- ✔ **Firing:** Perhaps the most difficult part of general contracting consists of firing subcontractors who perform substandard work or fail to show up.

- ✔ **Paying:** Paying your contractors the agreed upon amount on time keeps them with you on the next flip. Cheat a contractor, and your water tank may turn up missing. Paying your workers before they pull out of the driveway is a good practice. It guarantees future business and gives you a good name in the industry. News, good or bad, travels fast.

When acting as contractor, obtain a permit before starting work on any project that requires a permit, such as a room addition, a deck, a garage, or even installing a pool. If you don't obtain a required permit and something bad happens, you may ultimately be responsible, even after you sell the property.

Chapter 13 has the full scoop on planning and prioritizing your renovations.

Tracking down top-notch contractors and subcontractors

Good help shows up on time, performs quality workmanship, charges reasonable fees, and completes the job on time or ahead of schedule. Finding good help is one of the main challenges of successfully flipping properties. Fortunately, you can network your way to the best available help in your area by doing the following:

- ✔ Ask for referrals at your local hardware store. Word-of-mouth is better than advertisements or a name on a grocery store bulletin board.

- ✔ Ask real estate agents, investors, and other real estate professionals for references. When they're not working, real estate people talk . . . a lot. Good contractors and subcontractors have a solid reputation.

If your real estate agent volunteers to act as your general contractor, think twice about hiring him; good agents typically make horrible contractors. If your agent is good, he's serving his clients well and has neither the time nor the desire to get involved in construction. Besides, agents don't like to get their hands dirty; contractors do.

- ✔ Contact your insurance company. Most insurance companies have a database of contractors who do everything from installing carpet to cleaning up after floods and are happy to steer you toward the right person, especially if they're footing the bill. However, these contractors are often a little pricey.

- ✔ Talk to friends, relatives, and neighbors who live in the area and find out who they hire for specific jobs.

- ✔ Contact a referral service such as Angie's List at `www.angieslist.com`, which provides ratings and comments from homeowners.

Contracting with contractors and subcontractors

When you're hiring a contractor or subcontractor, you have three goals. You want the job completed to your satisfaction, on budget, and on schedule. To achieve these goals, here's what you do:

- ✔ Draw up a one-page agreement stating when the contractor is to start and finish, with a built-in fee of $50 for every day beyond the scheduled completion date. When you get the contractor's estimate and proposal, attach your agreement to it. The contract should specify a start and end date and how you want extras handled. Your agent or lawyer can help you draft a suitable contract.

✔ Let them know when the For Sale sign is going up.

✔ Give them what they need to succeed, including deposits and supplies.

✔ Have them furnish you with receipts of their purchases.

✔ Show up unannounced at the worksite to see whether they're working.

✔ If the workers are doing a good job, tell them so, and do it often.

✔ Don't strive for perfection. If the work is 90 percent satisfactory, shut up about the 10 percent that's not quite perfect.

Beware of the following issues when contracting workers:

✔ When hiring a contractor or subcontractor, make sure that the person is insured against both property damage and personal injury. An average hospital bill can wipe out your profit.

✔ Be careful about deposits, especially when you're dealing with a contractor you don't know. Contractors have been known to take the deposit and disappear. A 25 to 50 percent deposit is normal — generally, the smaller the contractor, the larger the deposit. You can pay most handymen on a week-to-week basis.

To lessen the risks of getting ripped off, do your due diligence: check references, workmanship, and the amount of time the contractor has been in business; ask the contractor whether he's licensed and insured; and check with the state or your local Better Business Bureau to see whether anyone has filed complaints against the contractor.

Your contractor should supply you with a separate *proof of insurance* form, attached to the bid that verifies that the contractor and his workers are insured for this particular job. If you're hiring a subcontractor who's moonlighting from his day job, he may be covered under his company's insurance policy, but he may *not* be covered during his stint as a moonlighter. When hiring a contractor or handyman who can't provide you with proof of insurance, contact your insurance company and take out a separate workman's comp policy (or add coverage to your current policy on the house you're flipping) that covers anyone who's working on your house. Added insurance takes a little extra time and costs a few hundred dollars, but if you're not covered and a worker is injured on the job, he may sue you and you may lose your entire profit and even some of your own personal savings. I estimate that only about 5 percent of the people who flip houses follow this advice — those who don't are vulnerable to suffering a big loss.

Finding a handyman and other helpers

You don't necessarily need a licensed subcontractor to do odd jobs around the house. A *handyman* (someone who's handy with power tools and hand tools) can often complete small jobs for a fraction of the cost that you pay a subcontractor. If the house needs all new wiring or plumbing or has structural damage, pay a little extra for a licensed expert. For smaller jobs, such as leaky faucets, clogged drains, replacement windows, and new doors, a good handyman is the more affordable choice.

Word-of-mouth is still the best way to find a handyman, but your neighborhood newspaper provides additional leads in the classifieds. (The local paper is also a good source for finding general laborers and trash haulers — perfect for cleaning out that cluttered basement, attic, or garage.) The handyman with the fanciest truck and flashiest ad isn't always the best or most affordable. Look for a worker with paint-stained pants and worn hands. Performance and reputation carry more weight than marketing glitz.

In the summer, consider hiring neighborhood high school and college students who are off for the summer. Many of these kids work hard, especially with the lighter stuff, like painting, cleaning, and yard work. Just be sure you're there to supervise and make sure that your eager students are taking sufficient safety precautions.

Part II

Fiddling with the Financials of Property Flipping

The 5th Wave   By Rich Tennant

"Can you explain your mortgage program again, this time without using the phrase 'yada, yada, yada'?"

In this part . . .

Flipping properties can be a lot of fun, but it's rarely so much fun that people would pay money to do it. You flip houses because you want to make money. How much money can you make? Well, that depends on several factors way beyond my control, but I do show you in this part how to project your profit by guesstimating the final sales price, subtracting expenses, and accounting for the unexpected. In addition, I offer advice on how to convince lenders and other generous people to give (or at least loan) you some money to get started and how to keep more of your money by taking full advantage of several legitimate tax breaks. After you master the mundane money matters, you can begin to focus on more entertaining activities associated with flipping — buying, fixing, and selling properties.

Chapter 5

Guesstimating Your Potential Profit

Whether you're dealing in antiques, collectibles, or houses, the trick to making a profit is no secret — know the cost of the item and how much you can sell it for *before* you buy it.

When you're flipping houses, the formula becomes a little more complex. You should have a pretty good estimate of how much you can get for the house after improvements, and then subtract the purchase price of the house and all expenses related to buying, owning, rehabbing, marketing, and selling the property. The chunk of change that remains is your gross profit — in IRS parlance, your *capital gains* or in some cases your *ordinary income*. Subtract any taxes due, and the rest is yours to keep . . . or invest in your next house flipping venture.

This chapter gives you what you need to answer the big question you face every time you're about to make an offer on a property: How much money will I make flipping this house?

Knowledge is power. Only by knowing how much you can get for the house, how much it costs, and how much fixing it up and selling it costs can you determine whether the purchase is worth your investment of money, time, and aggravation. Chapter 2 has more information to help you gauge whether flipping is right for you.

Making Money in Any Market

The housing market, like the stock market, fluctuates. Home values can steam ahead, stay put, or spiral down out of control. You make your money when you buy a house at less than market value. By adjusting your purchase price based on market conditions, thus lowering your total investment in a property, you can make money in any market. The following list offers some general guidelines for gauging your total investment in the three main types of housing markets:

- ✔ **Increasing:** When home values are rising, your total investment in the property, including the purchase price, closing costs, renovation costs, holding costs, and selling costs, shouldn't exceed 80 percent of its estimated resale value (I cover resale values later in this chapter).

- ✔ **Flat:** When home values are steady, limit your total investment in the property to 70 to 75 percent of the estimated resale value.

- ✔ **Decreasing:** When homes in the area are decreasing in value, invest no more than 60 to 65 percent of the property's estimated resale value.

For example, to flip a house you expect to sell for $200,000 in a flat market, you may buy the house for $120,000, spend $20,000 fixing it up, and use $10,000 for other expenses (such as mortgage payments, insurance, utilities, selling costs, and unexpected bills). Your total investment is $150,000, which is 75 percent of the estimated resale value. In an increasing market, you can invest a maximum of $160,000 (80 percent of $200,000) in the property. In a decreasing market, you can invest a maximum of only $130,000 (65 percent of $200,000) in the property. After you decide how much you can afford to invest overall, adjust the purchase price accordingly. Don't expect to make up the difference in your other expenses (including renovation and holding costs).

On their surface, these numbers suggest that you stand to make more in a declining market. You invest a maximum of $130,000 in the hopes of selling the house for $200,000, but in a declining market, you can't count on selling the house for $200,000. You may have to drop the price to $180,000 or less to price it competitively. By adjusting the total investment down in a down market, you simply reduce your exposure to risk.

In any market, you want to earn at least a 20 percent profit for your time and effort.

Don't let a slow market slow you down. If you see a gaggle of homes for sale with recently reduced asking prices, the market in that particular neighborhood may be starting to soften. This softening may signal a great buying opportunity, but you need to re-evaluate your resale estimate as well. Head to Chapter 8 for more details on determining the type of real estate market that any given neighborhood is in.

Ballparking a Realistic Resale Value

You start house hunting by looking at neighborhoods and houses in your price range (see Part III for the scoop on house hunting). When you're guesstimating profits, though, you start your journey at the end by determining a realistic ballpark figure for the home's resale value after improvements. The key term here is *realistic*. Overestimating the resale value of the house can be as devastating as discovering termites in the floorboards; it can cause you to overpay for a house and almost guarantee a financial fiasco.

To estimate a realistic resale value for a house, imagine the house all fixed up and then research the actual sales prices of comparable homes that have recently sold in the same neighborhood. Assuming that you're comparing apples to apples — this house to comparable homes in the same area with the same amenities — you should come away with an accurate estimate. What if the market takes a nose dive? By following the guidelines in the previous section, you're already taking into account potential market fluctuations.

Your goal as a house flipper is to purchase the worst house on the street for the lowest price possible and convert it into the best-looking house on the street at the highest price the market can bear. Anything you can do to add WOW to the home, especially in terms of curbside appeal, can boost your bottom line.

Devilish devaluations

When you purchase a property, you get much more than a lot with a house on it — you get neighbors. I once purchased a home at a sheriff's sale and waited patiently through the redemption period, only to discover during the possession process that the house was haunted, and the local gossipmonger was determined to keep all passersby well informed.

The next-door neighbor wasn't about to relinquish her reporting job after I took possession. In fact, she stepped up her efforts to broadcast the news to anyone and everyone who looked at the house. Her intrusions completely undermined my marketing and sales efforts.

If this sort of intrusion happens to you, nip it in the bud. Better yet, become proactive in establishing positive relationships with your neighbors. Let them know that your intention is to rehab the property and improve the neighborhood, which ultimately increases the value of their homes. Invite your neighbors over for an open house, make light of any nasty rumors, and use the opportunity to highlight the main features of the house. In addition to helping you sell the home, positive neighbor relationships often generate future leads.

Estimating the resale value of a house can be tricky, because you may not know what you're getting into until you take possession. Houses have histories, and dramatic events, such as murders, suicides, and drug busts can give a house a bad rep, making it a tough sell. The only way to battle back is to shake off any of your own superstitions right away and put a positive spin on the property. Superstitions, as demonstrated in the nearby sidebar, can get into your head, muddle your thinking, and slash your bottom line.

Subtracting the Purchase Price and Closing Costs

Your biggest financial outlay in any house flip is the cost of acquiring the property — the purchase price and closing costs. Fortunately, these are the two items over which you have the most control. You're always free to walk away from a deal if the price exceeds your budget, and you can often negotiate to have the seller pay a portion of the closing costs.

Your maximum purchase price depends on several factors, including the estimated sales price, cost of renovations, and holding costs. When you complete the Profit Projector in the later section "Ka-Ching! Projecting Your Potential Gross Profit," you can tell immediately whether the purchase price is too high for your budget, and you can adjust your offer accordingly. For now, you can determine a ballpark maximum purchase price by completing the following formula:

Estimated Sales Price:	$_____
Closing Costs:	- $_____
Renovation Costs:	- $_____
Holding Costs:	- $_____
Costs to Sell:	- $_____
Maximum Purchase Price:	= $_____

Set a minimum offer and maximum purchase price. Use the maximum purchase price in your calculations to give yourself additional wiggle room.

Next, subtract the estimated closing costs. Your real estate agent, lending institution, or title company can provide a detailed estimate of closing costs, which, if you're taking out a typical loan to finance the purchase, typically include the following items:

✔ **Loan origination fee:** If you finance the purchase through a bank or other lending institution, it may charge a fee for establishing the loan. (See Chapter 6 for more details about financing your purchase.)

✔ **Discount points:** Some lending institutions charge discount points — a percentage of the total amount borrowed — to provide you with a lower interest rate or wring another few hundred (or thousand) bucks out of you.

Avoid loans with discount points. You usually have to hold a property for several years to justify the monthly savings, and when you're flipping houses, holding a property for several years isn't your goal.

✔ **Appraisal fee:** The lending institution charges you this fee to have an appraiser ensure that the property is worth at least the amount you're borrowing to purchase it. (See Chapter 11 for more about appraisals.)

✔ **Title insurance:** Even if you researched the title or hired a title company to do it for you (see Chapter 4), the bank may require you pay for title insurance or a mortgage policy (sometimes called a mortgagee policy).

✔ **Insurance and taxes:** If you take out a loan that requires you to pay taxes and insurance out of an escrow account, you may need to pay a prorated share of insurance and taxes upfront.

✔ **Deed recording fee:** Whenever a property changes hands, the name on the deed changes and must be recorded. Yes, you're charged for this, too.

✔ **Credit report charge:** The lending institution does a financial background check on you called a *credit report* and then charges you for the privilege. (See Chapter 6 for details about credit reports.)

✔ **Closing fee:** The title company typically charges a closing fee.

Most closing costs originate with the bank or other lending institution. By financing the purchase through the seller or with money from private investors, partners, friends, or family members, you can trim closing costs considerably. See Chapter 6 for details on these options.

Subtracting the Cost of Repairs and Renovations

Eager house flippers often underestimate the cost of repairs and renovations. They're so enthusiastic about purchasing the house, selling it, and counting their money that they forget how much a carpenter or plumber charges per hour and the cost of materials at the local hardware store. Repairs and renovations are costly, and if you wait until you take possession of the house before obtaining estimates, you're already too late.

If you're still interested in a house after you take a quick tour of it, do a second, more thorough inspection of the premises to determine the repairs and renovations you want to make. (See Chapter 10 for details on the process of inspecting a potential flip.) List all the repairs and improvements needed to bring the property in line with your projected resale price (which we cover earlier in this chapter). Estimate the cost of repairs by doing the following:

- ✔ Flag any repairs you can do yourself. These are zero-labor repairs, but you may need to visit your local hardware store to check out prices for materials.

- ✔ Ask a member of your team who has more experience with construction projects to walk through the house with you and offer estimates and advice. (See Chapter 4 for details on building your flipping team.) To prevent the negativity of naysayers from undermining your vision, keep in mind that you're taking the risk and making the final decisions.

- ✔ Call one or two local contractors to obtain ballpark estimates for any repairs or improvements you can't do yourself. You may be able to hire a general contractor to walk through the house with you and provide a professional opinion.

If you can't look at the wiring in a house and come up with a pretty good guess at what it would cost to bring it up to code, you'd better consult somebody who can.

- ✔ Research estimated costs online. Contractors.com at `www.contractors.com` features a tool for estimating the costs of bathroom and kitchen renovations, room additions, decks, roofs, and other improvements. LetsRenovate.com at `www.letsrenovate.com` offers a toolbox packed with calculators for estimating the costs of repairs and renovations and the return you can expect on your investment.

Tally the estimated costs of repairs and renovations and multiply the total by 1.2 to add 20 percent for unexpected expenses.

You can trim the costs of repairs and renovations in several ways:

- ✔ Trade your services for free labor. Bartering (or trading services) may have tax consequences, so check with your accountant. Chapter 4 has info on finding an accountant to work with.

- ✔ Do some of the labor-intensive work yourself.

- ✔ Negotiate with the property owner to share the costs.

Chapter 13 has more details on planning and prioritizing your renovations, including tips on tagging do-it-yourself projects and knowing when to hire professionals for certain tasks. Chapter 23 is full of great tips on cutting your renovation costs.

Subtracting Your Holding Costs

As a homeowner, you're well aware of the monthly costs of owning a home, but when you first begin flipping properties, you tend to overlook the monthly expenses of holding onto the property, such as your house payment, homeowner's insurance, and property taxes. Reality hits after you've owned the property for four or five months and begin running out of cash. By then, your 20/20 hindsight leads only to panic and despair.

To keep the property, you need money to pay the mortgage, property taxes, and insurance. And if you plan on using any power tools on the premises, you'd better pay your electric bill, too (in addition to other utilities).

TIP

If you're using the home you're flipping as your primary residence, you can safely skip this section. For you, holding costs are actually *living expenses* — the normal amounts you pay to have a roof over your head.

TIP

A great way to project holding costs is to assume, on average, an amount of $100 a day. This amount works for most houses and provides for any surprises along the way. If it takes you a total of six months to flip a property (including rehab and resale time), total closing costs would break down as follows:

- $100 per day
- 6 months × 30 days per month = 180 days
- 180 days × $100 per day = $18,000 (in other words, $3,000 per month)

Of course, holding costs vary depending on several factors. To establish a more accurate estimate of your monthly holding costs, add your total estimated monthly bills for each of the following items:

- **Loan payments:** Mortgage payments and payments on any home equity loans you used to finance renovations comprise a significant chunk of your monthly holding costs.

- **Homeowner's insurance:** Ask your insurance agent for a quote and explain your plans, including whether or not you plan on living in the house, to properly insure the property. (A typical homeowner's policy allows for a home to be vacant only a certain number of days.)

- **Property taxes:** Set aside enough money per month to pay the property taxes when they're due. If you pay property taxes out of an escrow account, this amount may already be part of your mortgage payment.

- **Utilities:** Gas, electric, water, sewer, and trash bills are all part of your monthly holding costs. The seller should be able to provide averages for last year's bills.

- ✔ **Neighborhood association fees:** You may prepay these fees at closing and chalk them up as part of your closing fees, but if that's not the case, be sure to include them (if applicable) as part of your monthly fees.

- ✔ **Maintenance:** If you pay somebody for mowing the lawn, watching the house, and letting real estate agents inside to show the home, include this amount as part of your holding costs.

Err on the safe side. Budget sufficient funds to hold the house for three to six months beyond the date on which you expect to place the house back on the market. Few experiences are more demoralizing than renovating a house and then losing it in foreclosure because you underestimated your holding costs and can't make the monthly payments.

Holding costs can be a great motivator in completing the project on schedule. The faster you flip, the less you pay in holding costs.

Subtracting the Cost of Selling the House

When you place your rehabbed house back on the market, you incur additional expenses for marketing the house before you sell it and selling the house when you close the deal. These costs vary depending on whether you sell the home yourself or through a real estate agent:

- ✔ **Agent fees:** Attempting to sell your home without the help of a real estate agent can backfire, drastically restricting your number of potential buyers. Even if you choose not to use an agent, the agents hired by prospective buyers may not show your home unless they can get their 3 percent cut at the time of sale. Count on paying 3 to 7 percent of the sales price in agent fees. If you don't use an agent, add $250 to $1,000 for attorney fees.

- ✔ **Marketing fees:** If you choose to sell the home yourself, you can count on investing 1 to 2 percent of your list price in marketing fees. Whether you list your home in the classifieds or on a For Sale By Owner (FSBO) Web site, you pay for advertising. You also need a few bucks for a For Sale sign and for finger foods for your open house. (See Chapter 19 for more about marketing and Chapter 20 for more about staging and showing the house.)

- ✔ **Home warranty:** Supplying a warranty for the house can make it an attractive deal while protecting you against any lawsuits in the event that some undiscovered defect in the property rears its ugly head after the sale. If you decide to offer a warranty, budget enough to cover its cost. A typical home warranty costs between $300 and $500.

✔ **Closing fees:** A title company typically manages the closing and charges $150 or more for the service. Ask your title company for a more specific estimate.

✔ **Title insurance:** Insuring the title ensures that you're not liable for any hidden liens against the property. Title insurance can cost hundreds of dollars, so shop around for the best price and service. You can trim this cost by asking the seller to pay for the owner's policy of title insurance.

✔ **Deed preparation:** The cost of preparing the deed usually goes to the seller and is typically about 50 bucks.

✔ **Transfer tax:** Your state, city, or town may levy a transfer tax on the exchange of property. The amount varies depending on your location, so consult your accountant.

✔ **Delinquent water bills or tax bills:** At closing, you must pay any water bills or tax bills that are in *arrears* (overdue or unpaid).

Don't list your house while you're rehabbing it, but feel free to talk to people during this time and pass out your business cards. If a buyer falls into your lap through your neighborhood contacts, contact a real estate agent or attorney to complete the transaction. Check out Chapter 21 for more details about negotiating the sale of your rehabbed house.

Ka-Ching! Projecting Your Potential Gross Profit

As you gather estimates for each item related to purchasing, rehabbing, holding, and selling the house, complete the Profit Projector form shown in Figure 5-1.

To complete the Profit Projector, jot down the property's address, its estimated resale price, the maximum price you can afford to pay for the property (and still turn a profit), estimated closing costs, the cost of repairs, monthly and total holding costs, and the estimated expenses for marketing and selling the house (including agent commissions). These calculations determine your gross profit from which you can subtract your estimated taxes to determine your net profit (see the following section).

If your gross profit is less than 20 percent (or 25 percent in a flat market or 35 percent in a declining market) of your total investment in the property, you may need to lower your purchase price or simply pass on the property. Don't raise your estimated sales price just to make the numbers work — this approach has led to the ruin of many a poor house flipper by leading them into the trap of paying too much for a property.

Profit Projector

Property Address: _____

Estimated Resale Price		$_____
Maximum Purchase Price		$_____

Estimated Closing Costs

	Cost	$_____
_____	Cost	$_____
_____	Cost	$_____
_____	Cost	$_____
_____	Cost	$_____
_____	Cost	$_____

Total Closing Costs	$_____

Estimated Repairs

	Cost	$_____
_____	Cost	$_____
_____	Cost	$_____
_____	Cost	$_____
_____	Cost	$_____
_____	Cost	$_____
_____	Cost	$_____

Subtotal Repairs	$_____

Subtotal Repairs x 1.2 (for 20 percent unexpected costs)	**Total Repairs**	$_____

Monthly Holding Costs

	Cost	$_____
_____	Cost	$_____
_____	Cost	$_____
_____	Cost	$_____
_____	Cost	$_____

Total Monthly Holding Costs	$_____

Months to Hold	**Months**	_____

Monthly Holding Costs x Number of Months	**Total Holding Costs**	$_____

Cost of Marketing and Selling Property	**Sales Cost**	$_____

Estimated Gross Profit (Resale Price - Purchase Price - Total Closing Costs - Total Repairs - Total Holding Costs - Sales Cost)	**Gross Profit**	$_____

Taxes on Profit	**Taxes**	$_____

Net Profit (Gross Profit - Taxes)	**Net Profit**	$_____

Figure 5-1:
This Profit Projector is a handy tool to figure out your potential profit on a flip.

After doing the math, estimate the number of hours you intend to work on the project and divide that into the projected profit to determine your hourly pay rate. If you can make more by taking on a second job at a fast food restaurant, this house probably isn't worth the time and effort you would put into it. Keep looking. Repeat the exercise after completing the project to determine your actual hourly rate. You may discover that flipping burgers is more lucrative and less aggravating for you than flipping houses. . . at least nobody ever lost money flipping burgers.

Subtracting Uncle Sam's Cut (in Some Cases) to Get Your Net Profit

The taxes you owe on the profit you make from flipping houses are ambiguous at best. Of course, you pay taxes only on the money that remains after expenses, but the percentage you owe on your profit varies depending on several factors:

✔ If you flip your primary residence in which you lived two of the past five years and you earn $250,000 or less ($500,000 or less for a couple), you walk away with your entire profit scot-free, at least according to the tax laws that were in effect when I was writing this book.

✔ Owning the investment property for at least one year and one day qualifies your profit as a *long-term capital gain,* taxable at a rate of 15 percent. *Long-term* is longer than one year plus one day. *Capital gain* is whatever you make on the sale of an asset that has increased in value.

✔ Owning the investment property for less than one year and one day qualifies your profit as a *short-term capital gain,* taxable at the rate you normally pay in income tax.

✔ If you flip houses for a living, the IRS considers flipping to be your career and considers profits to be your income, subject to income tax. You may find yourself paying 35 percent or more in taxes!

✔ If you lease the property, any income you receive from the rental, minus the cost of owning and maintaining the property is considered ordinary income taxed at the rate you normally pay in income tax.

The tax figures provided here are accurate during the writing of this book, but tax rules can change at any time. Consult your accountant for accurate estimates on the amount of taxes you can expect to owe on your profits.

House flippers often boast about how much they make flipping properties, but the real measure of success is not your gross profit but your net profit — how much you get to keep *after taxes*. To determine your net profit, simply subtract your taxes from your gross profit. Chapter 7 discusses tax issues in greater depth and offers techniques for trimming your taxes to keep more of your earnings and boost your net profit.

Chapter 6

Securing the Funds to Fuel Your Flip

Flipping houses is an expensive habit. You need money — *investment capital* — to finance the purchase of a house, perform renovations, pay the utilities and taxes, sell the home, and cover your living expenses while you're hard at work. The good news is that it doesn't all have to be *your* money. You can borrow against the equity in your home, hunt for the best loan, finance the purchase of the house through the seller, and even find eager investors who are willing to finance your venture in exchange for your expertise and sweat.

Lining up financial resources in advance of your house hunting enables you to pounce on a bargain and gives you leverage in negotiating the price you ultimately pay for a property. When you place an offer on a house and other bids come in, the seller may accept your offer of thousands of dollars less, simply because you have the financing in place to quickly close the deal. Ready cash also frees you to plan and begin rehabbing the property immediately rather than waiting around for sluggish loan approvals and credit checks.

Lining up financing can never be done too soon, and it's something you should continue to work on. Always be on the lookout for additional sources of investment capital — cheaper money that's more readily available.

If you're thinking that you can't possibly get your mitts on enough cash to finance your house flipping venture, this is the chapter for you. Here you find out what you're really worth — financially speaking, of course — and investigate the myriad sources of house flipping investment capital.

Grasping the Power of Working with Borrowed Money

Some people have a natural aversion to debt for good reason — you can afford less stuff if you have to pay interest on it. As a house flipper, however, you quickly find out that debt can be either good or bad. *Bad debt* is any money you borrow to purchase something fleeting that leaves you with "nothing to show for it," such as a boat, a vacation to Bali, or a pair of designer shoes. *Good debt* consists of money you borrow to acquire items that increase in value at a rate that exceeds the interest you pay on that debt.

As a real estate investor, good debt gives you *leverage*. It enables you to use other people's money to make money. Sure, borrowing money means you have to pay interest, and it carries some risks (if you don't turn a profit, you stand to lose money), but if you do everything right, you stand to earn considerably more than what the loan costs you in interest.

With house flipping, your goal is to move as much house as you can with as little of your own money as possible. If you invest $100,000 of your own money in a property, for example, and you flip it for a profit of $20,000, you make a 20 percent profit on your $100,000 investment. On the other hand, if you invest $20,000, borrow $80,000, and flip the property for a profit of $20,000 ($20,000 more than your investment), you earn a 100 percent profit.

To look at it another way, say that you have $100,000 to invest. Many people assume that using that $100,000 to finance a single flip is the smart thing to do, because you avoid paying interest on borrowed money. However, by leveraging that $100,000 with borrowed money, you stand to earn a bigger profit. For example, you can combine that $100,000 with borrowed money to flip a higher-priced property — perhaps a $500,000 house that you know you can sell in the $575,000 to $600,000 range.

Borrowing money is always risky, but you have to take some risk to earn the big bucks. Throughout this book, I show you ways to reduce the risk, but unforeseen events can undermine the best laid plans. As a flipper, you need to decide for yourself whether the potential benefits outweigh the risks.

The following sections show you how to gain leverage by using other people's money to finance your flips. And if you don't have money, I show you how to convince private lenders to put up some initial investment capital to get you started.

Unleashing the Equity of Your Current Home

Your home is more than just a place to live — it's an investment, perhaps the best-performing investment you have. As you pay down the principal on the mortgage and as the house appreciates, equity in the home grows. *Equity* is your home's net worth — if you sold the home today and paid off the mortgage, equity is the money you stuff in your pocket.

You don't have to sell your home to pocket the equity. By refinancing the home or taking out a home equity loan, you can unleash the equity and use it (or a portion of it) as investment capital to finance your house flipping venture. I cover both of these options, along with the risks of unleashing equity in your home, in the following sections. Further on in this chapter, I show you how to work with banks and other lending institutions to unlock the equity in your home.

You don't have to tap into the equity in your home to flip houses. Tapping into your equity can place your home at risk, and if you and your spouse both sign the loan documents, you're both at risk. If you're uncomfortable placing your home and other positions at risk, consider borrowing *hard money* — high-interest loans that typically require an upfront payment and scheduled balloon (lump-sum) payments. Hard money loans often finance the purchase of the property along with the cash needed to repair and renovate the property. The property and any future improvements function as collateral for the loan. Banks, mortgage companies, other lending institutions, and private lenders often offer hard money loans. The drawback is that hard money isn't cheap — lenders may charge two to three times as much in interest as banks and other lending institutions along with 3 to 10 percent in closing costs.

Recognizing the risks

In many ways, equity is funny money . . . or fuzzy money. Nobody really knows how much you can sell your home for until you actually sell it, so borrowing against equity is a bit risky. Before taking the leap, be well aware of the risks:

- ✔ If real estate values drop, you may owe more on your home than it's worth.

- ✔ Unlike other types of loans, mortgage and home equity loans use your home as collateral. If you can't afford the higher house payments on your new loan, you can lose your home.

✔ If interest rates rise, refinancing at a higher rate or for a longer term results in your paying more for your current home — potentially tens of thousands of dollars more.

✔ Frequent refinancing can cost you thousands in *closing costs* that may take you years to recoup.

Refinancing your mortgage

The easiest way to unlock a chunk of equity is to refinance your home, giving you a whole new mortgage, paying off the old mortgage, and leaving you the rest. (I cover the basics of mortgages in the later section "Winding your way through the mortgage maze.") Ideally, you refinance a mortgage not only to cash out equity for investment capital but also to snag a lower interest rate or shorter term.

Suppose, for example, that you currently have a $200,000, 30-year mortgage at 8 percent with a monthly house payment of $1,467.53. You've owned the house for 10 years and still owe $175,000 on the mortgage. If you refinance for $250,000 (the home's current appraised value) and take out a 20-year mortgage at 6 percent, now you have a house payment of $1,791.08 and you walk away with the $75,000 equity that was locked up in the house (the refinanced amount of $250,000 minus the $175,000 to pay off the old mortgage) to use as investment capital.

Well, that certainly looks pretty rosy, but what have you lost in the transaction?

✔ You now owe $250,000 on your home and have no equity built up in it.

✔ Your new house payment is $323 more than your previous house payment.

✔ Over the life of the loan, you're scheduled to pay $77,651 more than you would have paid by sticking with your original mortgage.

In short, you're pretty much getting money now and paying it later. But think of it this way — by putting your equity to work for you in successful flips, you can eventually profit enough to pay off your mortgage in much less time. If you can make ten times what it cost you, you earn $750,000 by putting your equity to work for you.

Of course, you don't have to unleash all the equity in your home. To build on the previous example, you could take out a 20-year, $225,000 loan at 6 percent, with a monthly payment of $1,611.97, freeing up $50,000 in equity or a 20-year, $200,000 loan at 6 percent with a monthly payment of $1,432.86, freeing up $25,000 in equity. Your choice depends primarily on your comfort level and risk and debt tolerance. The more equity you leave in the house, the greater your cushion, but the less investment capital you have to work with.

Lending institutions often order their own appraisals, which can be somewhat inflated so that they can loan you more money. Don't borrow more than the current market value of your home, no matter what the appraiser and loan officer tell you. Other caveats about refinancing include the following:

- ✔ Don't refinance into a loan that has a prepayment penalty.
- ✔ Don't refinance if you have to roll the closing costs into your new mortgage — thus increasing the principal.
- ✔ Don't refinance a fixed-rate mortgage into a new adjustable-rate mortgage.

Taking out a second mortgage with home equity loans and lines of credit

Taking out a second mortgage, in the form of a home equity loan or line of credit, unlocks the equity in your home without affecting your current mortgage:

- ✔ A *home equity loan* provides you with a single chunk of money — a one-time payment to you. Lenders may not charge closing costs on home equity loans. Some banks even pay for the credit report and appraisal.
- ✔ A *home equity line of credit* enables you to borrow only what you need and pay interest on only what you borrow, making this option attractive for financing renovations. It's sort of like a credit card line of credit, often with a lower interest rate.

Home equity loans and lines of credit often come with adjustable interest rates, which carry additional risks, as I explain later in the section "Riding the waves with an adjustable-rate mortgage."

A second mortgage separate from your first mortgage may be a better financial choice in the following situations:

- ✔ The interest rate on your first mortgage is low compared to current interest rates. Refinancing a home at 8 percent when you already have a loan at 4.5 percent is usually a poor choice.
- ✔ You've been paying on your first mortgage for several years. With every payment you make, you pay more on principal and less on interest, so if you've been paying 15 years on a 30-year mortgage, refinancing now may cost you in the long run.
- ✔ You can quickly flip the property you're investing in and pay off the second mortgage. Assuming the loan has no early-payment penalty, if you can unlock the equity in your home and then quickly pay back the money, you retain your home's equity.

Home equity loans are almost always preferable to taking out a second mortgage, assuming you can get a low-cost, low-interest, fixed-rate loan, because they're reusable. That is, after you pay off the loan, you can usually take it out again at the same rate. That's something you can't do with a second mortgage.

Making Yourself Look Good to Prospective Lenders

After you establish yourself as a successful house flipper, private investors will stuff your pockets with cash, because you have a proven track record. Until then, you better look good on paper. That means you have to have money in the bank, investments, or assets that you can sell. It means you pay your bills on time. It means you're not so heavily burdened by debt that one more loan is likely to push you into bankruptcy.

Before you begin flipping houses, examine your financial position as carefully as any lender would examine it. Pretend that you're the lender. Would you loan yourself the money? Lenders look at your four C's: Collateral, Character, Credit, and Confidence:

- ✔ **Collateral** is the property you intend to purchase. When you're flipping houses and attempting to obtain loan approval before looking at houses, you're not in a position to describe the collateral, but you can put together a plan that shows the price ranges of the houses you intend to purchase, appreciation percentages for the area, and how you plan to renovate and sell the properties for a profit. See "Pitching your plan" later in this chapter.

- ✔ **Character** is the way you present yourself to the lender. You need to convince the lender that you have the knowledge and resources available to profit from your investments. A strong plan and presentation can convince the lender that you have the right stuff.

- ✔ **Credit** is your credit report and credit score. A clean credit report shows that you pay your bills and aren't over your head in debt. See "Checking and correcting your credit score," later in this section.

- ✔ **Confidence** is the confidence you and the lender have that you can deliver what you promise. Pitching a solid plan can build the lender's confidence.

The following sections take a snapshot of your financial picture and highlight the details that lenders commonly consider before approving a loan. By identifying areas of improvement, you can airbrush out any imperfections to make yourself look as good as possible to prospective lenders.

Determining what you're worth in dollars and cents

Net worth is simply whatever money you would have if you sold all your stuff and then paid off all your debts, including your taxes. Officially, the equation goes like this:

Net Worth = Assets – Liabilities – Taxes

A strong positive net worth indicates that you:

- Own more than you owe.
- Don't borrow more than you can pay for.
- Can pay off a loan by liquidating assets, if needed.
- Pay your taxes on time.
- Probably know more about net worth than you realize.

To prove to a lender that you're net worthy, type up a page that lists your assets and liabilities and presents your net worth. The following section shows you how to calculate your net worth. If you have a spreadsheet program or a personal finance program, such as Quicken, you can use the program to do the math for you.

A strong net worth can help you borrow money at competitive interest rates, but a low or even a negative net worth is not a death knell. If you have a solid investment strategy and the energy and commitment to implement it, you can secure the capital you need to get started. See "Pitching your plan" later in this chapter for tips on how to prove to a lender that you have a solid investment strategy.

The following sections explain how to calculate and boost your net worth.

Tabulating your net worth

Nobody has much trouble subtracting liabilities from assets to determine their net worth. The tough part is identifying assets and liabilities. First, jot down a list of everything you own, including cash, savings, and investments. The following list of items may stimulate your brain cells:

- **Home:** If you sold your home today, what could you get for it? If you recently had an appraisal, use that number, assuming the appraiser assigned it an honest value. (See Chapter 11 for more about appraisals.)
- **Car:** The bluebook value (current value), not what you paid for it.

- ✔ **Savings account:** Whether you have $5 or $50,000, it counts.

- ✔ **Checking account:** The current balance as recorded in your check register. No cheating. If you just wrote five checks that haven't cleared yet, you don't really have that money.

- ✔ **Retirement savings:** 401(k), IRA, SEP, or other account that you don't dip into for your daily living expenses.

- ✔ **Investments:** Stocks, bonds, and mutual funds that aren't part of a retirement account.

- ✔ **Jewelry, antiques, and artwork:** If you're not sure what this stuff is worth, have it professionally appraised and insured. People often think that their stuff is worth much more than it really is.

- ✔ **Furniture:** If you sold all your furniture at an auction or garage sale, what could you get for it?

- ✔ **Cash value of life insurance:** If you have term life insurance, that would be $0. If you use a life insurance policy as an investment, how much is it worth today?

If you don't have it, don't count it. The money you stand to inherit when Aunt Millie kicks the bucket doesn't count.

Now for the painful part. Jot down a list of liabilities, such as the following:

- ✔ **Mortgage principal:** The amount you owe on your house today and on any other loans you've taken out on the house.

- ✔ **Car loan:** How much would it cost to pay off your car loan today? Write it down.

- ✔ **Student loans:** If you're paying off any student loans from your old college days or are named as a co-signer on any of your kids' student loans, record the amounts as liabilities.

- ✔ **Credit card debt:** Dig out your credit card bills and tally up the total you currently owe on them.

- ✔ **Taxes owed:** Do you owe any back taxes or property taxes? Total the amount.

- ✔ **Personal loans:** Did you borrow $5 from the neighbor to buy candy from the neighborhood kids? Write it down.

You can get most of the liability information you need from your credit report, as I discuss later in this chapter in the section "Checking and correcting your credit report." However, if you know that you have a debt that doesn't appear on the credit report, be sure to include it in your calculations.

Chapter 6: Securing the Funds to Fuel Your Flip **87**

Now, add up your assets, subtract your liabilities, subtract any back taxes you owe, and the next time someone asks, "What's your net worth?" you're prepared to answer.

Boosting your net worth

As a general rule, net worth grows about as fast as an oak tree. Unless you score big in the lottery or inherit a couple hundred thousand dollars, you can do little to jack up your net worth in a hurry. By becoming fiscally responsible, living within your means, and paying down credit card debt, however, you can improve your net worth over time.

Some companies can set you up with phony savings accounts and lease assets to you to make you look like Ritchie Rich, so you can qualify for loans you can't qualify for legitimately. Don't get sucked into asset rental scams. You can end up in jail. Boost your net worth the old fashioned way — earn it.

Checking and correcting your credit report

Good credit is gold. Without it, you have access only to your money. With it, you can put other people's money to work for you. Whenever you apply for a loan, the lending institution performs a *credit check* — sort of a background check to make sure that you're not up to your gills in debt, that your income covers expenses, and that you pay your bills on time.

To ensure success at obtaining loans, become proactive. Check your credit report every three months or so, correct any errors, and take steps to improve your credit rating, as instructed in the following sections. No irregularity is too small to correct.

The following sections show you how to obtain, review, and correct your credit report. I also explain how to improve your credit score.

Obtaining a credit report

As of September 1, 2005, the Federal Trade Commission has made it mandatory for the three major credit reporting companies to provide you with a free credit report once every 12 months. To obtain your free credit report, do one of the following:

- Submit your request online at www.annualcreditreport.com.
- Phone in your request by calling toll-free 877-322-8228.
- Download the Annual Credit Report Request Form from www.annualcreditreport.com/cra/requestformfinal.pdf, fill it out, and mail it to Annual Credit Report Request Service, P.O. Box 105281, Atlanta, GA 30348-5281.

If you already obtained a free credit report this year and want something more recent, you can order a credit report for less than ten bucks from any of the following three credit report agencies:

- ✔ **Equifax:** 800-685-1111 or online at www.equifax.com.
- ✔ **Experian:** 888-397-3742 or online at www.experian.com.
- ✔ **TransUnion:** 800-916-8800 or online at www.transunion.com.

Inspecting your credit report

When you receive your credit report, inspect it carefully for the following red flags:

- ✔ Addresses of places you've never lived.
- ✔ Aliases you've never used, which may indicate that someone else is using your social security number or the credit reporting agency has mixed someone else's data into yours.
- ✔ Multiple social security numbers, flagging the possibility that information for someone with the same name has made it into your credit report.
- ✔ Wrong date of birth (DOB).
- ✔ Credit cards you don't have.
- ✔ Loans you haven't taken out.
- ✔ Records of unpaid bills that you either know you paid or have good reason for not paying.
- ✔ Records of delinquent payments that weren't delinquent or you have a good excuse for not paying on time.
- ✔ Inquiries from companies with whom you've never done business. (When you apply for a loan, the lender typically runs an *inquiry* on your credit report, and that shows up on the report.)

An address of a place you've never lived or records of accounts, loans, and credit cards you never had may be a sign that somebody has stolen your identity. Yikes! Contact the credit reporting company immediately and request that a fraud alert be placed on your credit report. For tips on protecting yourself against identity theft and recovering from it, check out *Preventing Identity Theft For Dummies* by Michael J. Arata, Jr. (Wiley).

Last but certainly not least: Your credit report should contain your credit score. If it doesn't, contact the credit reporting agency and request your score.

Understanding what your credit score means

To give your credit rating an air of objectivity, credit reporting agencies often assign you a credit score that ranges roughly between 300 (you never paid a bill in your life) and 900 (you borrow often, always pay your bills on time, and don't carry any huge balances on your credit cards).

Your credit score determines not only whether you qualify for a loan but also how much you're qualified to borrow and at what interest rate. A high credit score lets you borrow more and pay less interest on it. A high score can also lower your home and auto insurance rates — just another reason why the rich get richer and the poor stay poor.

Cranking up your credit score

If you have a credit score of 700 or higher, pat yourself on the back. You're above average and certainly qualified to borrow big bucks at the lowest available rates. Anything below about 680 sounds the warning sirens. This number is the point at which lending institutions get out their magnifying glasses and begin raising rates and denying credit. If your credit rating dips below 700, take steps to improve it, such as the following:

✔ Dispute any erroneous items on your credit report. Disputing a claim doesn't always result in a correction, but you can request to have a paragraph explaining your side of the story added to your report.

✔ Apply for fewer loans and credit cards. When you apply for a loan or credit card, the lending institution typically orders an inquiry that shows up on your credit report. Evidence that you're applying for several loans or credit cards in a short period of time can make you appear financially desperate.

✔ Pay off your credit card balances or at least pay off enough so the balance is 50 percent or below your available credit limit. If you have enough equity in your home, you can refinance to consolidate high-interest credit card bills into your mortgage payment, but avoid the temptation to begin racking up more credit card debt after refinancing. (I cover refinancing your mortgage earlier in this chapter.)

Avoid credit enhancement companies on the Web that claim to provide seasoned credit within 90 days. Law enforcement authorities are shutting down these sites on a regular basis. Legitimate credit counselors can help you repair your damaged credit, but it takes some work and a little belt-tightening. Quick fixes are typically fraudulent fixes.

For additional tips on boosting your credit score, check out *Credit Repair Kit For Dummies* by Stephen R. Bucci and Terry Savage (Wiley).

Credit score stats

Credit reporting agencies rely on one or more statistical models to determine your credit score. One of the most popular models is the Fair Isaac Company (FICO) rating system. The credit company assigns numerical values to particular pieces of data in your credit history, such as the length of your credit history and the various types of interest you're paying. They then plug these numbers into the statistical model, which spits out your credit score. It's basically a numbers game that weighs the data on your credit report in the following manner:

✔ 35 percent of the score is based on payment history

✔ 30 percent is based on outstanding debt or how much you currently owe

✔ 15 percent is based on the length of your credit history or how long you've been borrowing

✔ 10 percent is based on recent inquiries on your report (whenever a lending institution requests a report)

✔ 10 percent is based on the types of credit, such as mortgage or credit card interest

Avoiding mistakes that can sabotage your loan approval

After you apply for a loan, resist the urge to make any life-changing decisions that negatively affect your current financial status. Major changes can undermine your efforts to secure a loan, so follow some sage advice:

✔ Stay married.

✔ Don't apply for other loans or credit cards.

✔ Avoid buying big-ticket items.

✔ Don't make any major purchases on credit.

✔ Don't co-sign for any loans.

✔ Don't withdraw or move substantial amounts of cash.

✔ Pay your bills on time.

To simplify the loan process, supply your lender with copies of your last three bank statements and last three federal tax returns.

If your financial situation changes between the application and the time of closing, you are legally obligated to inform the loan officer and lender of the change.

Bargain Hunting for Low-Interest Loans

When money is readily available and you have a credit score in the mid- to upper-700s, lending institutions trip over themselves to win your business by offering bigger loans at lower interest rates. By shopping around and haggling a little, you can often convince a lending institution to loan you money at a rate lower than advertised.

Smart shoppers are well aware of the market and the various factors that make one loan more attractive than another. The following sections bring you up to speed on mortgage-speak, show you where to look for the best deals, and help you compare loans that appear to be similar but can be drastically different. For the full scoop on mortgages, be sure to check out *Mortgages For Dummies,* 2nd Edition, by Eric Tyson, MBA, and Ray Brown (Wiley).

Winding your way through the mortgage maze

Before you start loan hunting, brush up on the five main types of loans that I cover in the following sections: fixed-rate, adjustable, interest-only, balloon-payment, and minimum-payment. Although one loan type isn't necessarily better or worse, each has unique characteristics that make it better suited for a particular house flipping strategy (I cover these strategies in Chapter 3).

When financing a flip, having access to cash is the most important consideration, followed closely by the cost of the money. Ask yourself:

- ✔ Can I afford the payment?
- ✔ Are the rates reasonable?
- ✔ Will I be able to make a profit in the end?

Holding steady with fixed-rate mortgages

A fixed-rate mortgage is a loan whose interest rate remains unchanged throughout the life of the loan. If you take out a 30-year loan at 6 percent today, you still pay 6 percent interest 25 years down the road. Fixed-rate mortgages are most attractive under the following conditions:

- ✔ Interest rates are low.
- ✔ Your house flipping strategy hinges on holding the property for several years.
- ✔ You expect interest rates to rise suddenly in the next few years.

For quick flips of one year or less, the benefits of a fixed-rate mortgage are typically negligible. If you're a buy-and-hold-'er, fixed-rate is probably the way to go. If you're doing a quick flip and have the stomach for a bit more risk, an adjustable-rate, interest-only, or minimum payment mortgage may be a better choice, as I describe in the following sections.

Riding the waves with an adjustable-rate mortgage

Adjustable rate mortgages (ARMs) have interest rates that fluctuate. You may take out a loan for 5 percent and find yourself paying 9 percent the following year. When shopping for adjustable-rate mortgages, examine the following factors to determine the worst-case scenario:

- **Initial interest rate:** The interest rate when you sign for the loan. This rate is usually lower than the rate for a fixed-rate mortgage (see the previous section).

- **Adjustment period:** The frequency at which the rate can go up or down. This period is typically 1, 3, or 5 years, but can be in months rather than years.

- **Index:** Adjustable-rate mortgages are tied to an index that typically rises or falls based on government lending rates. Ask which index the lender uses, how often it changes, and how it has performed in the past.

- **Margin:** The percentage above the index that the lender charges. Think of it as a markup. For example, if the index is at 3 percent and the margin is 2 percent, you pay 5 percent interest. If the index rises two percentage points to 5 percent, you pay 7 percent interest.

- **Cap:** The cap is the highest interest the lender charges, no matter how high the index rises. So, if the lender sets a lifetime cap at 9 percent, you never pay more than 9 percent interest. If the lender sets an adjustment period cap of 2 percent and the adjustment period is one year, the interest can rise a maximum of 2 percent each year. ARMs typically specify an adjustment period and a lifetime cap; for example, for an ARM with a cap of 2 and 6, the rate can jump a maximum of 2 percent per period but no higher than 6 percent over the life of the loan.

Don't dismiss an ARM just because you have an innate aversion to it. I often hear people say that they'd never take out an adjustable-rate mortgage because interest rates could skyrocket, but if you can get a lower rate with no early-payment penalty and know that you'll pay off the loan before the first adjustment period, an ARM can save you, well . . . an arm and a leg.

Don't bite when a bank dangles an unbelievably low-interest ARM in front of you. Lenders often use this marketing ploy to snag unwary borrowers and then hit them with huge interest rate increases a few months down the road. By knowing the adjustment period and lifetime caps, you have a clear idea of the worst-case scenario.

Paying later with interest-only loans

An interest-only loan is just what it sounds like; if you take out an interest-only loan for $100,000, in 2 years, you still owe $100,000. Sound like a bum deal? If you plan on living in your home for 15 years and the value of the home doesn't appreciate significantly, it may be a bum deal, but if you're using the loan for a quick flip, it may be perfect. You pay off the loan in full right after you sell the house. In the meantime, you have more investment capital for buying properties and financing renovations.

When considering interest-only loans, be aware of the following:

✔ Most interest-only loans are ARMs (see the previous section), so check the adjustment period, index, margin, and caps.

✔ Make sure the loan doesn't come with an early-payment penalty. You may be able to pay off the loan early by flipping quickly, but if you have a 3 percent early payment penalty, a $100,000 loan can cost you an additional $3,000.

✔ Rarely is an interest-only loan interest-only for the life of the loan. Read the fine print to determine when and how you must pay the principal. Some loans require a lump-sum payment three to five years down the road. They suck you in with low monthly payments early and then sock you with huge bills later.

Interest-only loans are great for quick flips or for homeowners who have jobs with wildly fluctuating monthly incomes, such as CEOs who receive fat seasonal bonuses and can pay off the principal in huge chunks. For the average homeowner, however, interest-only loans can be quite risky, especially in an inflated housing market.

Reducing interest with balloon payments

You can often find loans with lower interest by committing to pay off the principal after a fixed period of time with a *balloon payment* — a lump sum payment due at the end of the term. Balloon-payment loans are often acceptable for quick flips, especially if the balloon payment is scheduled to coincide with the sale of the house.

Don't commit to balloon payments if you have any doubts that you can make the payments — you may set yourself up for failure. If renovations take longer than scheduled and payment is due before you can sell the property, you may have to refinance or get another loan to cover the balloon payment. If you can't secure additional loans, you may lose the property.

Flexing your finances with minimum-payment loans

Minimum-payment or *reverse amortization* loans specify the absolute least you can pay each month. When you're strapped for cash, you pay just enough to cover the interest, and the principal remains unchanged. When you have a cash surplus, you can increase the payment to reduce the principal. When you're buried in bills, you can make the minimum payment, which doesn't quite cover the interest and increases the principal.

Minimum-payment loans aren't the most financially sound for the average homeowner, but they're attractive to flippers who need more flexibility in their financing. If you're running short on cash because renovations are running a little high, you can make the minimum payment and have more money to pay for renovations.

Playing the numbers game when you compare loans

When considering any type of loan, carefully examine interest rates and other factors to determine what's best overall and which loan is most suitable for your situation. An interest-only loan may offer lower monthly payments, but it may not be the best choice. A fixed-rate loan at a slightly higher interest rate may be better.

The best way to compare loans is to determine the total cost of the loan over the life of the loan:

1. **Start with the amount the bank charges you upfront in loan origination fees, discount points (interest you pay upfront, typically a percentage of the loan, to lower the interest rate), and other fees.**

2. **Multiply the monthly payment times the number of months you plan to pay on the loan.**

3. **Add the two amounts to determine your total payment.**

4. **Total the amount of each payment that goes toward paying the principal of the loan. (Your lender can tell you how much of each payment goes toward principal.)**

5. **Subtract the total you determined in Step 4 from the total in Step 3.**

Say that you're considering two loans, each for $100,000. You plan on using the loan to buy and renovate a home over two years and then sell it and pay off the remaining principal on the loan. You have a choice between a 30-year, fixed-rate mortgage at 6 percent or a 30-year interest-only loan at 5 percent. Look at the 6 percent, fixed-rate mortgage first:

Loan origination fee and discount points:	$1,000.00
Plus monthly payment of $599.55 × 24 months:	$14,389.20
Equals total payment:	$15,389.20
Minus total paid toward principal:	$2,531.75
Equals total cost of loan:	$12,857.45

Here are the numbers for the 30-year, interest-only loan at 5 percent:

Loan origination fee and discount points:	$1,000.00
Plus monthly payment of $416.67 × 24 months:	$10,000.08
Equals total payment:	$11,000.08
Minus total paid toward principal:	$0.00
Equal total cost of loan:	$11,000.08

If you're fixed on fixed-rate loans thinking that you're paying down the principal while you own the property, the numbers compel you to reconsider. With the fixed-rate mortgage, you're not only paying over $180 more every month, but by the time you sell the house, you've paid $1,800 more for the privilege of borrowing the money!

As a general rule for quick flips, opt for loans with low (or no) closing costs, low (or no) discount points, and low interest rates. Avoid any loans that have early-payment penalties.

Finding eager lenders online and off

To secure investment capital for flipping properties, you need to know where to look. Obvious sources, such as banks, may be a little reluctant to loan money to a novice for investing in real estate, so you may need to poke around a little to find willing lenders and investors. The following sections show you where to start looking. Your agent can also help steer you toward lenders.

Don't request quotes from more than a couple of lending institutions. When several lending institutions query your credit report in a short period of time, it shows up on your credit report and can lower your credit score and jeopardize your ability to qualify for a loan. Shop around first and then apply for a loan with only one or two lenders who offer the best rates and services.

Sticking close to home with local institutions

Small, local banks often run loan specials in an attempt to lure you into doing all your banking with them. But they may offer low-rate loans whether or not you open a checking or savings account with them. Check your local newspaper for ads, call around to four or five banks in the area to check out their loan offerings, or check with your current bank, which may offer an even better deal because you already have an account there.

If you have the choice, obtain your loan from a lender that doesn't sell its loans. Some smaller banks and mortgage brokers sell to larger, out-of-state banks, which can foul up the handling of your *escrow account* (the account from which the lender pays your taxes and insurance), resulting in unpaid property taxes and insurance.

Expanding your search through the Internet

You've probably seen those commercials in which a couple goes online to submit a request for quotes from various lenders. The lenders descend on the house like a flock of fawning suitors and grovel to win the couple's favor. Funny, yes, but realistic? Not quite. You still have to perform due diligence by checking the numbers, as I explain earlier in this chapter.

I recommend that you stay close to home when borrowing money to finance your flip, especially when you're first starting out. Local lenders are typically more motivated and capable of servicing your loan, and can work with you more effectively if something goes wrong.

Exploring Other Creative Financing Options

You have a credit score pushing the 500 mark, you just got divorced and your spouse got the house, you hate your day job, and house flipping, as you see it, is the only ticket out of tinsel town. You have the time, skills, and pent up angst to power a successful flip. You just need to get your mitts on some moolah. What do you do?

With the right attitude and a strong work ethic, you can hop on that train out of town by tracking down alternative sources of investment capital. The following sections show you where to start looking for your pot of gold.

Passing the hat among friends and family

Charity should begin at home. If you have a rich Uncle Jeb and Auntie Emily who have a stash of cash they're willing to invest, and you don't mind calling in some favors, hit them up for the money. With family members, you may be able to get a short-term, no-interest loan, assuming you're not considered the black sheep of the family.

Borrowing from a private investor

Lots of people have money to invest and are disenchanted with returns on their stocks and bonds. Convince them of your ability to turn a profit flipping properties, and they just might provide you with the investment capital you need to get started. I show you what to do in the following sections.

Loans from private investors often come in the form of hard money, as discussed earlier in this chapter.

Finding private investors

You can often locate private investors (or private lenders) through the newspaper, real estate agents, and mortgage brokers; by attending landlord meetings or investment seminars; or by joining a real estate investment group (I cover these groups later in this chapter) and doing a little networking. Most private investors loan money through mortgage brokers, because most states require that lenders be licensed.

Pitching your plan

Before approaching a private investor, do your homework and draw up a small business plan showing that you know what you're doing. Here are a few ideas on how to proceed:

- ✔ Show the investor a sample of a property that someone else recently flipped in the area — for example, a property that the person bought for $80,000 on August 8 and sold for $146,000 on November 16. Convince the investor through your knowledge and enthusiasm that you can do the same.

- ✔ Present a property you would purchase now if you had the money and explain how you would fix it up and sell it.

- ✔ Tie up a property on paper (either through a purchase agreement or an option to buy) and present this property as an opportunity. Sounds risky, but it often works, and it definitely forces you to find the money to close on the deal! (Your agent or attorney can help you acquire the necessary paperwork.)

If you're not comfortable drawing up a plan yourself, ask your agent and attorney for help. Not only can they assist you in creating a plan, but they can also steer you toward private investors they know.

If at first you don't succeed, try, try again. If a lender rejects your proposal or gives you the cold shoulder, figure out why, change your package or presentation, and give it another shot. When I first started, a lender told me "No" and explained that I didn't have enough experience. I added my father, an experienced carpenter and builder, to my proposal and pitched it to the same lender, who eventually loaned me the money I needed. My perspective has always been that "No" means the person I'm dealing with doesn't "know" enough information to say "Yes."

Calculating the splits

When you're just getting started and you have no money and no solid track record, your negotiating muscle is a little flabby. The person with the cash usually calls the shots. A 50/50 deal is about the most you can expect, but even that can be a little iffy at first. With each successful flip, you strengthen your position and eventually can offer investors slightly more than what they can make by investing their money elsewhere, so you keep most of the profit.

Remain cautious of experienced investors, landlords, or real estate gurus who may try to sell you their don't wanners. As a house flipper, you typically look for properties that owners don't want, but properties that these guys don't want could be real lemons.

Establishing effective partnerships for the long haul

Partnering with one or more friends or family members may be an option, especially if you have rich friends whose house-flipping skills complement your own. With their financial backing and your combined knowledge and skills, you may be able to form a long-lasting and financially rewarding partnership. You may also consider taking on a partner in the following situations:

- ✔ Your credit is damaged and you need someone who has a better credit rating to help you secure the loan.
- ✔ You can obtain the loan for purchasing the property but you need a partner to provide funds for renovating it.

Granny and me

My first partner was my grandmother. She put up the money for my investments. We made a deal — every time I sold a house, I had to take her out for lunch. When we started having lunch regularly, I was able to obtain traditional financing.

Partnering with friends or family members can be one of the most fulfilling experiences, but when it comes to money, friends and family can be more brutal than bankers, especially if your flip flops. In most cases, I discourage investors from taking on a partner, but with Granny and me, the partnership turned out to be a rewarding experience for both of us.

Taking on a partner is like getting married, so if you don't trust a person as much as you trust your spouse, you probably shouldn't become partners. Great partnerships are rare, but when they work, they enable both parties to achieve more than they could achieve individually. All too often, however, a partner runs off with the cash, fails to pay the contractors, cashes checks made out to the water company or building supply store and pockets the money, files an insurance claim to collect for damages without your knowledge, or figures out some other way to pick your pocket.

If you partner with someone, have your attorney write up a contract that details the responsibilities of each party and how profits are to be divided. Need an attorney? Head to Chapter 4 for help in finding one.

Investing your retirement savings in real estate

Newcomers are often attracted to real estate investments because they may result in a higher percentage return than stocks or bonds. In addition, real estate gives you more control over the performance of your investment. In the case of flipping houses, if you do it right and the housing bubble doesn't burst, you stand to earn 20 percent or more on each house you flip. You're not likely to see that sort of return on your IRA investments.

Because real estate is an investment opportunity that's as legitimate as stocks and bonds, some real estate investors are choosing to structure their IRAs (or at least a portion of them) around real estate investments. In other words, you can convert your IRA into a *self-directed IRA* and use the money in your retirement account to fuel your flips. Consult your accountant and your personal finance specialist to determine whether this option is one you want to explore and to work out all the details if you choose to go this route. It's risky, but so is the stock market.

Steer clear of using your retirement money to flip houses until you've achieved some success with flipping houses. I've been in real estate for over 30 years and I'm just beginning to look at this personally. My father-in-law and my attorney have been real estate investors for a number of years and they use this strategy successfully.

Chapter 7

Trudging Through Some Taxing Issues

You start flipping houses with the confident presumption that you're finally working for yourself. Instead of kowtowing to an overbearing boss and trading the best years of your life for a skimpy paycheck, you get to be your own boss and pocket the entire profit from your labors.

After you flip your first house, however, you may start to feel like you're working for the government. Unless you're careful, taxes can wash your profits downstream faster than a gully gusher. If you hold the property for a year, the 15 percent capital gains flush your profits, but if you opt for quick flips of less than a year, the 35 percent short-term capital gains tax — or even worse, income tax — can send you scampering for the lifeboats.

Evading taxes is always a choice, assuming you don't mind bunking with your fellow inmates at a federal prison, but I'm not about to recommend tax evasion as a viable alternative. Instead, in this chapter, I show you how to take advantage of legal tax exemptions and deductions to which you're legally entitled and structure your deals to pay as little tax as required under the law.

Shameless Disclaimer: I'm no CPA, accountant, or tax attorney, so I'm not providing advice in this chapter. Besides, tax laws are constantly changing, and state and local taxes vary depending on where you live, so even if I could offer you some sage advice, I couldn't possibly guarantee that it would be accurate for you and where you live. The information I offer in this chapter merely provides you with a stepping off point that can help you communicate more effectively with your CPA or tax specialist. See Chapter 4 for finding an accountant to add to your flipping team. For general tax information and forms, visit the IRS Web site at www.irs.gov.

Estimating the Tax Man's Take from Your Flipping Profits

You can get yourself into a real tax jam when flipping properties if you don't know upfront how the Internal Revenue Service (IRS) and your state and local taxing authorities classify your profits. If you go in thinking that the most you have to pay is 15 percent in capital gains tax, you may find an unpleasant surprise in your mailbox when tax time rolls around.

To avoid any future shock, know the tax man's cut upfront and how your house flipping strategy affects the percentage you pay in taxes:

- ✔ You owe 0 percent if you flip a home in which you lived for two of the past five years. See "Maximizing Tax Savings from the Sale of Your Principal Residence" later in this chapter for details.

- ✔ You owe 15 percent if you take at least 12 months to flip the property. By holding a house for 12 months, the IRS considers your profits to be long-term capital gains, taxed at a rate of 15 percent.

- ✔ You owe 35 percent if you sell the property in fewer than 12 months. Because you flipped the property in less than a year, profits qualify as short-term capital gains, taxable at 35 percent.

- ✔ You owe standard income tax if you flip houses for a living. When profits from flipping houses are your sole income, the IRS may consider flipping to be your job and tax your profits as income, complete with an additional 15 percent in self-employment tax. (See "Paying Income Tax: When Flipping Houses Becomes Your Occupation," later in this chapter, for details.)

Never postpone a sale in the hopes of improving your tax position. Take the sale when you have the sale. If the buyer backs out because of your delay, you stand to lose a lot more than you stand to save on taxes.

Maximizing Tax Savings from the Sale of Your Principal Residence

Living in the house you flip provides you with much more than a roof over your head. It qualifies you for a whopper of a tax exclusion. If you're married and you sell the house you've lived in during the past two years for a profit of $500,000 or less, you can stuff the money in your pockets and purse tax-free, at least according to the tax rules in place during the time I was writing this book. If you're single or married filing separately, you can deduct only $250,000, a comparatively paltry sum, but better than nothing.

Here's how it works: The profit from the sale of a house you owned for more than 12 months is subject to a 15 percent capital gains tax plus any additional taxes that your state or local taxing authorities lump on top. If you and your spouse live in the home for at least two years, however, the IRS excludes the first $500,000 of the proceeds ($250,000 if you're single) from capital gains tax. Any amount over that is subject to tax.

To take advantage of this exclusion, your home must be your principal residence, you have to own it (duh!), and you must have lived in it for two of the past five years. The following sections help you determine whether you qualify for this most generous tax break.

Knowing the tax rules before you flip

A woman I know just flipped her first house — a shabby two-bedroom job that she purchased for $120,000, renovated to the tune of $20,000, and sold for $175,000, walking away with a cool $35,000 in profit. And it took her only a little over ten months. She was ecstatic! But when she visited her accountant to tell her the great news, ecstasy quickly turned to agony.

The woman's accountant informed her that because she owned the home for less than a year, her profit qualified as a short-term capital gain, taxable at the rate of 35 percent, which cost her $12,250 in federal taxes alone. If she had held the home for an additional two months, the profit would have qualified as a long-term capital gain taxed at the much lower rate of 15 percent, and she could have saved $7,000!

As I say in the section "Estimating the Tax Man's Take from Your Flipping Profits," earlier in this chapter, you should never postpone a sale in order to take advantage of a tax break. The woman may have held onto her house for two more months only to find out that buyers were no longer interested in it, and she could have lost more money by having to sell the property for less later than she actually lost in having to pay higher taxes. However, this particular seller could have saved taxes by leasing the property to the new buyers until after the one year was up and then closing at that time. Know the tax laws, so you can establish a well-informed plan and avoid surprises that may lead to unnecessary regret.

Consider buying two houses. Pick the one that promises the most profit and takes the longest to rehab as your principal residence, and plan on spending at least two years fixing it up. While you're taking your time slowly renovating that property, do a quick flip on the other property. When you're done flipping that one, do a quick flip on another property. Following this approach, you can take advantage of the tax exclusion on your most profitable property (the long-term flip), while generating income with lower-profit, short-term flips.

Proving "principal residence"

Government officials like to quibble about the meanings of words. To close any loopholes in the tax law that applies to using your home as your *principal residence,* they carefully define the term "principal residence." For your home to qualify as your principal residence, you must:

- ✔ Live in the home instead of rooming with friends or relatives.
- ✔ Have your mail and utility bills delivered to this address.
- ✔ File your homestead exemption for this property with your county and state.
- ✔ Use this address on your driver's license, voter registration, tax returns, car registration, and so forth.
- ✔ Bank and shop in the vicinity of your home. No, the government doesn't really care where you bank or shop, but in close calls, the auditor may want to see grocery receipts that prove you live in the neighborhood.

A good rule of thumb for determining the location of your principal residence is this: If your mom's coming to visit you, which house does she come to?

Qualifying for the two-out-of-five-years rule

The two-out-of-five-years requirement is fairly straightforward — over the course of five years, you have to use the house as your principal residence for at least two years. If you spend a year island-hopping in the Caribbean, that year doesn't count, but a year in which you're away on vacation for six weeks counts as a full year. Check with your accountant or tax specialist to determine the exact amount of time you can be away from your home and still qualify as having lived there for a full year.

You can claim the exclusion only once in any two-year span. If you have two residences, both of them may qualify for the exclusion in the span of four or five years, but if you already claimed the exclusion, you have to wait two years before claiming it again.

Many times people want to keep their personal residence because it has already appreciated and they think that it's going to appreciate more. That can be a costly mistake. If possible, take full advantage of this generous tax break while it's available. You could conceivably own three homes — your principal residence, a summer home, and a winter home. You could sell your principal residence, move into your summer home for two years, sell your summer home, move into your winter home for at least two years, and then sell your winter home to take advantage of the tax benefit three times in a little over six years.

Taking the ownership test

Owning a property means having your name on the deed. If your generous parents let you live in the second home they own, fix it up, and then sell it, neither you nor your bighearted parents qualify for the tax exclusion. You don't own the home, and they don't live there.

If you're married and only you or your spouse is named on the deed, as a couple you still qualify to exclude the full $500,000 from your taxes. This rule applies to your principal residence — where you live — and it doesn't necessarily matter whether both names are on the deed.

Splitting hairs: Special circumstances

What if you *have to* sell the house before the two years is up, perhaps because of a job change? Is that just tough luck? Nope. The tax code accommodates for circumstances beyond your control, including the following:

- ✔ Divorce or legal separation
- ✔ Multiple births from the same pregnancy . . . fertility drugs gone wild
- ✔ Death of the homeowner, spouse, or co-owner, making the home unaffordable
- ✔ Serious health problems that require you to move in order to obtain proper treatment
- ✔ Loss of employment that results in your receiving unemployment compensation
- ✔ Military duty that calls you away from home for an extended period
- ✔ Involuntary conversion of your home — when the government takes possession of your home by claiming imminent domain

In these and similar instances, you may qualify for a prorated exclusion. In other words, if you and your spouse live in the home for a year, you may qualify for half the exclusion or $250,000 rather than the full $500,000.

Slashing Your Capital Gains Through Careful Deductions

You buy a house for $250,000, fix it up, and flip it for $300,000 in under 12 months. Now you're stuck paying 35 percent short-term capital gains tax on your $50,000 profit, right? Wrong. The $50,000 is your gross profit, but you pay tax only on your net profit — the actual profit you make after deducting all your expenses. This tax rule applies to any house you flip — the property need not be your principal residence.

Carefully log all your expenses related to the purchase of the property, holding costs, repairs and renovations, and the sale of the house, including the following:

- **Closing costs:** You can deduct the appraisal fee, title search, deed reporting fee, and credit reporting fee. No double-dipping. If you paid discount points, deduct them as mortgage interest, not as closing costs.

- **Cleanup:** Deduct any expenses for house cleaning, landscaping, or trash removal.

- **Repairs and renovations:** All expenses for improving the property for resale are deductible.

- **Utilities:** Gas, electric, water, sewer, and trash bills for this residence for the entire time you own the property are deductible expenses.

- **Property taxes:** Property taxes you pay out of pocket or out of an escrow account are fully deductible as expenses.

- **Insurance:** Calculate the total amount of insurance you paid on the property during the time you owned it.

- **Agent fees:** Any fees you paid to a real estate agent to purchase or sell the house are expenses you can deduct from your gross profit.

- **Other expenses:** When you flip houses, you're essentially running a business out of your home, so you can deduct all expenses related to flipping — mileage, phone bills, paper, ink, and so on. If you have an office in your home, you may be eligible for the home office deduction, as well.

According to tax laws in effect during the writing of this book, you also can deduct the mortgage interest you pay on a loan of up to $1 million on your first and second homes. In effect, unless you neighbor with royalty, all or at least most of the mortgage interest on your first and second homes is deductible.

The $1 million cap on deductible borrowing applies to both married and single tax payers; if you're married filing separately, the deduction is limited to interest on a home loan up to $500,000 for each of you.

When you're flipping houses, you can deduct your mortgage interest in either of the following ways:

✔ On a monthly basis, so you can keep track of your profit and the taxes you owe per month.

✔ By property, so it appears on your books either as an interest deduction or an expense you can deduct from your gross profit.

Consult with your CPA or tax specialist on the best way to keep track of your interest payments and claim the deduction.

Deducting your expenses can make a big difference at tax time. If you flip a house for a gross profit of $50,000 but pay $20,000 fixing it up and selling it, instead of paying 35 percent of $50,000 or $17,500 in taxes, you pay 35 percent of $30,000 or $10,500!

Don't be a dupe. Save all your receipts and pay taxes only on the profit you pocket.

Deferring Taxes: Rolling Your Gains into Your Next Purchase

You don't always have to pay capital gains tax upon the sale of a house. You may be able to roll your profit into the purchase of your next investment property. Rolling the profit over doesn't eliminate the tax. It defers payment until you pocket the profit. Rollover regulations can be a little tricky, but they boil down to the following two rules:

✔ You can roll over the profit from the sale of your principal residence into the purchase of a pricier house. With the $500,000 exclusion I discuss earlier in the chapter, this rule won't help the average homeowner, and it won't help when you're doing a quick flip (holding the property for less than two years).

✔ For rental/investment properties, you can file for a 1031 exchange that enables you to roll the profit from the sale of a rental property into pricier rental property.

Selling Your Home at a Loss (Ouch!)

Paying taxes on a profit is always preferable to the alternative — saving taxes on a loss, but if you have one bad apple in your bunch, you can sell it at a loss and deduct the loss from the profits you make on other properties. As a flipper, losing money on a property isn't your goal, but if you know that the longer you hold a property, the more you're going to lose on it, sometimes cutting your losses on one property so you can focus on other more profitable investments is a wise move.

Don't rush to take a loss on a property. Sure, if the property shows no signs of appreciating and it's sucking money, now may be the time to cut your losses and move on. However, if the area's in a housing slump and you think that it has potential, consider holding and renting the property until the market improves (see Chapter 3 for more about this flipping strategy and Chapter 25 for tips on surviving in a slow market). Analyze the situation and do what's best for your bottom line.

Paying Income Tax: When Flipping Houses Becomes Your Occupation

You decide to keep your day job and moonlight as a house flipper, buying and selling one or two properties a year to supplement your income. In such cases, the IRS considers your profits investment income subject to capital gains tax. When you begin earning big bucks flipping houses and quit your day job, you suddenly become a house flipper, and your profits become self-employment income — subject to income tax and a whopping 15 percent self-employment tax.

If your annual income places you in the 28 percent tax bracket, for example, you can expect to pay about 40 percent in federal taxes alone. Why not 43 percent (28 percent tax bracket plus 15 percent self-employment tax)? Because you can deduct the 15 percent self-employment tax when figuring your income tax, which gives you a tiny break.

Because everyone's tax portrait is unique, I can't tell you whether the IRS earmarks your profits as capital gains or self-employment income, but I can provide you with a list of determining factors:

✔ The purpose for which you purchased the property

✔ The amount of time you held the property

✔ The number of deals you did over the course of the tax year

✔ Your total sales over the course of the tax year

✔ Amount of income from the sales of property compared with income from your day job

No hard-and-fast rules govern the way the IRS (or your state or local taxing authority) looks at these numbers. What's most important is that you follow the rules to the best of your ability and accurately report your income and expenses. Consult your CPA or tax specialist for details to ensure that you meet the federal, state, and local tax requirements.

I hear plenty of stories about tax preparers who creatively underreport income and over report expenses. If you bump into someone like this, turn around and start running in the opposite direction. If they're willing to do it for you, they're probably doing it for dozens of other clients already, and eventually they'll get caught.

Right after you close on the sale of a property, visit your tax expert and find out how much of your profit you owe to Uncle Sam. Remit that amount as an estimated payment or at least keep it in a separate account so it's there when you need to pay your taxes.

Part III
House Hunting with an Eye for Flipping

The 5th Wave   By Rich Tennant

Before we go in, let me ask you— do you like to bowl?

FOR SALE

In this part . . .

The key to success in flipping houses is buying the right house — the house with the most potential. Buy the nicest house on the nicest block for the sticker price, and you've already lost the game before it even starts. Buy the worst house on the nicest block for way less than it's worth, and you're almost assured a profit, even if you make a few minor mistakes along the way.

In this part, you take on the role of treasure hunter, discovering the secrets to sizing up the best neighborhoods, unearthing undervalued gems, evaluating a property's profit potential, and then negotiating with the owner to acquire the property at a bargain-basement price. You also pick up some tried-and-true techniques for a special kind of purchase: foreclosure properties.

Chapter 8

Scoping Out a Fertile Neighborhood

In This Chapter

▶ Identifying the hot residential districts in your town or city

▶ Checking important indicators in a market

▶ Distinguishing the signs of good and bad neighborhoods

▶ Researching school performance, crime statistics, and business climate details

*I*nspiration for flipping properties often comes from real estate muses on late-night infomercials. Some guy posing in front of a private jet on the tarmac convinces you that you can become a multi-millionaire real estate investor simply by following his advice and making house flipping your week-end hobby. Of course, he fails to mention that the jet in the background really isn't his and that he makes most of his money from selling his books and CDs rather than from flipping real estate.

Probe the background of these real estate gurus, and you often discover that, if they're legitimate, they hit pay dirt in very affluent areas with red hot real estate markets. They're working their magic in Phoenix, Arizona; Venice, Florida; and Washington, D.C. All they have to do is buy, hold, and sell, and they make $100,000 snoozing in their recliners. In the meantime, you're trying to eke out a modest profit in an area where home prices top out at $150,000, and you're wondering what you're doing wrong.

You don't have to pack up and move to Phoenix to make money flipping houses, but farming a fertile market improves your chances of reaping boun-tiful profits. This chapter shows you how to dig up pertinent information so you can pinpoint potentially profitable real estate markets in your area.

As you begin researching neighborhoods, create a three-ring binder for each area complete with all the information you dig up, including names and addresses of schools and school administrators, local politicians, local law enforcement organizations, the names and phone numbers of the crime watch committee members, and so on. This information can come in handy later and even help you market the property when you're ready to sell. You can hand prospective out-of-town buyers a relocation package that contains all the information they need to successfully navigate the neighborhood.

Pinpointing House Flipping Hot Spots

Whether you're an average home buyer or a seasoned real estate investor, every search for the right home begins with a search for the right neighborhood. After all, location is everything. In the following sections, I help you zone in on a neighborhood. First, I introduce you to a few basic traits that help you choose a range of neighborhoods. Then, I help you narrow the search to the top neighborhoods on your list. And finally, I help you scratch a few neighborhoods off your list that aren't quite in your price range. By the end of the process, you should have one to three top candidates.

Tagging neighborhoods with the right basic traits

You can make money in any real estate market, but some markets are more profitable than others. Trying to target flippable properties in an area where all the homes are immaculate and people tend to stay put is tough. Stable areas that have their fair share of ugly or unkempt homes provide enhanced opportunities. Look for areas that exhibit the following qualities:

- ✔ Steady or rising real estate values
- ✔ Multiple offers on recently sold homes and homes currently for sale
- ✔ An influx of homeowners moving in from other areas
- ✔ A decrease in the number of homes for rent
- ✔ An increase in the number of homeowners in the neighborhood moving into bigger homes rather than moving out
- ✔ Older homes — homes built at least 20 years ago — and homes that generally require more rehab

✔ Areas with aging homeowners — homeowners who may be downsizing or retiring

✔ Visible updating in older neighborhoods — new roofs, aluminum replaced with vinyl siding, replacement windows, modern earth tone trim paint

✔ City improvements including street repaving, new street lights and street signs, and repaved sidewalks

Although agents in your area can steer you toward hot markets, an agent may try to steer you toward *her* market instead. Talk with several agents who work in different areas you're considering before selecting an agent so you have a better feel for which areas are most conducive for flipping houses. Then, pick one of the top agents who knows the area inside and out, as I discuss in Chapter 4.

Don't dismiss a neighborhood simply because it has few homes for sale. Every neighborhood has property for sale and people who need to sell it. In a tight market, you may just have to look a little longer.

Finding your focus

As you explore various neighborhoods in your town or city and evaluate their potential for flipping, you can save time by narrowing your focus to particular types of property or a specific area:

✔ **New construction:** When an area is growing rapidly, purchasing a newly built home where property values are rising provides an excellent opportunity to flip, especially if you can get a great deal on the property. (The people who stand to make the most money are the first 20 percent to buy into the area.)

✔ **Depressed area that's on the rebound:** An older neighborhood where homeowners are currently renovating their properties provides ample opportunities to buy, fix, and sell homes at a profit.

✔ **Farm area:** Pick a limited geographical area, which real estate insiders often refer to as a *farm area*. This area can be your ZIP code, a school system (see "Grading local schools" later in this chapter for more about finding school information), your town or city, four major intersections that define your perimeter, or whatever else you want to use to set your boundary. Agents commonly use this technique to become experts in a particular area. As a flipper, you can take advantage of this same tactic. As an expert, you know the values and can spot a deal instantly.

In the following sections, I give you a few additional pointers on keeping your search focused and manageable.

Dissecting your city or town

Given about 30 seconds to mull it over, most residents of a town or city can name the upscale areas — neighborhoods where everyone would live if they could afford it. The selection of homes for sale may be slim pickings, but when you put the house back on the market, you have little trouble moving it.

Grab a map of your town or city and highlight the hot spots — areas where the rich people live, the artists hang out, or people gather for activities and entertainment. These are the happenin' places. Here you see a lot of new construction or older, well-kept homes. People walk or ride their bikes through the neighborhood and keep an eye out for any riffraff.

Run-down neighborhoods where the community center is the corner liquor store or a triple-X movie theater don't draw families and first-time home buyers.

You can resuscitate a dying neighborhood by investing heavily in it and changing its reputation over the long haul, but don't try to go it alone, and don't expect it to improve overnight. If you decide to rebuild a run-down area, work with other investors, town officials, local businesses, and neighborhood residents, and plan on sticking around for quite awhile.

Sticking close to home . . . or not

Pinpointing the hottest real estate market across town doesn't mean that's where you should set up your home base. Setting home base closer to home offers several advantages:

- ✔ You have a vested interest in the community.
- ✔ Getting up to speed on property values is less of a chore.
- ✔ Your neighbors can turn you on to great deals.
- ✔ Commuting distances are shorter.
- ✔ Neighborhood news and gossip are within earshot.

Farm your own neighborhood only if it makes financial sense to do so. If property values are falling without the hope of recovery, investing in your neighborhood can lead to your own financial demise and further deterioration of the neighborhood. If the neighborhood housing market is less than promising, you may need or want to prospect in more fertile areas, but try to stay within an hour's drive of your house.

Identifying areas in your price range

Your financing dictates where you can shop and how much house you can afford. Anyone who's played Monopoly knows that you need a wad of cash to build hotels on Boardwalk and Park Place. To score that kind of money, you may need to start out earning some investment capital on Kentucky Avenue.

When you spot an attractive area, a neighborhood you would consider farming, check real estate values in the area to make sure they're in your price range. Don't worry if you're eliminating neighborhoods that you thought were your best prospects. The process of elimination is necessary to establish a realistic focus.

Check the fringes of areas where homes are outside your price bracket. Adjacent areas often ride the coattails of their pricier neighbors. If you can time your purchase just right, you stand to earn a profit as the neighboring areas increase in popularity.

Chapter 5 has full details on determining a suitable price range and estimating your potential profit. Refer to Chapter 6 to find sources of capital to fuel your flip. You need enough cash on hand to purchase, renovate, hold, and sell the property while turning a profit of at least 20 percent in a healthy market. How much money you can gather dictates your price range.

Taking the Pulse of the Real Estate Market in a Neighborhood

You identified two or three housing markets that look promising, but now you have to pick the area in which you want to buy a house. Your choice boils down to two questions:

 ✔ Which of the few areas I've selected has the best deals?

 ✔ Where can I resell the home for the highest profit?

The ideal real estate market is an area with rising property values, a few homes available at below-market prices, and a strong market or desire for homes in the area. With the help of your real estate agent — who can provide you with exact numbers on prices, homes for sale, and average time on the market — you can research various areas to identify signs of a healthy real estate market or warning signs of a market turning sour.

Research not only neighborhoods but also specific areas in those neighborhoods. You can discover two different real estate markets right across the street or across the tracks from one another. Just because two homes are within 100 yards of each other doesn't place them in the same market.

What's the annual appreciation percentage of the average home?

One key indicator of the health of the real estate market is the rate of appreciation — the percentage that properties increase in value from one year to the next. To determine the appreciation percentage, look at the prices of two comparable homes — one that sold recently and one that sold approximately one year ago. Use the following formula to determine the appreciation percentage:

$$(P2 - P1)/P1$$

In this equation, P2 (property 2) is the price of the home that recently sold and P1 (property 1) is the price of a comparable home that sold one year ago.

For example, if a home recently sold for $175,000, and a comparable home sold for $160,000 one year ago, the annual appreciation percentage would be:

$$(\$175{,}000 - \$160{,}000)/\$160{,}000 = \$15{,}000/\$160{,}000 = .09375 = 9.375\%$$

So, what's considered good? Anything in a range of 5 to 10 percent is good. Lower percentages may indicate a stagnant market or a market that's taking a downturn. Appreciation in the 15 to 20 percent range is bubble burst material — buying in to this market is highly speculative.

Don't get too excited about a 10 percent appreciation rate. Just because your calculations show that a home sold for 10 percent more this year than a comparable home sold for last year doesn't mean that homes in the area are selling like hotcakes. Check the sales prices of several comparables and examine other statistics, as I explain in the following sections, to determine the overall health of the market.

How many homes are currently for sale?

The number of homes for sale can often help you size up the real estate market. Of course, the number is relative, so I can't give you a specific number of homes that indicate a healthy or unhealthy market. You have to define the geographical location of your market (for example, a zip code or an area that sits inside four major intersections) and then compare the number of homes currently for sale to past numbers. A change in the number of listings from one year to the next indicates a shift in the market. If, for instance, you see a 20 percent increase in homes for sale from 2006 to 2007, the numbers indicate a shift from a seller's market to a buyer's market. You may be able to buy a house for less, but reselling the house in the near future may be more of a challenge.

By including sales volume in your calculations, you can determine whether a market is slowing, remaining steady, or on the upswing. If plenty of houses are listed and plenty are selling, you have another sign that the market is shifting. Combine this data with the data you have on appreciation percentages (see the previous section), and you can determine whether the shift is positive or negative. If lots of homes are selling and prices are declining, you can readily see a flight pattern. If homes are selling briskly and property values are increasing, the neighborhood may be turning over in a positive way.

How long is the average home on the market?

The time it takes to sell a house varies according to several factors, including the location and condition of the house, the asking price, and market conditions. A good house in a healthy market with the right asking price should sell in 30 days or less. If the average house sells in 60 days or less, the market is cruising along at a good pace. If most homes are lingering on the market for 90 days or more, the market may be slowing. Price range also affects time on the market — higher-end properties typically take longer to sell.

Markets often appear slower than they really are. When the market begins to cool, agents and sellers take awhile to pick up on the shift, and they continue to set asking prices that are higher than what the market can bear. Because the houses are overpriced for the current conditions, they remain on the market for much longer. When agents and sellers begin adjusting their list prices down, the market begins to pick up, and houses sell quicker.

Adjust your strategy as needed for the current market conditions, as I explain in Chapters 5 and 25. In a slow market, housing values can decrease while your holding costs increase (because your house may be on the market longer). To reduce your risk in a flat or declining market, you need to purchase homes for less than you'd pay in a strong market.

Evaluating the Good and Bad in a Neighborhood

The housing market in a particular area may look good on paper — property values are rising, demand is high, and home sales are brisk — but you should compare these indicators with what you observe on the ground. Is the neighborhood on the upswing or the downswing? Is the entire neighborhood turning into a don't wanner?

The following sections help you distinguish a neighborhood that's an excellent target for flipping properties from a neighborhood that's not.

Spotting the signs of a good neighborhood

Good neighborhoods look nice. Residents mow their lawns, trim their trees, fix any cracks in the sidewalks, and keep their roofs and gutters in good repair. You can see the neighbors out working in their yards when the weather's nice. After work, you see neighbors strolling, jogging, and riding bikes. At sunset, the neighborhood quiets down, and by 10 p.m. or so, it slips into its knapsack and settles in for the night.

To spot the signs of a good neighborhood, don't just drive around the area after work. Take a walking tour. Visit the neighborhood in the morning, afternoon, and evening. Check it out on weekends. If you happen to bump into somebody, introduce yourself and ask him why he moved to this neighborhood, how long he's lived here, and what he likes and dislikes about the area. The attitude of the residents often determines the future course of the neighborhood.

The perfect neighborhood is one in which almost all the homes are in excellent condition, you see few or no For Sale signs, and the block has one don't wanner — a run-down property that nobody wants. This is the grand slam of opportunities.

Seeing the warning signs of a declining neighborhood

Broken windows; dangling gutters; weedy, overgrown lawns; and wandering gangs of pimple-faced hoodlums are all signs of a neighborhood in decline. The residents gave up long ago. Maybe the major employer in the area moved out, leaving its workforce to deal with unpaid mortgages, or perhaps declining schools and increasing crime triggered a mass exodus. Here are some additional warning signs:

✔ A large number of For Sale or For Rent signs

✔ Eviction notices on doors with belongings and debris piled along the curb

✔ Broken down cars in the streets or alleys or on lawns

✔ Security bars on many doors and windows

✔ Wild dog packs. This may sound funny, but I've seen it!

Whatever the reason, don't buy into a declining market, unless you have the scoop on some imminent change that promises to turn the neighborhood around. Perhaps a new company is planning on moving in or a state-of-the-art medical center is in the works.

Even if you do hear of a neighborhood improvement, approach with caution. Good news can take many years to impact an area, so if you're considering buying in, be prepared to hold onto the property for several years.

Taking Other Neighborhood Factors into Consideration

Local politicians obsess about three things — schools, crime, and business. If the schools are top notch, the crime is low, and the business climate is healthy, people like to live in the area, property values rise, the tax base grows, the town or city can afford to pay for improvements, and the citizens reelect the politicians or promote them to higher offices.

When you're scoping out an area to flip, you should obsess about these same three factors, because they strongly influence the resale value of the property. The following sections show you how to research and evaluate school performance, crime rates, and the business climate. I also show you how to find the scoop on upcoming neighborhood improvements.

Having the neighborhood scope you out

While you're scoping out neighborhoods and deciding which area you want to farm, don't simply focus on your target. Make yourself a target. Increase your visibility, so you won't have to work so hard at discovering leads. When people know who you are and what you do and you've established a solid reputation for sticking to your word, they begin coming up to you and providing you with additional leads and prospects.

Don't be the invisible man or woman. Let people know every day who you are and what you do — first by word of mouth, possibly by advertisement, and best of all by reputation.

Grading local schools

Great schools boost more than just test scores — they increase property values, sometimes by as much as 10 to 20 percent. Real estate agents have known this for years, but recent studies prove a direct correlation between student performance on standardized tests and the percentage that homes in the area appreciate. So when you're comparing housing prices, be aware of the dividing lines between school districts. The following sections show you how to research area schools.

Don't rely on the name of a housing addition to determine which school district it's in. Sly builders often name their additions after popular school districts in an attempt to confuse home buyers who are moving into the area.

Researching school systems online

Quantifying the quality of education is difficult, if not impossible, but standardized test scores, low student-to-teacher ratios, and other statistics are the only measures we have to compare schools. You can find much of this information by visiting any of the following Web sites and searching for schools by name or location:

- ✔ SchoolMatters at www.schoolmatters.com
- ✔ GreatSchools at www.greatschools.net
- ✔ HomeGain at www.homegain.com
- ✔ eSchoolprofile at www.eschoolprofile.com
- ✔ SchoolMatch at www.schoolmatch.com

To compare schools using standardized test scores, you can obtain most of the information you need from local newspapers (either in print or on the Web). Almost all schools in the nation publish their scores at least once a year. You may also find this information posted on school Web sites, especially if the students did particularly well.

Picking the brains of teachers and school administrators

Visiting local schools in person is often a better way to evaluate schools than by researching online. In person, you can get a feel for the atmosphere of the school — how orderly and how well organized it is. Meet with the principal and find out how long she's been in the system. Ask the name and phone number of her predecessor, and then call him and find out whether he liked the school and why he left.

When you meet with the principal, be prepared to ask some probing questions, such as the following:

- ✔ What's the student-to-teacher ratio? A ratio of 30-to-1 is a little high; 25-to-1 is more in the average range, and 20-to-1 and lower ratios are good.

- ✔ How long does the average teacher remain on the job? If teachers stay five years or more, the system is fairly stable. If most of them move on after a year or two, you should be a little concerned.

- ✔ How do students perform overall on the standardized tests compared with students in nearby school systems? Are scores on the upswing or downswing?

Strike up a conversation with a teacher or one of the school's secretaries. Administrators are often overly optimistic PR people. Teachers and secretaries are typically more willing to offer an unbiased analysis, assuming they know you, of course. If you're a stranger to the area, they may be a little tight-lipped, too.

Gabbing with parents and students

Before you buy a home in a particular neighborhood, talk with parents and students, if their parents allow it. They usually know which elementary school in the area is considered the best, whether discipline is getting out of hand at the junior high or middle school, and how well the high school students fare after graduation.

Insider information from teachers, administrators, secretaries, parents, and students is often much more valuable and timely than the statistics you can obtain online. Don't expect your agent to provide this information — an agent can quote facts and statistics, but if he offers opinions, he may just get slapped with a "steering" lawsuit for steering you toward or away from a particular school system.

Digging up crime statistics

In addition to dragging down property values, high crime rates can directly slash your bottom line. If you're rehabbing a home, theft of tools and materials can significantly increase your expenses and cut into your profits. (Tools and building materials may disappear from houses in *any* area, so avoid leaving anything of value in your flip overnight.) To be safe, research crime statistics using the info in the following sections before you buy.

Checking crime statistics online

Online research into crime statistics is somewhat limited. You can visit the following Web sites to compare crime rates in major cities, but the sites don't break the numbers down by neighborhood:

- ✔ Crime Comparison at www.bestplaces.net/crime/
- ✔ Relocation Crime Lab at www.homefair.com/homefair/calc/crime.html

Grilling local law enforcement

Local law enforcement officials can provide much more detailed information on crime than you can get online, and they're usually pretty willing to talk with concerned citizens. Call or visit the law enforcement department that serves your target area and ask the following questions:

- ✔ Is crime a problem in this area?
- ✔ What types of crimes are most prevalent — violent crimes, theft, vandalism?
- ✔ Are crime rates rising, falling, or remaining about the same?

If your target area has a crime watch program, contact one or more of the organizers and ask the same questions. (You can ask a local law enforcement agent or a resident in the area about any neighborhood crime watch programs.) Find out what the community is doing to fight back and how successful they've been. Community activism can significantly lower crime rates. In Detroit, the international press had stamped the city with a scarlet letter for the Devils Night incident — the Detroit burning. Since then, thousands of volunteers have succeeded in turning Devils Night into Angels Night.

Exploring the business climate

Just as the health of the national economy drives new home construction and development, local businesses drive local economies and influence population growth and eventually real estate values. Local employers not only provide income-producing jobs, but they also draw families to the area, increasing the demand for housing.

When a large employer moves out of an area and nobody moves in to fill the gap, real estate values commonly take a nose dive. By exploring the business climate and talking with business owners in the area, you can get a good feel for the health of the local economy and become aware of any impending developments — positive or negative. I give you a few helpful pointers on researching a neighborhood's business climate in the following sections.

The health of area businesses played a larger factor in real estate values in the horse and buggy days. Nowadays, people think nothing of driving 30 minutes or an hour to work, one way. However, if you're buying and selling real estate in a small town that's a considerable distance from a major city, the business climate can have a strong influence over property values.

Contacting the local chamber of commerce

The local chamber of commerce can fill you in on the business environment and local resources available to residents. Don't go in expecting to hear anything negative, however; one of the organization's primary goals is to promote development in the area. Ask the following probing questions:

- ✔ How many new businesses have moved into the area in the past year?
- ✔ How many businesses have moved out of the area in the past year?
- ✔ How many new jobs have come to the area?

Talking to business owners

When you want to know about the business climate, call around and talk to the business owners. To get the ball rolling, try opening with one or more of the following questions:

- ✔ How long have you owned a business in this area?
- ✔ Does business seem to be picking up or tapering off?
- ✔ What do you think of the mayor? (If the other questions don't generate some conversation, this one usually works, especially if businesses are suffering.)

Getting the lowdown on planned neighborhood improvements

Community centers, shopping malls, new schools, and other neighborhood improvements can boost property values, so if you're planning to flip houses in a particular neighborhood, keep abreast of the latest developments by using the tips in the following sections. If the town is planning on building a new health and fitness center near the park, you're more prepared than other investors to capitalize on the plan.

Perusing the neighborhood newspaper

Read the neighborhood newspaper from front page to back. Reporters in small towns and neighborhoods have little to report, so they usually broadcast every minor incident . . . DUIs, petty thefts, lovers' quarrels. When news leaks out about something big like a city beautification plan, reporters splash it across the front page. Neighborhood newspapers also announce all the important meetings scheduled for the coming weeks.

Sitting in on town meetings

To listen to people gripe, hear the local gossip, and discover all the petty and important problems that set the community abuzz, sit in on town meetings. Here, you get the lowdown on everything from planned sewer projects and street repairs to complaints about inappropriate content on billboards.

Even if you find no enlightenment in the meeting itself, you can usually plug your ear into an errant discussion to pick up some interesting bits of news on property issues, such as abatements and plans to tear down houses. Town meetings are also a great forum for networking and finding leads on property for sale. I've attended several meetings in which I've picked up on leads that have turned into transactions.

If you have cable TV, you may have a local channel that airs the town hall meetings. The broadcast is usually delayed, but if you can't attend the meeting, you can still watch it. But keep in mind that by not attending the meeting in person, you stand to miss out on any networking opportunities.

Chatting it up with the locals

Chat it up with the locals to discover what's really going on in the community and establish a feel for the local sentiment. Are people pretty positive about where they live, or are they getting fed up with the conditions? Who's died recently? Who's moving out and why? Who's been laid off?

Donut shops, coffee houses, and greasy spoon joints are great places to pick up leads as well as general information. I often visit the local eateries in my farm area, and I usually walk out with at least one new lead or prospect. Of course, I tip a little high, hand my business card to the server, and leave a few additional cards at the counter. Pharmacists and butchers are often tuned in to the local gossip channel, as well.

Chapter 9

Hunting for Houses in Your Target Area

In This Chapter
▶ Staying focused on a certain price range and house style
▶ Exploring key resources for information on bargain properties
▶ Spotting potential flips in special areas of the market
▶ Spreading the word to generate additional leads

*B*uried in every neighborhood are hidden treasures offering real estate investors the opportunity to turn a handsome profit. You just have to dig a little to discover these buried treasures; to figure out where to dig, you need a map. The real estate market offers an entire atlas full of treasure maps, ranging from the all-important MLS (Multiple Listing Service) to classified ads and real estate publications. You have to dig a little to find these valuable resources, and then you need to know how to read them to discover key words that identify the most promising properties.

In this chapter, I point the way to the plethora of publications, Web sites, and other resources that provide information on properties for sale, and I show you how to use the information they provide to hunt for buried real estate treasures in your target neighborhood. By the time you finish this chapter, you should have a list of at least ten promising prospects from which to select the most qualified candidate.

Focusing Your Search on Affordability and a Particular Property Type

When you go hunting for a home you want to live in, you don't look at every house in the neighborhood that has a For Sale sign out front. You narrow your list of prospects by stipulating your selection criteria. You typically begin with a price range and style of home — say a ranch-style house between $120,000 and $150,000. You may not consider a home that has fewer than three bedrooms and two baths (or even three baths if you have more than one teenager). Or you may insist on an oversized garage with a tile floor, where you can safely park your new Hummer. You specialize in order to prevent becoming overwhelmed by the wide selection of homes on the market.

When you begin looking for investment properties, take a similar approach. Settle on a price range and style of home; I cover both topics in the following sections. Depending on the predominant features in your target neighborhood, you may focus further by considering only brick homes or only two-bedroom homes that have attic space that you can covert into a third bedroom. You don't want to specialize to the extent that you limit yourself to only one or two properties, but try to limit your prospects to the number of houses you can realistically consider in your allotted time frame and price range.

Specializing can help you master a narrow market, search more efficiently, and establish an edge over your competition. The fewer houses you have to look at, the quicker you can inspect the property, make your offer, and begin renovations.

How much house can you afford?

You don't have to start counting your pennies yet, but before beginning a serious search for properties, you should have a ballpark figure in mind — how much you can afford to spend on a property. (Chapter 8 can help you zone in on affordable neighborhoods with promising prospects.) Several factors influence your price range, including the following:

✔ Amount of *financing,* or how much money you can get your hands on (see Chapter 6)

✔ Type of financing, such as cash, bank loan, personal loan from a relative, or *hard money* — a high-interest, short-term loan from a private investor (see Chapter 6 to discover more about acquiring hard money)

✔ Cost of renovations

✔ *Holding costs,* or monthly costs of owning the property while you're renovating it

✔ Cost of purchasing and selling the property

✔ Additional (and often unforeseen) costs, such as unpaid back taxes or utility bills, major appliances that break down a day after closing, and residents who refuse to move out

You're not purchasing the house yet. You're simply determining a realistic price bracket for the houses you want to consider. If you have the financing to make a $100,000 purchase (and an additional $20,000 on hand for renovations and other costs), you may consider looking at homes in the $90,000 to $130,000 range. Because you need enough to cover purchase costs, renovations, and holding costs, you probably don't want to pay more than $100,000 for a house in this case, but you should extend your range a little higher — you may stumble on a property that's way overpriced or a motivated seller who's willing to accept significantly less than the asking price or is willing to pay for some of the essential repairs.

Don't overextend yourself, especially on your first deal. Calculate the total amount of money you need with enough padding to cover the costs of buying, holding, renovating, and selling the property. To come up with this total, you need the following:

- ✔ Enough money to cover your current living expenses
- ✔ The cost of buying and selling the property and making renovations
- ✔ A buffer of about six months worth of payments on the new property, including taxes, insurance, and utilities
- ✔ Enough money to cover the cost of cheeseburgers for you and your crew

See Chapter 5 for advice on estimating your total investment.

What style and features do you want in a house?

When evaluating investment properties, a common mistake is to purchase a home you like rather than a home that everyone else likes. You may think that ranch style homes are a blot on the American landscape, but if 99 percent of the home buyers in your area disagree, then you'd better acquire a taste for ranch style homes. Your focus should include the following features:

- ✔ **Style of home:** Victorian, Tudor, Cape Cod, ranch, split-level, townhouse, bi-level, colonial, or contemporary. (Be careful here. Not all homes fit into a neat category, and you don't want to miss a golden opportunity because you and the seller couldn't agree on the style of the house.)
- ✔ **Total square footage:** If the hot properties sport over 2,000 square feet of living space, you want to look for homes in that range or homes that you can add on to.
- ✔ **Floor plan:** Are home buyers looking for roomier rooms or more rooms? Make sure the floor plan conforms to what home buyers are currently looking for or that you can easily adapt it by erecting or knocking down walls or building additions (see Chapter 18 for more about these types of renovations).

- ✔ **Number/size of bedrooms:** If the homes that are selling most briskly have three or four bedrooms, don't consider purchasing a home that has fewer than three bedrooms or the potential for creating another bedroom. Ideally, the smallest room (excluding laundry rooms and bathrooms) should be no smaller than 10 x 10 feet.

- ✔ **Number/size of bathrooms:** A bathroom can be a humdinger to add to a house, especially an older, smaller house. Consider only properties that have the number of bathrooms required to make the property marketable.

- ✔ **Basement:** A clean, dry basement can be a big plus. It doesn't add to the official living space of the house unless it has a separate walk-out, but it does add significant storage space and options for unofficial living space.

- ✔ **Lot size:** Lot size can significantly influence the value of a home. The lot size should be similar to the size of lots for other comparably priced property.

- ✔ **Garage size and type:** In some areas, an attached, three-car garage is a necessity. In other areas, a small, detached garage (or even no garage) is sufficient.

Don't rule out a house just because it lacks one or two essential features. A missing feature is often a sign that you've found the perfect house to flip. Add the feature, do some cosmetic renovations, and you can often spin straw into gold. Check out Chapter 13 and consult your agent to find out what's hot and what's not in your target neighborhood.

An old saying claims that "There's no arguing taste." When you're looking for properties to flip, that should be your motto, but keep in mind that it's not *your* taste that counts. What's most popular and in highest demand should dictate your choice.

Digging Through Property Listings, Ads, and Publications

When homeowners decide to sell their property, they do what any good capitalist does — they market and advertise. It's all about supply and demand. They can't do much on the supply side, so they try to increase demand by getting the word out and catching the interest of as many buyers as possible.

The most comprehensive marketing blitz begins by listing the property with a real estate agent, who advertises the property through various publications online and off and markets it through a network of motivated real estate agents. When you're scoping out a neighborhood for properties to flip, start your search with the valuable and easily accessible resources that I present in the following sections.

Searching MLS listings with the help of your real estate agent

The *Multiple Listing Service* (MLS) is like a dating service for home buyers and sellers. Through a real estate agent, a home seller can post a complete description of the property, including the asking price, total square footage of the house, room specifications, and a host of other details about the home's layout and construction. Prospective buyers can search the MLS (or, in some areas, multiple MLS listings) with the assistance of a real estate agent to find the ideal match for their needs.

If an area has more than one local MLS board, more than one MLS may list homes for sale in the area. Choose a real estate agent who has access to all MLS listings for your target area, or use two or more agents. To access MLS listings, an agent needs to be on the local MLS board or be a member of the National Association of Realtors. In other words, for access to the most comprehensive database of homes for sale, you're going to need some real(tor) help. Chapter 4 has more information about selecting the right agent for your needs.

In the following sections, I show you how to maneuver the MLS listings to locate and assess basic information, sniff out important clues, and weed out potential time wasters.

The National Association of Realtors at www.realtor.com offers a searchable database of more than 2.5 million listings. Consider this database the Cliffs Notes version of the MLS.

Checking out MLS basics

Ask your agent to supply you with the listing and listing history of all properties for sale that match your search criteria, including the following:

- Location
- School district (see Chapter 8 for the importance of school districts)
- Asking price
- Style of home
- Construction materials
- Total square footage
- Number of bedrooms
- Number of bathrooms
- Presence (or not) of a basement

The *listing history* indicates when, how long, and for how much the home has been on the market. And it provides you with the following key information:

- ✔ All transactions on the property in the past few years.

- ✔ How much the seller paid for the property.

- ✔ Whether the seller listed the property with another agency in the past — and how long it was listed and for how much. (This information is helpful in determining actual time on the market. The current listing shows only the time that the seller listed the property with the current agent.)

- ✔ The amount the property has appreciated from one sale to the next.

- ✔ Whether the seller has dropped the asking price and by how much.

- ✔ How much trouble the seller is having trying to unload the property.

Through the MLS, your agent can also look up the number of homes that have been on the market in the area and have sold in the last three years. By looking at sales over the most recent six-month period, the agent can clue you in to the health of the housing market. If ten homes are on the market and six sold in the past six months, that's a good sign. If 20 homes are on the market and only three have sold, that could mean trouble. Chapter 8 has more on taking the pulse of the real estate market in a particular neighborhood.

Keep an eye on sale-pending properties. Often, someone makes an offer that ties up the property but then fails to close on the sale. The property is typically placed back on the market at a reduced price. The law forbids your agent from disclosing the sales price of a pending sale, because if the transaction falls through, the seller would have a tough time negotiating the next offer, but you can compare the new asking price with the old one to determine whether the seller has become more motivated.

Ask your agent to print out five listings of homes that have recently sold in the same price range, so you can comparison-shop. Ask for five listings of homes that have sold in the next higher price bracket, so you can determine the types of modifications you need to make in order to sell the property at a higher price. With MLS materials in hand, you're ready to begin your search.

Sniffing out clues on a listing

Each MLS listing contains a deluge of details about the property, all of which can be very helpful in your search (see Figure 9-1 for a sample listing). Some of these details, however, are more useful than others. Focus your search on the following golden nuggets:

- ✔ **List price:** Now that you're looking at listings of only those homes in your price range, examine the list price and compare it to that of other comparable houses in the same area. An inordinately low price can signal a buying opportunity, or it can raise a red flag, making you (and others) wonder, "What's wrong with this one?"

✔ **List date or time on market:** How long has the home been on the market? You typically find your best opportunities in homes that recently have been listed (in the past couple days) or in homes that have been on the market for a couple of months. A home that's not selling may be over-priced for the current market. In many cases, the longer the seller holds out, the harder it is to sell, and the more desperate the seller becomes. This cycle could signal a buying opportunity in the near future. Your agent can tell you the average time a home is on the market in any given neighborhood, so you can properly gauge what's considered "a long time."

✔ **Remarks:** Near the bottom of every MLS listing is a Remarks or Property Description section that offers additional bits of information. Look for key terms, such as "Sold As Is," "Handyman's Special," "In Need of a Little TLC," or "Needs a Little Work." These phrases translate to "You'll get the house for less, because the current owner doesn't want to clean, paint, or tear out carpeting."

Nothing on the MLS is the gospel truth. Sellers and real estate agents alike often estimate room sizes or make mistakes when entering details. Approach all prospects with a discerning eye.

Weeding out potential time wasters

Just as an MLS listing contains words and phrases that highlight potential buying opportunities, listings commonly contain details that function as red flags, such as the following:

✔ **Inordinately high list price:** If the price is way out of line with respect to comparable properties in the same area, the seller may be delusional. Sellers who are emotionally attached to their homes can be difficult in negotiations. Keep an eye on the property to see whether the price drops.

✔ **Super cheap:** Either something is terribly wrong with the property or somebody made a typo.

✔ **Flowery description of the property:** Under the Property Description or Remarks section of the MLS, watch out for any phrases like "Nicest Home in the Neighborhood" or "A Real Show Stopper." When you're flipping a house to make some quick cash, the nicest, highest-priced house on the block isn't the best investment.

✔ **Neighborhood that's outside your farm area:** Don't be tempted by properties outside your farm area — the neighborhood you decided to target. These properties may look like great deals at first glance, but if the property is on the wrong side of the tracks, it may not be such a great deal in that area.

Ralph Roberts
Ralph Roberts Realty LLC
30521 Schoenherr

Warren MI
48088

PH: (586) 751-0000
FX: (586) 751-2177

~~6363 OLD COACH TRAIL~~
WASHINGTON TWP , MI, 48094--

$289,900

R 30339148 A

Click Photo for More Photos

AGENT REMARKS: To set a showing appointment please call Ralph Roberts Realty at 586-751-0000! For any further questions/concerns please contact ~~Sarah Hodges @ 810-217-8318~~

PUBLIC REMARKS: This House has it all!!Country setting on over 1/2 acre wooded lot in family neighborhoodLG eat-in kitchen with bay wndw & ceramic tile.Grt Rm w/ ntrl frplc. Fin. bsmt, circular drive, 2 1/2 car garage, nice decking/pavers & hot tub. Updates Include: Furnace, Central Air, Gutters, Siding, Roof, Most Wndws, Garage door opener, R/O System and extra insulation in both attic and outside walls!! Make this your next home!!

LOCATION INFORMATION

County: 50 Macomb	MLS Area: 50006 WASHINGTON TWP	Lake Name:
Twp:	Legal: CARRIAGE HILLS SUB #5 LOT 278	
Map Coor: C 20	Directions: WEST OF CAMPGROUND & S OFF 28 MILE	
Acres: .55	Cross Str: CAMPGROUND / 28 MILE	
School Dist: ROMEO	Elem/Mid/High: INDIA / POWEL / ROMEO	
Property ID: 0428126013	Tax(yr)=S(yr)+W(yr): $ 3,772.36(2005) = $2,176.03(2005) + $1,596.33(2004)	
Section:	SEV/Yr: $ 135,400. / 2005 Principal Residence Exemption: YES	
Lot Size: 118x204	Subdivision: CARRIAGE HILLS 5	
Frntg: 118		

PROPERTY INFORMATION

Rooms: 10	Bed Rms: 4	Bath F/H: 2.1	Yr Blt: 1979
Built On: BASEMENT		Garage: 2.5	Sq Ft: 2,500
Style: 13 2 STORY RES	Exterior Finish: Full Masonry	Site Condo: NO	Manufactured: NO
Water: WELL	Sewer: SEPTIC	Certified Inspection: Y	Inspection Date: 10/13/2005

Room	Dimensions	Level	Room	Dimensions	Level	Room	Dimensions	Level
Bedroom	17-00x14-00	2	Bedroom	14-00x12-00	2	Bedroom	14-00x10-00	2
Bedroom	12-00x12-00	2	Bedroom			Bedroom		
Breakfast Nook			Dining	14-00x12-06	1	Great Rm		
Kitchen	21-00x14-00	1	Living			Lib/Den	15-10x12-07	1
Laundry	08-06x05-00	1	Sun/Florida			Family	18-00x14-00	1
Sitting			Other			Other		

LISTING INFORMATION

List Date: 01/10/2006	Exp Date: 01/10/2007	
L-Agt llm: 336323 Ralph Roberts	L-Frm llm: 749 Ralph Roberts Realty LLC	L-Frm Phone: (586) 751-0000
Show: CALL FOR APPT.		

Lease(y/n): N	Comp SA: Y P 3.00	Contract: ERS	
Signed Discl: Y	Comp BA: Y P 3.00	DOM: 41	
List Excptn: N	Comp HA: Y P 3.00	Occup: 0Days @:$ 0 / day	Assoc: $ 25 YEARLY
Ownership: PRIVATE	Assessments: $ 1,800		

No Additional Required Fees, Forms, or Addendums

FEATURES

BRICK	VINYL	SHINGLES	100-199 FT FRONT
PORCH	OUTSIDE LIGHTS	CONVENTIONAL	CASH
GAS FORCED AIR HEAT	CENTRAL AIR CONDITIONING	CEILING FAN	2+CEILING FANS
GAS HOT WATER HEATER	FP IN FAMILY ROOM	INTERCOM	HUMIDIFIER
WATER SOFTENER	SMOKE ALARM	LIVING ROOM	BREAKFAST ROOM
WASHER	DRYER	MICROWAVE	FIRE PLACE-SEE REMARKS
POSSESSION 30 DAYS/LESS	ATTACHED GARAGE	FAMILY ROOM	GARBAGE DISPOSAL
1st FL LAUNDRY	1st FL BATH/LAV	EATING SPACE IN KITCHEN	FORMAL DINING (3 WALLS)
SPA/HOT TUB	FINISHED BASEMENT	RECREATION ROOM	SIDEWALK
PAVED STREET	MSTR BDRM W/BATH	MORE THAN ONE BATH	SIDE ENTRANCE GARAGE
IN GROUND SPRINKLERS	2ND FLOOR BATH/LAV	DEEP LOT/OVER 150 FT.	STORMS & SCREENS
PATIO	DECK	OVEN/RANGE	DISH/WASHER
REFRIGERATOR	CABLE TV	SURVEY	SUMP PUMP
VINYL TRIM	ACCESS BY APPOINTMENT	CALL LISTING BROKER	COLONIAL
RESIDENTIAL			

CONFIDENTIAL INFORMATION: Information deemed to be reliable but not guaranteed.

Figure 9-1:
An MLS listing contains a lot of useful information.

Scanning the classifieds for key words

Local newspapers (and the Web sites of local newspapers) typically carry classified advertisements of homes for sale. When scanning these ads, look for words or phrases that clue you in to the fact that the property is a "don't wanner" as in "The owner don't want her." As a flipper, you want the houses that current homeowners don't want because the homeowner is more motivated to sell and is likely to offer you a better deal. Phrases like "Needs Work," "Must Sell, Owner Relocating" and "Fixer-Upper" are like billboards broadcasting that the owners want to get out, move on, and cut their losses. To you, these billboards are telling you to "Look at this house!"

Beware of the following subliminal messages that warn you of potential trouble ahead:

- ✓ **Glitzy $100 ads:** The more money the seller invests in advertising, the less likely the person is to negotiate price. Give more consideration to the tiny $10 ads.

- ✓ **Words indicating a reluctance to negotiate:** If the ad includes the word "FIRM," the owner has probably set a steep asking price and is unwilling to haggle. Don't waste your time with an owner who thinks his bungalow is worth a million bucks.

- ✓ **Ads that promise "Cash Back at Closing":** Translated into plain English, this phrase means "con artist at work." The property owner or the front man is using the house as a pawn in his or her scam. Don't be the sucker who gets hooked into an illegal transaction. Don't even call. (See Chapter 1 for information about additional real estate scams.)

Poring over real estate magazines

Walk into just about any grocery store, restaurant, or gas station, and you see a rack of Homes for Sale magazines. Grab an armful of these publications and head to your local café to peruse the offerings. Most magazines organize the homes by area — North, South, East, West — and may contain listings for well-known areas, such as homes around a local lake or reservoir.

Although Homes for Sale magazines may steer you toward a hidden gem, listings are often two to three weeks old — after all, printing and distributing the magazine takes time. Other real estate investors very likely have picked over the properties already. These ads, however, can help you locate a quality real estate agent, check out the asking prices for comparable properties in your target area, and acquire tips on how to make a property more marketable.

Panning for Gold in Special Markets

During the Gold Rush, miners headed to California to pan for gold. After all, that's where all the gold was. When you're flipping houses, limiting your focus in this way can often increase your chances of finding a great deal. The real estate market has several areas that hold more promise than others. These areas include For Sale By Owner (FSBO) properties, foreclosures, probate properties, and government-owned properties. In the following sections, I show you how to pan for gold in these markets.

Homing in on homes "For Sale By Owner"

Drive through any neighborhood, and you're likely to see some crummy-looking signs that say "For Sale" or "For Sale By Owner." No self-respecting real estate agent would ever think of planting one of these signs on a client's lawn, but for aspiring real estate flippers, these signs are like flashing Vegas neon. People who sell their own homes are often highly motivated and willing to deal with a serious buyer.

People commonly try to sell their own homes for one of three reasons:

- ✔ To save the sales commission they would have to pay a real estate agent.
- ✔ To get rid of the house when they don't really know or care about the value of it.
- ✔ To sell the house for a price that's so far above a realistic market value that no agent in her right mind would consider listing it.

If you like the property, pull over and jot down the number or grab your cell phone and start dialing. If you're not comfortable approaching the property owner yourself, call your agent. The only wrong way to approach a FSBO that catches your eye is not to approach it at all.

Avoid overpriced property. If you run into a seller who's convinced that his run of the mill shack is the neighborhood Taj Majal, don't waste your time.

For Sale By Owner at www.forsalebyowner.com is a commercial site where property owners can list their properties online without going through a real estate agent. If you're interested in FSBOs, check this site and similar Web sites.

Getting the scoop on foreclosures

Easy credit and an unpredictable job market have led many homeowners to assume more debt than they can handle. If the homeowner misses one or more mortgage payments, the bank or other lending institution that holds the mortgage typically begins the process of *foreclosing* — taking possession of the property. (See Chapter 12 for more information on finding, evaluating, and purchasing foreclosure properties.)

Probing probate properties

When someone who owns some stuff dies, the stuff often goes into *probate,* where the courts decide what happens to it. Because a house divided cannot stand, probate often results in the process of selling a house to turn it into liquid assets (cash), which the courts can more easily use to pay off outstanding debts, taxes, and administration fees. The court divides any remaining crumbs among the beneficiaries of the estate.

The best way to discover more about houses in probate is to contact probate attorneys. They handle estates, and they want to get paid, so they need the services of real estate investors. You can also check the classifieds and your county clerk's office for any information about estate sales, or check the Yellow Pages, under Auctions, for auctioneers who specialize in estate sales. Be sure to ask for references and check those references to find a reputable attorney.

Add the names and contact information of helpful probate attorneys to your Rolodex and keep in touch with them, so when good deals cross their desks, you're the first person they call.

Probate sales can be a little tricky, especially in states that allow *overbids.* An overbid occurs when the property sells to the highest bidder at an auction and then another investor bids higher than the winning bid. The overbid typically must exceed the winning bid by 5 percent or more, so someone can't just bid an extra dollar and get the property. Still, if you're bidding on a probate property, overbids are a concern. If you're in a state that allows overbids (ask a probate attorney), don't assume the sale is final just because you were the high bidder at the auction. Keep tabs on the property until the sale is final.

Scouting for government-owned properties

Government, at the county, state, and federal levels, frequently acquires and disposes of property. For example:

- Federal agencies, such as *Housing and Urban Development* (HUD) and the *U.S. Department of Veterans Affairs* (VA), obtain houses when borrowers fail to make their mortgage payments.

- The U.S. Justice department seizes the homes of convicted criminals and drug dealers. States and counties often seize homes for the nonpayment of taxes.

- When the military closes a base, the federal government ends up with surplus property it must dispose of.

As a real estate investor, you can bid on these properties. I show you how in the following sections.

Shopping for HUD homes

First-time buyers often finance their homes through the federal government, primarily by way of *Federal Housing Authority* (FHA) and VA loans. When the property owner fails to make mortgage payments on the property, the FHA or VA initiates a foreclosure (I cover foreclosures earlier in this chapter and more fully in Chapter 12), which commonly results in the agency taking possession of the house and reselling it through HUD registered real estate agents. HUD properties are residential and include single-family homes, townhouses, and condominiums.

Many real estate investors specialize in buying and flipping HUD homes, but before becoming involved with HUD homes, be aware of the following:

- HUD homes are often sold at market or just below market value, so they're not always the best deals available. You need to assess the potential profitability of these properties as you would any property you consider buying.

- You may qualify for FHA financing on the purchase of a rehab. The agency often offers special interest rates for loans used to purchase and rehab run-down property.

- You may need to purchase the home through a HUD-registered real estate agent and pay a sales commission.

- HUD homes are sold as is, so have the home professionally inspected before placing your bid (see Chapter 11 for details on home inspections). After you buy it, you own it, my friend . . . and all the defects with it.

If you're interested in investing in HUD homes, hook up with a real estate agent who specializes in these properties. The right real estate agent can supply you with a steady stream of leads along with tips on how to best profit from your investment. Also, check out HUD Homes Listings at www. hud.gov/offices/hsg/sfh/reo/homes.cfm.

HUD sells homes "owner occupied." If you purchase a HUD home, you must sign a document stating that you'll live in the home for at least 12 months before selling it. You may be tempted to stretch the truth a bit and sign the document even though you have no intention of living in the house, but that's fraud. If you're caught and convicted, you may face a hefty fine and some jail time. Be patient and do the right thing. Also keep in mind that sales of owner-occupied houses fall through more often than investor deals, so don't give up just because someone "bought" the property you wanted. Keep an eye on the pending sale and be prepared to pounce if the sale falls through.

Tracking down government-seized properties

Various government agencies at all levels seize or purchase property. None of these agencies is interested in the property itself. They want to unload it quick for whatever they can get for it. In other words, the government is the ultimate motivated seller.

A land-grab boondoggle

The department of transportation was selling patches of property, 1 to 10 feet wide, along a 15-mile stretch of expressway in Michigan. A real estate investor swooped in and purchased the properties, thinking he could sell the parcels to adjoining property owners, so they could expand their acreage and move their fences out closer to the road. He calculated carefully. Through an initial investment of $10,000 for the land and a truckload of For Sale signs, he stood to earn nearly $100,000!

Unfortunately, none of the property owners along the highway were too interested in paying big bucks for additional slivers of land, and none of the properties sold. Eventually, the investor lost the properties to the local taxing authorities, the city gave the properties to the adjoining property owners for free, and the department of transportation billed the investor for weed cutting. What initially appeared to be a chance at $90,000 easy money turned out to be a $20,000 boondoggle.

The moral of this story is that clever, get-rich-quick schemes can often backfire and cost you money. Keep this fact in mind when you're scouting for great deals, and make sure you consider any and all problems that may arise. Most importantly, examine the numbers and make sure they work.

You can find leads by contacting government agencies directly, especially at the state or local level. Go online or use your handy-dandy phonebook and your people skills to contact the following agencies:

- **Your state's department of transportation:** The department of transportation commonly purchases real estate when building or widening roads. If the property isn't destroyed during the construction project, the department of transportation puts it up for sale. You can often buy property directly from the department or through an auction at a deep discount.

- **Your state or county drug enforcement agency:** Drug enforcement agencies commonly seize property that has been purchased with ill-gotten gains, and then auctions off the property. Call the DEA to determine sales dates and locations.

- **Your county sheriff's office:** Your county sheriff's office may sell seized property directly, through an auction, or through real estate brokers. The sheriff is also commonly stuck with handling foreclosures (which I cover earlier in this chapter and more fully in Chapter 12). Contact the office and ask for the name and contact information of the person in charge of the disposition of seized property and foreclosures.

You can poke around on the Web to find Web sites of various federal, state, and local agencies that seize and dispose of real estate. Use your favorite search tool to look for "government seized property," "government seized properties," or "government seized real estate." Use your imagination to come up with other search phrases, such as your county or state followed by "seized property." And be sure to try the following sites:

- **Home Steps** at www.homesteps.com: This Freddie Mac site features a searchable online database containing information on thousands of homes all across the nation. This site is a great place to discover REO properties, which are essentially bank repos placed back on the market.

- **Office of Property Disposals** at propertydisposal.gsa.gov/Property/: This Web site provides access to information about properties owned and for sale by the federal government, such as land and buildings made available by base closings or federal marshal property seizures.

- **Real Estate for Sale from Government Surplus & Foreclosures** at www.firstgov.gov/shopping/realestate/realestate.shtml: It features several groups of links for Commercial Buildings and Land, Farms and Ranches, Single Family Homes, and State and Local Government Sales. Follow the trail of links to your desired destination.

✔ **Seized Real Property Auctions** at `www.treas.gov/auctions/customs/realprop.html`: This site features a list of properties that the U.S. government has seized and put up for auction online. Discover more about the auction process at this site.

✔ **USDA Real Estate for Sale** at `www.resales.usda.gov`: It displays links to single-family or multi-family properties. Simply click the link and follow the trail of maps to your state and county to find out whether any USDA properties are for sale in your neighborhood.

Generating Additional Leads

At this point, you likely have more opportunities to explore than you have time to research, but after you have a solid support team in place, you may find that your flippable property pool becomes overfished. To continue expanding your real estate investment business, you can either widen your net by reaching out to other neighborhoods (see Chapter 8 for details) or fish a little deeper by advertising for leads.

Unless you're afflicted with a bad case of tunnel vision, you've probably noticed ads, signs tacked to telephone poles, and billboards advertising in big bold letters We Buy Homes. Well-established real estate investors often post these ads to draw sellers to them instead of locating properties on their own. You can follow their lead by doing a little of your own guerilla marketing:

✔ Tack up flyers at local stores, but don't post them on telephone poles, vacant buildings, or lawns, because it's against city ordinances.

✔ Print and distribute business cards to people you meet in the area.

✔ Network with others by telling *everyone* what you're doing and asking lots of questions.

✔ Visit neighborhood churches; they often know people in the neighborhood who need to dispose of a property.

✔ Post an ad in the neighborhood newspaper — Private Lender Looking for Properties.

✔ Post your own billboard ad after you become well established.

I know one investor who goes to sporting events and throws his business cards into the air like confetti. He claims that this stunt has led to a host of successful transactions. Refrain from throwing cards out of a moving vehicle, however, because the authorities consider this littering. Don't ask me how I know this, but rest assured that it's true.

Zip code flippers

Several flippers find success in a five-digit number. They concentrate on a specific zip code, the neighborhood in which they live. That's where their church is. They know the neighbors. They're committed to improving the neighborhood, and they do it one house at a time.

One particular zip code flipper I know performs a combination of flipping and holding (for rental income), specializing in two-bedroom homes that he converts into three-bedroom homes. He updates the mechanicals — plumbing, electric, heating, and so on. All his rehabs have central air conditioning. Over time, this focused flipper has established a solid reputation, not only for successfully flipping properties, but also for single-handedly revitalizing a depressed neighborhood. After a couple of years, he has become so well known and respected that he no longer needs to search for properties. People who are interested in selling their homes come to him first. He always has the first crack at the best opportunities.

Advertise only after you become well established and are comfortable flipping multiple properties at once. Otherwise, you may be overwhelmed with calls that you're unable to follow up on. This inability to get back with potential leads can quickly damage your reputation as a real estate investor.

Chapter 10

Inspecting the Property with an Eye for Rehab

*B*efore you even consider making an offer on a property, you should examine the property inside and out to evaluate its potential and then draw up a preliminary list of improvements that would make the property marketable at an attractive, yet profitable price. You can inspect the property during an open house or showing or during a private visit with your agent, who can assist you in determining which renovations could add the most value to the home and help you decide whether the property is a good investment.

In this chapter, I take you through a preliminary inspection and point out the features of the landscape and house that should draw your focus. I highlight the types of defects you should avoid at all costs, areas of a home that are often packed with potential, and the types of renovations that really boost a property's resale value. By the end of this chapter, you should be able to walk through a house in 15 to 30 minutes, give it the thumbs up or thumbs down, and walk away with a to-do list that you can use to start planning the repairs and renovations. (For additional tips, see Chapter 13.)

No problem is a real deal breaker if you know about it. You can calculate the cost of fixing a problem into your offer, so you're not losing any money. The situation you want to avoid is buying a house when you don't know about an issue. A thorough inspection of the premises and estimates for repairs and renovations is critical in determining how much to offer for a house.

Packing for Your Inspection Mission

A house inspection isn't just a pleasure trip. You're on an information-gathering mission to find the property with the most potential. To complete your mission successfully, plan ahead and pack the following essential tools:

- ✔ Pen or pencil.
- ✔ Clipboard.
- ✔ Camera, preferably digital. Pack extra batteries.
- ✔ Flashlight, for checking dark nooks and crannies. Test it beforehand to make sure that it works. And pack extra batteries.
- ✔ Circuit tester (one of those plug-in jobs), to check the outlets.
- ✔ Step ladder. Throw it in your car, just in case.
- ✔ One copy of the home inspection checklist in Figure 10-1 for each house you plan to visit. This document lists every area of a house (both exterior and interior) and includes spaces for comments, estimated renovation costs, and the amount of time needed for renovations.
- ✔ Screwdrivers (Philips and flathead), just in case you need to open something.
- ✔ Tape measure, for measuring rooms, doorways, ceilings, and so on.

If you don't like the idea of writing everything down, consider carrying a small digital recorder in your pocket or purse so you can record comments during your walk-through. A house-inspection trip typically brings you in contact with at least three or four properties, and when you're done looking, you're too exhausted and overwhelmed to remember important details. Don't rely on your memory alone.

Home Inspection Checklist

Property Address: _____

Area	Comments	Estimated Costs	Estimated Time
EXTERIOR			
Roof			
☐ Shingles & Underlayment			
☐ Underlayment			
Gutters & Siding			
☐ Missing or Damaged Gutters			
☐ Aluminum Siding			
☐ Vinyl Siding			
☐ Brick			
☐ Other			
Windows			
☐ Glass			
☐ Screens			
☐ Frames & Sills			
Driveway			
☐ Trip Hazards			
☐ Gravel			
☐ Asphalt			
☐ Concrete			
Landscaping			
☐ Backyard			
☐ Front & Side Yards			
Doors			
☐ Screens			
☐ Storms			
☐ Entry Doors & Frames			
Porch			
☐ Front Porch & Stairs			
☐ Back Porch & Stairs			
Garage			
☐ Roof, Siding, & Gutters			
☐ Doors & Windows			
☐ Foundation & Floor			
☐ Electric			
INTERIOR			
Electrical			
☐ Fuses/Circuit Breakers			
☐ Wiring			
☐ Switches			
☐ Junction Box Covers			
☐ Faceplate Covers			
Plumbing			
☐ Water Pipes			
☐ Wastewater Pipes			
☐ Hot Water Heater			
☐ Floor Drains/Sump Pump (Basement)			

Figure 10-1:
A home inspection checklist is an essential inspection tool.

Heating & Cooling			
☐ Furnace/Radiators/Boilers			
☐ Duct Work & Vents			
☐ Filters			
☐ Air Conditioning			
☐ Humidifier/Dehumidifier			
Living Room/Family Room			
☐ Floor/Carpet			
☐ Walls			
☐ Ceiling			
Laundry Room			
☐ Floor/Carpet			
☐ Walls			
☐ Ceiling			
☐ Washing Machine Connect			
☐ Laundry Tub			
Kitchen			
☐ Floor			
☐ Walls			
☐ Ceiling			
☐ Light Fixtures			
☐ Cabinets/Countertops			
☐ Sink			
☐ Stove			
☐ Refrigerator			
☐ Dishwasher			
Bedrooms			
☐ Floor/Carpet			
☐ Walls			
☐ Ceiling			
Bathrooms			
☐ Floor			
☐ Ceiling			
☐ Walls			
☐ Tile			
☐ Cabinets			
☐ Countertop			
☐ Lights			
☐ Tub/Shower/Enclosure			
☐ Toilet			
☐ Sink & Vanity			
☐ GFIs (Ground Fault Interrupters)			
Basement			
☐ Stairs & Handrail			
☐ Watertight Foundation			
☐ Windows & Lighting			
☐ Finished			
Attic			
☐ Insulation			
☐ Vents			
Other			
Total Estimated Costs			
Total Estimated Time			
Additional Comments			

Figure 10-1:
Continued.

Finding the Perfect Candidate for a Quick Makeover

When you're flipping your first or second property, look for the easy score — a property that looks a lot worse than it is. These houses are typically sold below market value because nobody wants them and the owners aren't motivated enough to do what's necessary to make somebody want to buy them. In short, look for a good, solid house that requires no major repairs and looks ugly. The following sections help you spot the signs of an ideal candidate. For full details on quick-flip renovations, head to Chapter 14.

Poor but promising curb appeal

If you go to look at a property and your first impulse is to drive past, that's a good sign that curb appeal is lacking. Either the house looks ugly from the street or you simply don't see it. The house has no pop. Assuming the shell of the house is sound — the roof, gutters, windows, and siding don't need to be replaced — you can often improve the curbside appeal with a few quick and affordable do-it-yourself improvements.

Figure 10-2 shows a potentially perfect candidate, although a closer inspection could prove otherwise. The house appears to be in good shape, but it doesn't really stand out from the street. However, some landscaping and light touches on the exterior can change all that!

Cosmetically challenged, inside and out

Often, a homeowner's poor taste is enough to turn away prospective buyers. The owners paint their house with colors that should be illegal in most states. They install carpeting that clashes and tile that can turn your stomach. They install a pink bathtub and paint the walls yellow.

Fortunately for you, cosmetically challenged houses are often a good buy, assuming they're in good condition. Simply by decking out the house in a new, neutral color scheme, you can raise the resale price by thousands of dollars and attract a steady stream of house hunters who previously couldn't stomach looking at the property.

Figure 10-2:
This house
is a
potentially
perfect
candidate
for a quick
makeover.

A second-rate showing

Homeowners often lack the energy, motivation, and expertise required to properly *stage* their home for a showing. Staging, as I discuss in Chapter 20, is the process of beautifying your home for prospective buyers. Think of it as primping yourself for a hot date. A properly staged home draws more interested buyers and commands a higher sales price, which is exactly what you *don't* want when you're bargain hunting.

When looking for a property to quickly flip for a profit, keep an eye out for poorly staged homes. The poor staging reduces your competition as a buyer, enables you to make a low-ball offer, and provides you with the opportunity to raise the resale price just by doing a little clean-up and redecorating.

Assessing Potential Curbside Appeal

Poor curbside appeal isn't necessarily a bad thing. It's often one of the main reasons you can purchase a property below market value. What you're looking for at this point is potential. When you pull up to the curb, don't scramble out of the car and sprint to the front door. Linger for a few moments, observe the outside of the house, and ask yourself the following:

✔ **Is the house visible from the street?** If it's visible, good. If you can do something relatively easy and inexpensive to increase its visibility, that's good, too. If the house is hopelessly hidden, that's bad.

✔ **Is the house on a busy thoroughfare?** If it is, that can be a good thing if the location provides convenient access to stores, schools, and work. It can also be a drawback, because people may worry about the noise and traffic.

✔ **Is the house near a park, school, or golf course?** Each of these places can be a big draw.

✔ **Is the exterior of the house inviting?** Can you make it more inviting without spending too much money? A little landscaping, including trimming trees and shrubs, mowing, and edging, can do wonders and doesn't cost a lot of money.

✔ **Are the sidewalks and driveway structurally sound?** Sidewalks and driveways can be solid and still look awful. Pulling weeds, patching cracks, and resealing an asphalt drive are easy, inexpensive fixes. If you need to install a new concrete drive or sidewalks, that can get a little costly.

✔ **What's the garage look like?** If the house doesn't have a garage, you may be able to add one, depending on how much land you have to work with. If the garage looks worse than it is, some minor improvements can give it the pop it needs.

✔ **How does this house stack up to neighboring houses?** Can you make affordable adjustments to make it the prettiest peacock on the block?

✔ **Does the house look as though it requires a greater investment than you can afford, both in time and money?** Bottom line: If the house strikes you as a money pit, walk away. Don't try to play the hero and try to salvage a hopeless home.

Be sure to include the entryway in your curb appeal assessment. A home's entryway is the bridge to an oasis. When a visitor passes through the front door, he should feel as though he's entering a new and better world. If the front porch is cluttered, the doors are ugly, and you enter feeling as though you're getting shoved into a closet, the entryway could use a little work.

And don't forget the backyard! Homeowners often treat the backyard like a pristine nature preserve. This undeveloped space often provides you with the pure potential you need to unleash your creativity, add living space, and significantly boost the property value. You may want to consider adding or improving a patio, deck, or attached garage.

Don't waste too much time and effort evaluating what you already know to be a lemon. Know when to cut and run. Here are some obvious signs of a house you probably want to steer clear of:

- ✔ Leaning tower of Pisa.

- ✔ Soil in contact with siding. This combination could mean no foundation, in which you should cut and run, or it may be a simple matter of grading (shoveling the dirt away from the house). If you can't figure out the cause of the problem, walk away.

- ✔ Nuclear plant in the backyard.

- ✔ Two neighboring houses completely gutted from fire.

- ✔ Numerous vacancies on the block.

Check out Chapter 15 for full details on perking up a house's curb appeal.

Taking a Big Whiff, Inside and Out

Nothing turns away a prospective buyer like a foul odor, so when you start looking at properties, get your sniffer up to snuff. Take a big whiff inside and out to check for any of these foul smells:

- ✔ Gas smells may indicate a leaking gas line. Notify the homeowner to contact the gas company and have it checked out.

- ✔ Sewage odors outside may point to problems with a septic tank or nearby sewer line. Indoor sewer odors may indicate a plumbing problem.

- ✔ Doggy doo is a common fragrance in backyards populated with one or more dogs. A little scooping can fix this problem. In addition, watch out for indoor pet odors from cats, dogs, or other animals and for decaying flesh from dead animals somewhere in the house.

- ✔ Cigarette smoke is a real turn-off for many buyers.

- ✔ Mold and mildew may be in damp areas in the house. (The notorious black mold isn't typically black, but you usually can smell it.)

None of these malodorous problems is a deal breaker, assuming you can locate the source of the smell and remove it without too much expense. Don't dismiss a bad smell, however, until you know what's causing it. If the seller is trying to mask bad smells by burning candles and incense or by using an assortment of air fresheners, try to smell past the cover-ups and pick up the scent in other rooms of the house.

Inspecting the House for Big-Ticket Items

Almost every property that's flippable can use a fresh coat of paint, new carpeting, and a little tender loving care. You expect that, and you budget it into the cost of the property. Unexpected defects in big-ticket items, however, can quickly bust your budget and drastically cut into your potential profit. Many of these items are costly to replace and, unfortunately, they don't increase the value of the property.

Although you should have the property professionally inspected before you close on the deal (see Chapter 11 for details about professional inspections), you can often save yourself the time and money by catching any major problems on your first visit. The following sections point out the most common and expensive problem areas.

Focusing on the foundation

Every house rests on a foundation, typically a basement or concrete slab. Inspect the foundation, inside and out, for any of the following symptoms of a sick foundation:

- **Cracked foundation or walls:** Almost all foundations have cracks, but large cracks that run down the entire length of the basement wall or along the floor are symptoms of costly structural problems. Check inside the house for cracked walls that may also point to foundation problems.

- **Bowed walls:** Check basement walls for any signs of bowing.

- **Warped floors:** Uneven floors may be a sign of underlying structural problems. If a floor is sinking, you may see the tops of the walls separating from the ceiling.

- **Spongy floors, particularly under wall-to-wall carpeting:** Be mindful while you walk to discover any spongy areas that may point to trouble. If the house has a basement or crawlspace, check the joists and the condition of the floor from the underbelly of the house.

- **Mold/mildew:** Mold and mildew on basement walls is often a sign of a leaky basement. The basement may appear to be dry now, but when the rain starts pouring down, you may have an indoor pool in your basement.

- **Recently installed paneling:** Recently installed paneling or drywall may indicate a foundation problem that the owner is trying to cover up.

Dampness in a basement isn't always a sign of a serious problem. Clogged gutters or downspouts that fail to direct the water away from the house are common causes of dampness too. Note the problem and be sure to mention it when you have the home inspected.

Examining the siding

Visually inspect the outside of the house and note the type of facing — brick, wood, vinyl, aluminum, or stucco. Compare it to the neighboring properties. Inspect the facing and note any damage or signs of aging:

- **Brick:** Worn or missing mortar
- **Vinyl:** Cracked, warped, or peeling siding
- **Aluminum:** Dented or peeling siding
- **Wood:** Rotted, cracked, or missing boards
- **Stucco:** Cracked, bowed, or peeling stucco

Chapter 15 has information on retooling a house's siding.

Giving the roof and gutters the once-over

As you inspect the home's facing, let your eyes wander up a little higher to check out the roof and gutters. Note any of the following potential problems:

- Bowed or damaged roof, indicating a problem with the underlying structure of the roof.
- Damaged or aging shingles. Shingles curling at the edges are often a sign that the house needs to be re-roofed.
- Obvious patches. An obvious patch or an area with shingles that don't match the color of surrounding shingles may indicate that the roof leaked in the past and caused additional damage.
- Two or more layers of shingles. You can usually lay one layer of shingles over another, but if you have two or more layers of shingles, the roofers often need to strip off the old layers first, which can nearly double the cost of roofing the house.
- Gutters pulling away from the house. You may be able to re-attach the gutters, unless the facing board they're anchored to is rotten.

Head to Chapter 15 for additional details about new roofs and gutters.

Glancing at the windows, inside and out

Windows are not only a functional part of every house — letting in light while insulating the house and acting as a barrier against the natural elements — but they also play an aesthetic role — accenting both the interior and exterior. Inspect windows for both function and appearance, and note the following:

- ✔ Any broken panes
- ✔ Torn or missing screens
- ✔ Windows painted shut
- ✔ Rotted wood, especially window sills

Chapter 17 has information about updating windows.

Evaluating the plumbing

As you walk through a house, turn the faucets on and off, flush the toilets, and check for the following common plumbing problems:

- ✔ **Clogged drains.** Leave the faucets running for several seconds to see whether the water backs up.
- ✔ **Leaking drains or pipes.** Check under the cabinets for any signs of leaking drains or pipes. Water stains on the ceilings and walls are often a sign of leaking pipes.
- ✔ **Dripping faucets.** Drips are relatively easy and inexpensive to fix, but note them.
- ✔ **Leaking toilets.** Try rocking the toilet or press your foot down near its base to make sure that the floor isn't rotted.
- ✔ **Low water pressure.** Water should flow faster than a trickle, especially if the house has an upstairs bathroom.
- ✔ **Broken water heater.** Make sure that you're getting hot water and visually inspect the water heater for rust, leaks, and other signs of damage.

Exploring the electrical system

A home's electrical system delivers power to every light, appliance, and gadget in the house. Fortunately, most homes built in the last 30 years or so have reliable electrical systems built to code. If the outlets function, the lights don't flicker, and the home was built in the last 30 years, you can be fairly confident that the electrical system is acceptable. Even so, you always should check for the following:

- ✔ The condition of the electrical box. An old electrical box with fuses instead of breaker switches may need to be replaced.

- ✔ The type of wiring used. The best wiring is installed in conduit (metal tubes that completely insulate the wire). Many homes use flexible cables insulated usually in white plastic, which is also acceptable. Older knob and tube wiring strings the wires around porcelain knobs and usually doesn't meet modern building codes. Aluminum wire (sliver rather than copper) may also be a problem in some areas.

- ✔ The use of lots of extension cords, indicating that the house has too few outlets or outlets that aren't working.

- ✔ The functionality of the outlets inside and out.

- ✔ The functionality of the lights. Turn on all the lights to make sure that they work.

For less than $5, you can purchase a three-pronged outlet tester (often called a *circuit analyzer*) with lights that indicate a properly or improperly wired outlet.

Checking out the furnace and air conditioner

When examining a house for investment purposes, compare what the house has to what it needs to bring it up to standards in the neighborhood. If most homes in the area have forced-air heat and central air conditioning, and the house you're looking at has radiant heat with no ductwork, adding central air conditioning can be costly, but it can also add real value to the property.

Visually inspect the furnace and air conditioning unit to determine their approximate age and any obvious damage. You may not be able to test the air conditioning if you're looking at a house in the winter, but you can check the furnace year-round by turning it on and cranking up the thermostat.

Check the seller's disclosure for the approximate age and condition of the furnace and air conditioning system. (Ten years is considered old, but I've seen furnaces last up to 30 years if they're good and well-maintained.) Also, turn on the furnace fan at the thermostat, and check the vents around the house to make sure the furnace fan is working.

Adjusting your eyes to the lighting

Some houses feel more like caves than homes. Even on a bright, sunny day, little light penetrates, and the house has insufficient lighting to compensate. As your eyes adjust to the lighting in various houses, observe what well-lit houses have that ill-illuminated houses lack. Focus on the following items:

- ✔ **Windows:** Compare the number, size, and positions of the windows.

- ✔ **Window dressings:** Some drapes and blinds are more translucent than others. What style of window dressings are used in well-lit houses?

- ✔ **Colors:** Dark walls, trim, carpet, and furnishings absorb light, often making a house seem darker than it really is.

- ✔ **Floor plan:** A house that's chopped into tiny rooms often prevents outside light from penetrating into the inner recesses.

- ✔ **Landscaping:** Trees and shrubs can filter out just enough light while shading the house and improving privacy, or they can blanket the house in gloomy darkness.

- ✔ **Skylights:** Modern homes often incorporate skylights to draw daytime lighting into a room and make it appear more open.

- ✔ **Light fixtures:** Well-lit homes typically have plenty of overhead light fixtures, track, or recessed lights. Poorly lit homes rely on lamps, which tend to cast shadows and consume living space.

Discovering Some Promising Features

Some houses are like army barracks. They're neat and clean and well suited for sheltering a family, but they're no work of art. A handful of homes are more inspired. They have a couple features that take your breath away . . . in a good way — perhaps a lush garden in the backyard, a master bedroom with a fireplace and built-in entertainment system, or a huge kitchen that opens into a living and dining room area complete with a fireplace. Keep an eye out for the features that I note in the following sections.

A single overpowering feature can often sell a home, so as you tour homes, look for these hidden gems, and when comparing houses, give more weight to a house with character than a house that's simply neat and tidy.

Rooms with character and class

Real estate agents often use the word "character" to mean "old," and they're typically justified in doing so. Older homes tend to have more character — interior walls of brick, tin ceilings, hardwood floors, sculpted plaster ceilings ten feet high, and so on. But some newer homes have their own classy features, as well.

Note any rooms that set the standard for character in the house. These are the rooms that can help you when the time comes to market your renovated home. The bare hardwood floors and unique shelving in Figure 10-3 really catch your eye.

Also note any rooms that fall short of the standard. These are the rooms that you can improve to make the house more attractive to potential buyers.

Figure 10-3:
Character
sells.

Hardwood floors hidden beneath the carpet

All too many homeowners think that hardwood floors are a liability, because they make the home look old. To hide the eyesore, they install wall-to-wall carpeting, completely unaware that they're hiding one of the most attractive features of their homes.

Whenever you inspect a home with wall-to-wall carpeting, try to find out what's under it. Check the floor in a closet or cubby hole near the carpeted area; these areas are often left uncarpeted. You may be able to peel up a corner of the carpet to take a peek, but don't get caught.

Hardwood flooring costs two to three times as much as carpeting laid over plywood, so it's definitely a bonus in terms of the property's value.

Getting a Feel for the Kitchen

Whenever you look at a home, imagine yourself preparing a meal, microwaving a bag of popcorn, grabbing a midnight snack, and washing dishes. Does the kitchen layout seem conducive to kitchen activities? Does it feel cramped? Would it feel cramped with another person? In the following sections, I give you a few tips on features to look for in a kitchen. Check out Chapter 16 for additional details on upgrading kitchens.

Gauging the hangout factor

Most house hunters want a kitchen they can hang out in with their friends and family. When sizing up a kitchen, gauge its hangout factor on a scale of 1 to 5:

- **1:** A small kitchen that's walled off from the rest of the house like the servants' quarters.
- **2:** A kitchen that's walled off from the rest of the house but has room for a table and chairs.
- **3:** A kitchen that opens into a dining room.
- **4:** A kitchen that opens into a dining room and living room.
- **5:** A kitchen that opens into a dining room and living room and has an island with a built-in stove and oven — so you can visit while cooking.

A tiny kitchen is no reason to give up on a house. You may be able to knock down a wall or two to open it up and add real value to the property. At this point, you're simply looking for potential and noting the existing quality of the kitchen. On your home inspection checklist, note the kitchen layout and any renovations required to bring it up to snuff. Use the flip side of the form if you want to sketch a rough draft.

Noting what the kitchen already has

On your home inspection checklist, note the condition of the kitchen countertops, cabinets, hardware (knobs and handles), sink and faucet, light fixtures, floor, and ceiling. Also, jot down a list of all the appliances that the homeowner plans to leave, including the following, and note their condition:

- Stove
- Oven
- Microwave
- Refrigerator
- Dishwasher

If you decide to make an offer on the house, be sure to include all kitchen appliances and anything else that's not an integral part of the house in your purchase agreement. Otherwise, the sellers have every right to take these items when they leave. See Chapter 11 for additional tips on negotiating the purchase.

Paying Attention to Bathrooms

The number of bathrooms and each bathroom's size and condition are important factors in determining the sales price of a house. A house with a single bathroom is a tough sell, as are houses with outdated or mold-covered baths or showers. As you tour a home, pay particular attention to the features described in the following sections.

As long as a house has a bathroom and a half or preferably two full bathrooms and the plumbing is acceptable, a bathroom is rarely a lost cause. Chapter 16 can help you estimate the costs of repairs and renovations.

Understanding that size matters

The minimum size for a bathroom is about 5 x 7 feet, and no matter how you arrange the toilet, shower, and sink, that feels a little cramped. An extra foot (5 x 8) significantly increases your choice of tub or shower. Any additional space is a bonus.

If a house has only one bathroom, you may be able to add a half bath or powder room — a room with a sink and toilet. A powder room requires 54 x 48 inches of space.

Recognizing a diamond in the rough

With the right amount of negligence, a bathroom can look a lot worse than it really is. If the room is spacious and the toilet and tub are in good condition, you may discover a diamond in the rough, as shown in Figure 10-4 (note the amount of space and the roomy tub). A thorough cleaning, some fresh caulk, and a coat of paint may be enough to transform a vile health hazard into a sparkling, nearly-new bathroom. With a little extra money, you can retile the floor and walls, resurface the tub, or install a new shower stall.

Figure 10-4:
This bathroom is a diamond in the rough.

Spotting water damage in floors and walls

Walls and floors are particularly susceptible to water damage in bathrooms. To check for water damage in the floor, press your foot down near the base of the toilet or try rocking the toilet back and forth. The toilet moves if the sub-floor it's anchored to is rotting.

If the bathroom is tiled, press lightly on the tiles around the bathtub, shower, and sink. In homes with drywall, moisture often softens the drywall and causes it to crumble. Note any serious damage you find, but don't rule out the house just yet.

Roaming through the Rest of the House

Although the overall floor plan and the kitchen and bathrooms are the key features in most houses, don't ignore the other rooms in the house. The following sections show you what to look for in these lower-profile rooms. Chapter 14 has details on renovations you can make in just about any room in a house.

Touring the bedrooms

In the not so distant past, bedrooms were for sleeping. If the room was big enough for a bed, a dresser, and a nightstand, it was sufficient. Nowadays, a bedroom is a sanctuary, often containing the aforementioned items along with a computer, TV, and other accoutrements.

Consider a 10-x-10-foot bedroom the bare minimum. When you consider that a queen size bed hogs about 35 square feet of floor space and a small dresser consumes another 5 or 6 square feet, a 100-square-foot bedroom quickly fills up. Of course, the larger the better — and that goes for the closet space in each bedroom, too.

A master suite, complete with a walk-in closet and an attached bathroom, is a big plus, because it appeals to married couples who have or are planning to have children.

Spreading out in living rooms, dens, and other wide open spaces

Like kitchens, living rooms, family rooms, and dens are social hangouts that should be spacious, attractive, and comfortable. A fireplace is a big bonus, as long as it's in working order. Be sure to have the condition of the chimney inspected and an estimate of any required repairs before you close on the house.

Looking at laundry rooms

Step into the laundry room and perform the usual inspections of the ceiling, walls, and floor to look for any damage or water stains that could indicate plumbing problems. Make sure the water pipe connections for the washing machine are present and that the threads on the connector aren't stripped. If the room has a laundry tub, note its condition and whether it needs to be replaced. Also, note the size of the room. The room should be large enough to hold a washer, dryer, and a shelf for storing clothes, along with one or two people to fold the laundry.

A main floor laundry room is a big plus. Most buyers don't want to have to run up and down the stairs to do their laundry. In some cases, converting an extra small room on the main floor into a laundry room is a smart move.

Stepping into closets, attics, and basements

As you're inspecting the house, don't forget to poke around in the closets, attic (if the house has an accessible attic), and basement. Note the condition and features of each on your inspection sheet. The following list runs down the kinds of things to look for:

- ✔ **Closets:** You should already have noted the bedroom closet space. Hallway closets are also a big plus for storing linens, cleaning supplies, and other stuff. Again, the bigger the better.

- ✔ **Attic:** If the house has an accessible attic, climb up there and note whether it has a floor (yes or no), adequate insulation (which you may not see if the attic has a floor), and sufficient venting for the roof. Is the attic large enough to convert into another room? Also inspect the under-side of the roof for any damage and note it on the roof section of your inspection sheet.

✔ **Basement:** Head to the cellar to inspect the stairway and handrail. Carefully check the outside walls for water or structural damage (walls bowed in or covered with mold or mildew). Is the basement finished or partially finished? Note the types of improvements you could make to the basement to enhance its appearance and functionality.

Are These Walls Optional? Envisioning a New Floor Plan

Some houses are begging for restructuring. They're either too chopped up to allow smooth movement throughout or they have too few rooms to make them marketable. Always look for houses with great floor plans so you don't have to invest in any major surgery, but if you can't find a house with a good floor plan, look for one that has a floor plan you can reconfigure affordably. If you're debating between two houses — one with three bedrooms and one with two bedrooms that you can convert into a three-bedroom house — all other things being equal, go with the three bedroom house. See Chapter 18 for details on reconfiguring spaces and other structural renovations.

Chapter 11

The Art of Haggling: Negotiating a Price and Terms

*T*he housing market doesn't have a "no haggle" policy. You pay for a property whatever you can convince the owner to accept. You negotiate. You compromise. You make trade-offs. You haggle until all parties either agree on the terms of the deal or agree to disagree and part company.

Negotiating requires patience and persistence, excellent communication skills, and an ability to look beyond the sales price and grasp all the factors that affect the deal — including the closing costs, costs of necessary repairs, date of possession, which appliances stay with the house, and the seller's motivation for selling.

In this chapter, I show you how to prepare an initial offer that's reasonable enough to bring the seller to the bargaining table, yet low enough to give you some haggle room. I recommend adding conditional clauses to your offer to give yourself a safe exit if something goes wrong. And I reveal negotiating secrets that can add thousands of dollars to your bottom line and ensure your long-term success.

A house is worth only what a buyer is willing to pay and a seller is willing to accept. Your success at negotiating hinges on your ability to accurately estimate what you can afford to pay and what the seller will accept. For more negotiating techniques and tips, check out *Negotiating For Dummies,* by

Michael C. Donaldson and Mimi Donaldson. For information on purchasing a home, check out *Home Buying For Dummies,* 3rd Edition, by Eric Tyson, MBA, and Ray Brown (Wiley).

Planting the Seeds for Successful Negotiation

Negotiation begins long before you make an offer on the house. It begins when you choose a real estate agent to represent you.

When you choose an agent, make sure that the agent represents your interests; can keep the lid on sensitive information, such as how much you're really willing to pay for the property; and has a good poker face. An agent who represents both buyer and seller or one who tends to wag his tongue is a poor choice. See Chapter 4 for tips on selecting the best agent for your needs.

Negotiation continues when you start looking at and talking about a property. As you walk through a property to check it out, remain dispassionate. You may see a two-bedroom house with attic space that you can convert into a third bedroom for $5,000, adding $25,000 to the value of the house, but you don't have to yell "KA-CHING!" in front of the seller or his agent. Contain your glee until you get home.

You're better off letting the seller or seller's agent overhear a few mildly negative comments about the property, such as the following:

- ✔ Nice house, but the asking price is a little steep considering all the work it needs.
- ✔ The bathrooms need to be completely remodeled. That'll cost a few grand.
- ✔ The furnace looks old. It'll probably need to be replaced.
- ✔ Looks like the roof has two layers of shingles already. It'll have to be stripped first.

Don't trash-talk the house, because it may turn the owners against you. But making subtle comments about work that needs to be done can help prepare the seller for a lower offer. When you're looking at a house to flip, if you can't say something bad, don't say anything at all. And if you can't be chatty without disclosing sensitive information, zip your lips. See Chapter 10 for more details on carefully inspecting a particular property.

Digging Up Pertinent Information about the Seller

You researched the property thoroughly, but details about the property comprise only about half the information you need before you present your offer. The second half consists of information about the sellers and the reason they're selling. Talk with your agent and do a little detective work to obtain answers to the following questions:

- ✔ **Why is the homeowner selling?** The answer to this question can help you determine how eager the homeowner is to sell the property (and how low you can go on your offer). Maybe the seller has just been laid off or needs to relocate to keep her job. Perhaps the seller's busybody mother-in-law just moved in down the block. Maybe something's going on in the neighborhood that will convince you not to buy the property.

- ✔ **How soon does the homeowner need to move?** Did he already purchase another house? Has he scheduled a moving date? If he sells the house now, will he need additional time to find a new house or apartment? By knowing the current owner's situation, you may be able to present your offer in a way that goes beyond the seller's monetary needs, perhaps by highlighting the fact that you can move ahead immediately.

- ✔ **How much equity does the homeowner have in the property?** If the owner stands to cash out $70,000, she may be more willing to compromise on price if you can offer something in return, such as a quick, trouble-free closing. If, on the other hand, she has little or no equity in the house, she may be less willing to negotiate on the price. (Check out Chapter 6 for more information about equity.)

- ✔ **Did another buyer already bid on the property?** If so, how much did he bid? Why did the deal fall through? You can learn lessons from previous offers that can help you make your offer more attractive. For example, if the previous offer fell through because the buyer couldn't come up with the cash to close, you may be able to offer less with more earnest money to prove that you're serious and that you have the cash on hand to seal the deal.

- ✔ **If you're purchasing the property from a bank's REO department, do they have an addendum to the purchase agreement?** If so, obtain that addendum and review it in advance. The addendum can inform you of any special conditions that apply to the sale, such as types of financing permitted. (See Chapter 12 for more about buying an REO property.)

Don't expect your agent to supply you with information about previous offers on the property and details of why a particular offer fell through. Laws in most areas discourage disclosing sensitive information that may provide one party with an unfair advantage. Try to engage the homeowner in a conversation in which he discloses this information himself.

Real estate revenge

Every once in a while you happen upon a deal that's just too good to be true. I was looking at houses to flip and, while touring one couple's home, I noticed that the closets had only women's clothes. This is always a good sign that the marriage is on the rocks or the couple is divorced.

I visited the courthouse and obtained a copy of the divorce decree. The entire process, including the time I spent driving to the courthouse and back, took me less than an hour. From the divorce decree, I discovered that the wife and children were allowed to live in the house until the youngest child turned 18. The wife was then required to sell the house and send the husband 50 percent of the proceeds. She was given the sole right to determine the price of the house.

Well, the wife was getting remarried to a relatively wealthy man, and she didn't really care about the money. What she cared about was sticking it to her ex, so she was willing to sell the house for $20,000 less than it was worth!

Fortunately, I was in the right place at the right time and was able to cash in on the irrational vengeance of a messy divorce. The Freedom of Information act entitles you to public records. (Check out www.usdoj.gov/04foia for more information.) You can view these documents and sometimes have them printed for a small cost. When you're looking for an edge at the negotiating table, leave no stone unturned. You may just stumble upon a minor detail that saves you a major amount of cash.

You can learn a great deal about the seller's situation by looking around the house on your first walk-through. If the property seems a little run-down but the seller has two satellite dishes on the roof, a big flat-screen TV, and a boat in the backyard, he may value the latest toys and gadgets more than he values the house. To the seller, selling the house may be an opportunity for him to buy more stuff or pay off the stuff he already has.

Making an Offer They Can Refuse (but Will Consider)

Preparing an offer (also known as a *purchase agreement*) on a property is like deciding how much to raise the bet in a hand of poker when you're holding a royal flush. Raise too much, and everyone folds. Raise too little, and someone may see your raise and end the betting long before you suck enough chips into the pot for a big payout. You want the betting to go on long enough so you can get more of what you want.

When preparing an offer, your goal isn't necessarily to have your first offer accepted. If it is, you may be paying more for the property than you should. Your goal is to offer just enough to persuade the homeowner to counter your offer and to show you're serious. In other words, you want to make an offer they *can* refuse but will consider and counter.

If a seller accepts your opening bid, it doesn't necessarily mean that your bid was too high. Don't get the heebie jeebies and start second guessing your decision. You did your homework, you made an offer on a property that you know you can profit from, and you got lucky. The homeowner accepted your bid. Now it's time to move forward. Delay can lead to downfall.

The following sections highlight the most important factors to consider in preparing your offer, including price, earnest money, conditional clauses, and other enticements. I also explain the best ways to pitch your offer and steer you clear of common negotiation pitfalls.

All offers and counteroffers must be in writing. With real estate transactions, the written word rules. Verbal agreements are worthless. The saying in the industry is "Buyers are liars, and sellers are worse." Get everything in writing. Your real estate agent can supply you with the form you need to officially present your offer.

Calculating a price

Before you make an offer on a property, you already know the maximum amount you can pay for it, based on market conditions, required repairs and renovations, and your desired profit. (Chapter 5 shows you how to project your profit.) But your maximum price isn't necessarily the price you want to offer. When settling on a price, the following three strategies are most effective:

- ✔ **Leave a little haggle room.** Offer 3 to 5 percent below the price you're willing to pay to allow some room to negotiate. You don't want to offer a price so low that the owner dismisses the offer outright and refuses to sell — or even worse, goes with another investor's offer — but you don't want to pay too much for the property, either. This strategy works well in most cases.

- ✔ **Make a firm offer.** Make your best offer and stick to it. I've seen firm buyers remain firm, and have the seller reject the initial offer only to come back three weeks later, highly motivated to sell. If you can remain firm, this strategy may be the best for you. Some buyers stick to this strategy in every case. Others do it only when they know they can profit from the property even if their best offer is accepted and they're pretty sure that it's the best offer the buyer is likely to receive.

✔ **Make a low-ball offer.** A good time to make a low-ball offer is when you're already working on a project and don't really need another property. If you get the house for a steal, great. If you miss out, you really haven't lost anything.

Consider including a one-page letter that explains how you arrived at the price you're offering. For example, you may point out that comparable homes in better condition are selling for more, but that this house needs a new roof, which would cost about $8,000; a remodeled kitchen, which would run about $10,000; and new carpeting, which would cost about $3,000. You may actually be able to get the work done for a lot less by doing some of the labor yourself, but it's okay to quote what the seller would have to pay to have the work done professionally. Don't jack up your estimates — the seller may have estimates of her own, and you don't want to look like a swindler. Chances are you're telling the seller what she already knows. Your letter simply shows that you're no dummy — you've done your homework.

Proving you're earnest: Money talks

The old saying that "money talks" is especially relevant when you're pitching an offer on a house. Every offer should include earnest money that demonstrates how serious you are about purchasing the property. A $5,000 earnest money deposit speaks louder than a $500 deposit.

I can't offer you any hard and fast rules on what to offer in the way of earnest money. That depends on several factors, including how much cash you have on hand, how badly you want the property, and how much you're offering as a purchase price. In general, earnest money in the range of $1,000 to $5,000 is sufficient. The more you put down upfront, the stronger your position at the bargaining table.

As long as you deposit the earnest money with the title company (see Chapter 4 for more about title companies) or another reputable and insured real estate professional, your deposit is safe. In most cases, the seller's broker holds the earnest money. With REO sales (see Chapter 12), the bank may require that the listing broker or title company holds the deposit. Either way, the money is safe unless you default on the purchase agreement. When the deal closes, the money is credited back to you. If the deal doesn't close, you get the money back, assuming, of course, you lived up to your end of the bargain — you were diligent in seeking financing, you showed up for the scheduled closing, and you had a good reason to back out of the deal.

Another way to show that you're serious about the deal is to provide proof of your financing along with your offer. Proof of financing may consist of a preapproval letter from your lender. If you're offering cash, you may include a copy of your bank statement with your account numbers blacked out. A signed and notarized statement from a private lender can also function as proof of financing. Head to Chapter 6 for details on securing financing for a flip.

Dangling additional enticements

Although the purchase price is the high-profile part of any offer, a real estate transaction isn't always all about money. Sellers have other needs. They may need some extra time to move, a new place to move to, some ready cash, or maybe even a good used car to get to work. By knowing the seller's needs and her motivation for selling (see "Digging Up Pertinent Information about the Seller," earlier in this chapter, for details), you can often sweeten the pot by addressing her most pressing needs. Check out the following sections for tips on providing additional enticements to the seller.

Helping the seller move on

Instead of approaching a negotiation as a contest, consider it a collaboration between you and the seller with the goal of meeting both of your needs. You need to acquire a property at a price below market value. Find out what the seller needs most:

- ✔ If the seller needs more time to move, consider giving him 30 days free rent, and then start charging him if he stays any longer. Taking a loss of a few hundred dollars to gain thousands later is often a wise choice. In the meantime, you can start lining up your contractors and planning renovations (see Chapter 13 to get started).

- ✔ Help the seller find a new place to live if she doesn't know where to go. As you become more involved in real estate, you establish connections with other owners and landlords and can often refer sellers to other people who can assist them.

- ✔ Refer the sellers to a probate attorney if they need legal assistance.

- ✔ Advance the sellers some money, so they can secure alternative housing, or assist them with a section 8 voucher if they qualify for subsidized housing. (You can find out more about public housing vouchers and track down your local Public Housing Agency through HUD's Web site at www.hud.gov.)

- ✔ Call around to car dealers if the sellers need affordable transportation.

If the seller isn't ready to sell right away, don't get pushy. You may lose the house for good. Consider purchasing the property on contract, as I explain in Chapter 3. That takes the heat off the seller and provides you with a future project.

Do whatever you can — if it's aboveboard and reasonable — to help the sellers get on with their lives, but don't cross the line. Helping distressed sellers get on with their lives versus plying them with favors so you can steal their property may seem like a fine line, but it's a line between right and wrong, between legal and illegal.

Laying down cash

In real estate, cash is King. Think of it like a deck of playing cards. Cash is King. Fifty percent down is a Queen. Thirty percent down is a Jack. Twenty percent down is a Ten. Ten percent down is a Nine. Five percent down is an Eight. And zero percent down is a Seven. To have the winning offer, you want to lay down a King.

Offers with large down payments in cash always have an edge over other offers, because they have less risk of falling through at the last minute due to the buyer's failure to obtain loan approval.

You may be wondering — if cash is King, what's an Ace? Con artists consider an Ace to be an offer of cash back at closing, but that's actually the Joker, and if you get caught, that Joker can lead to jail time. Working out a deal in which the seller agrees to sell you the property for more than it's worth so you can get a big fat loan and split the proceeds with the seller is a form of fraud.

Convincing the seller to sweeten the deal

When you're offering less than market value for a house, asking the seller to throw in the stove and refrigerator sounds a little pushy. But sometimes, the purchase price is all the seller sees. He's so focused on getting that purchase price a little higher that he really doesn't care about those expensive appliances.

Before you present your offer, you may not be entirely sure about how stuck the seller is to the sticker price. So, when you present your offer, consider asking the seller for additional items. If he won't budge on the price, he may be willing to negotiate on these other items, which can boost your bottom line. Here are some ideas on what you can ask for:

✔ **Seller to pay for all or some of the repairs.** If the home is in need of some costly repairs, ask the seller to pay for all or a portion of the repairs. Whatever you save in repairs decreases your total investment in the property and increases your bottom line.

✔ **Seller to leave all appliances.** If the appliances are relatively new and in good condition, ask the seller to include the appliances. A refrigerator, stove, microwave, and washer and dryer can represent thousands of dollars. Whether you're planning to rent or sell the house, saving money on buying the appliances later can be a big plus.

✔ **Seller to pay a portion of closing costs.** The seller can legally pay up to 6 percent of closing costs. Although that may not represent a huge chunk of change, it can help you recoup a little if you have to give in on the purchase price.

✔ **Seller to waive reimbursement of tax prorations.** In some states, the seller pays property taxes in advance. When you buy the property, you normally pay back to the seller any taxes he paid for months that you will own the house. Because the seller already parted with this money, he often doesn't see it as a loss if you ask him to waive the reimbursement. This waiver could save you $1,000 to $3,000 dollars, depending on the time of the year and the tax amount on the property. In other states, homeowners pay taxes in arrears — the homeowner pays last year's taxes this year. In these states, the seller typically gives money to the buyer at closing to cover taxes for any months the seller lived in the house.

To the seller, everything that affects the bottom line — the amount of cash she walks away with at closing — becomes her main focus. Asking the seller to leave appliances and waive the reimbursement of tax prorations is often less of an issue for the seller than asking for a significantly lower sales price. These are items that are often open for negotiation.

You can often distract the seller by asking for something that you know the seller won't negotiate. Say the seller has a boat stored in the garage. He loves this boat, and you know that he probably doesn't want to sell it. List it on the purchase agreement. When the seller sees it, he says, "No way is he getting my boat!" You agree to take the boat off the purchase agreement, and the seller okays the deal, giving you what you really wanted in the first place.

Protecting your posterior with weasel clauses

Weasel clauses (more officially known as *conditional clauses*) are legal phrases in the offer that enable you to weasel out of the offer if something goes wrong. Although they're designed to help buyers back out of a deal when they can't get their financing approved or in the event that the home inspection uncovers a serious problem with the property, they're often used as escape clauses when a prospective buyer gets cold feet or finds a better deal. Make sure that your offer contains the following weasel clauses:

- ✔ **Financing must be approved.** If you're taking out a loan to pay for the property, make the purchase conditional upon your financing being approved. Buying property you can't pay for is a sure way to end up in foreclosure. If you have cash on hand to pay for the property, don't worry about this clause. See Chapter 6 for more about financing.

- ✔ **Sale is subject to closing on another property.** If you're counting on the proceeds from the sale of another property to finance the purchase of this property, stipulate that your offer is conditional upon the closing of the transaction on the other property. If you add this condition, include a copy of the offer you have on the other property, so the seller knows you're not making up this information.

- ✔ **Property must pass inspection.** To ensure that you don't get stuck with a termite-infested house or a house that has foundation problems, make your offer conditional upon the home passing inspection. Not only does this clause provide a safety net, but it also buys you time to obtain estimates on repairs and renovations. See "Inspecting the house from the ground up," later in this chapter, for more about inspections.

- ✔ **Property must have a clear title.** A clear title ensures that the property has no liens against it and that the person selling the property actually owns it. Never submit an offer without this condition. Chapter 4 has the scoop on hiring a title company to do a title search for you.

- ✔ **Property must appraise at the sales price or higher.** To ensure that the property is worth what you're offering, make your offer conditional upon the appraisal. See "Ordering an appraisal," later in this chapter, for details on the appraisal process.

- ✔ **Buyer's attorney must approve contract.** A clause that gives your attorney ten business days to inspect and approve the contract provides you with additional time to seek a qualified second opinion. See Chapter 4 for details on finding an attorney.

Conditional clauses may protect you, but too many of them can sink the deal. Many purchase agreements have built-in conditional clauses required by local governing agencies or associations. Familiarize yourself with the purchase agreement used in your area, so you're not adding redundant clauses that raise red flags. Your agent can provide you with a copy of the purchase agreement used in your area.

Pitching your offer

When you're ready to make an offer on a property, work closely with your agent to put the offer in writing, and then submit the offer through your agent. Pitching your offer through an agent provides you with several advantages, including the following:

- ✔ The agent can act as the bad guy, presenting a low-ball offer without making the homeowner despise you personally.

- ✔ You lessen the risk of communicating sensitive information, verbally or through your body language.

- ✔ You have more time to react. When a seller voices an objection or presents a counteroffer, the agent acts as a buffer and gives you time to compose yourself and offer a rational response.

- ✔ A skilled agent can often present your offer more effectively than you can. Agents are in sales.

- ✔ Your agent can provide you with a second, expert opinion.

- ✔ You can focus on the offer while your agent attends to the minor details of making sure that everything is properly recorded.

Representing yourself during negotiation is like playing Texas Hold'Em with your cards facing out to the seller. A savvy seller can gather a lot of information about you by what you say and how you act that can cost you thousands of dollars. Hire a real estate agent who's an experienced and gifted negotiator, and make yourself readily available to your agent during the negotiation process. Your agent may have a limited amount of time to present your counteroffer, and the more responsive you are, the more serious you appear to the seller.

Handling counteroffers

When the owner proposes a counteroffer, you have two more pieces of valuable information. You now know:

- ✔ That the owner probably hasn't received a much better offer.

- ✔ More about what the homeowner wants, as described in the counteroffer.

A counteroffer typically specifies the amount of time you have to respond. This amount of time can range from several hours to several days, but it's usually a day or two. If the counteroffer is reasonable and contains the price and terms you need to successfully flip the property, accepting it outright is always an option. Don't get greedy. If the numbers and terms don't meet your requirements for turning a profit (as discussed in Chapter 5), consider countering the counteroffer. You and the seller aren't limited by a set number of counteroffers, so you can go back and forth until you reach an agreement.

Use the guidelines I give earlier in the chapter for presenting your initial offer to structure your counteroffers, and keep your eye on the bottom line. If the seller doesn't budge on the price, counter with an offer that requests additional items — appliances, repair costs, closing costs, and so on. Look at the whole picture, and make sure that after all is said and done, you can pay for the house, flip it, and still walk away with a profit of 20 percent or better.

Having another prospective property lined up can also help you during the negotiation. Tell your agent that if you can't come to terms on this property by a certain deadline, you want to look into making an offer on a second property. This tactic applies some gentle pressure on the seller. You make your offer, but you also let the seller know that you can take it away at any time.

Ducking common negotiating pitfalls

Some people are terrible negotiators. They're too open. They get rattled by uncertainty and silence. They overreact. They get emotionally involved. They convey a sense of eagerness and enthusiasm that prevents them from thinking straight. And then, they make critical errors. Following is a list of common negotiating pitfalls that you should avoid:

- ✔ **Overbidding:** Don't present everything you have to offer on your opening bid. If the seller says "No," you have nothing more to offer. However, some investors do well by presenting their best offer upfront and then sticking with it. If you're going to make your best offer upfront, make sure you're the type who can stick.

- ✔ **Excessively underbidding:** A low-ball offer is one thing, but make sure that your pitch doesn't end up in the dirt. It can turn the seller against you, make any competitive offers look that much better, and if you do it often enough, it can make your agent wonder whether it's in her best interest to work with you.

- ✔ **Bidding against yourself:** Don't submit another, higher, offer until the seller responds to your initial offer. Some buyers get the jitters when they don't hear back immediately from the seller, and they submit a higher offer. When you do this, you're bidding against yourself and often pay more for the property than you have to.

✔ **Making a take-it-or-leave-it offer:** An ultimatum is counterproductive in negotiations. You want to open the lines of communication, not shut them down.

✔ **Talking too much:** You have two ears and one mouth, so listen twice as much as you talk. Ask questions, but don't offer information about why you're buying the property or what you intend to do with it. If you can't restrain yourself, you're better off saying nothing — just smile and talk about the weather. If you're just making chit-chat, never talk about sex, religion, politics, or schools.

✔ **Responding to an unofficial counteroffer:** To be official, a counteroffer must be recorded on the purchase agreement and the seller must initial any changes. If the seller or seller's agent comes back with a note or phone call saying he'll consider the offer "if . . . ," make him put it in writing.

Keep a copy of all offers and counteroffers. If the seller rejects your offer, keep a copy of that, too. Write "Rejected" across it and file it with any other information you have on the house. If a seller comes back later claiming that you agreed to purchase the property, you want to have proof that you didn't.

Tending to the Details: Inspections, Appraisals, and Walk-Throughs

Just because the seller accepted your offer doesn't mean that you have a done deal. Now's the time to test those conditional clauses I tell you about earlier in this chapter. You need to schedule a home inspection, have the property appraised, and do one final walk-through before closing, as discussed in the following sections.

Inspecting the house from the ground up

Immediately after the seller accepts your offer, schedule a home inspection. (Chapter 4 explains how to find and select a home inspector.) The inspection ensures that the house doesn't have any hidden surprises, such as foundation problems, a faulty electrical system, or substandard plumbing. In the following sections, I explain different areas of concern to examine and show you how to put the inspection results to good use.

Although some experts recommend staying out of the inspector's way during the inspection and waiting for the written report, I strongly recommend that you schedule the inspection for a time you can be present, preferably during the daylight hours, so you have a clear view of the external features of the house. You should be there to hear specifically what the inspector has to say during the inspection. Take notes or carry a recorder for later reference, and pack a digital camera so you can take a picture of any defects the inspector points out and reference them later.

Examining areas of concern

If the inspector raises any doubts about a big-ticket item, such as the condition of the roof or furnace, or if she recommends additional tests or inspections, schedule follow-up inspections. For example, if the furnace is old, call in a heating and air-conditioning contractor to inspect it more thoroughly. (Chapter 4 has information on finding contractors.) The cost of repairs to any of these items varies depending on the nature of the problem and material and labor costs in your area. Areas of concern often include the following:

- **Foundation:** The entire house rests on the foundation. If it shows signs of water damage or serious settling, have it professionally inspected. Fixing the problem may be a simple matter of repairing the gutters to direct more water away from the foundation (inexpensive) to jacking up the house and pouring a new foundation (extremely expensive).

- **Electrical system:** If the home inspector points out any concerns about the electrical system, have a licensed electrician inspect it. An electrician can tell you whether the system is up to code and, if it's not, provide an estimate on the cost to bring it up to code.

- **Plumbing and septic:** A home inspector typically checks the plumbing to ensure that the water pressure is sufficient, nothing is leaking, and drains are freely flowing. If the plumbing appears to be substandard, have a licensed plumber inspect it. If the septic system is over ten years old, have that inspected, as well.

- **Aging, big-ticket items, including furnace, A/C, and roof:** If something is old but working, don't assume it's okay. Have a licensed contractor check it out. Even if a furnace is heating the house, it may be leaking carbon monoxide or have other problems that the inspector doesn't notice.

- **Attic and insulation:** Make sure that the inspector checks the attic. Does it have sufficient insulation? Does the insulation contain asbestos? Does the underside of the roof show any signs of damage or leaking?

- **Grading:** Does the ground slope down away from the house as it should? Poor grading can funnel water right into the home's foundation and is costly to fix.

✔ **Lead-based paint:** In some homes built before 1978 and many homes built before 1960, lead-based paint may be present. You can pick up a test kit at your local hardware store to test for lead. In some cases, correcting this problem can be cost-prohibitive — because you must disclose the presence of lead-based paint on your Seller's Disclosure, it can drive a lot of potential buyers away.

✔ **Asbestos:** Commonly used to insulate furnaces and water pipes, asbestos is a health hazard that's costly to deal with. If it turns up in a home inspection, obtain a couple of estimates on having it removed, and then calculate that into your rehab costs.

✔ **Radon:** Radon is a known cancer-causing gas that can be a problem in some areas of the country, and often requires that the foundation be sealed and vented or even completely replaced, which can cost thousands of dollars. Your local environmental protection agency can tell you whether Radon is a problem in your area.

✔ **Toxic mold:** If the home shows any signs of moisture damage or mold stains, have it tested for toxic mold and determine the cost of eliminating the mold and its cause. The presence of toxic mold (often called *black mold,* even though it's not always black) is enough to kill a deal — fixing the problem can cost as much as the purchase price of the house. If you suspect mold to be a problem, call a certified mold remediation specialist for additional testing and any necessary treatment.

✔ **Lead pipes or lead in water:** Some homes built before 1940 have lead pipes or copper pipes joined with lead solder. If lead is a concern, call your local water company to have the water tested. The cheap fix is to install a water filter for the drinking water. More expensive fixes call for replacing the pipes or installing a whole-house water filtration system.

The home inspector is sort of like your family doctor. She can give you a quick examination to tell whether you're generally healthy or not, but if you have any specific complaints that she's uncertain about, she refers you to a specialist. The home inspector can tell whether everything is functional, but if you or the inspector has a specific concern, consult a specialist.

If you're buying a property that the seller winterized, the gas, water, and electricity may be shut off, preventing an inspector from doing a thorough job. In this case, request that all utilities be turned on for the inspection.

Moving forward with the inspection results

You can use the home inspection results to your advantage in the following ways:

- ✔ If the home inspection turns up serious, expensive problems that the seller refuses to fix, you can back out of the deal.

- ✔ If the home inspection identifies required repairs, you can lower your offer to accommodate the cost of those repairs both in terms of time and money or demand that the seller pay for those repairs.

- ✔ You can ignore the little stuff and further endear yourself to the seller by avoiding the urge to nitpick.

If the inspection uncovers some issues that tempt you to submit a new counteroffer, realize that a counteroffer essentially places the property back on the market. I've seen many investors lose out on a good deal by over-negotiating.

Ordering an appraisal

If you're borrowing money from a bank or other lending institution, you don't have to worry about ordering an appraisal. The lender does it for you and adds the cost to the closing costs. Actually, the lender does the appraisal not to protect you but to protect the lender's investment. Even so, you should request a copy of the appraisal. The appraisal can either confirm or refute your belief that you're not overpaying for the property. Submit your request in writing; normally, the form you need in order to request a copy of the appraisal is in the package you receive at closing.

When you're purchasing the property with your own cash or with money from a private lender, consider ordering an appraisal to ensure that the property is worth what you think it's worth (an *as-is appraisal*) or what it will be worth after repairs and renovations (an *as-repaired appraisal*). An as-is appraisal is useful for helping you determine whether you offered too much for the property. An as-repaired appraisal can help you guesstimate your potential profit (as I explain in Chapter 5). In most cases, your agent's advice is sufficient, assuming he has a thorough knowledge of the market, but if you have any doubts, an accurate appraisal can put them to rest. I give you tips on finding an appraiser in Chapter 4.

If the appraisal shows that the house is worth way more than you offered, pop the cork on that bottle of champagne and start celebrating. If the appraisal comes back showing that you offered too much for the house, you then have several options:

- ✔ Ignore the appraisal, because you're sure that the property is worth more.

- ✔ Back away from your original offer and submit a new, lower offer. (This action places the property back on the market, so it's a little risky.)

- ✔ Ask the seller to throw in an added enticement to get you to go through with the offer.

Taking one final walk-through

The day before closing, walk through the house one last time to make sure that it's in the same condition or better than when you placed your offer. Until you close on the deal, the seller owns the house, and anything that happens to it is his responsibility. If the hot water tank bursts the day before closing, you're entitled to a new hot water tank at the seller's expense. If the wind picks up and the roof blows off, that's on the seller's tab.

Pack your digital camera and a notepad and document anything that looks out of the ordinary — any new problems that arose after the inspection.

Crossing Your Eyes and Dotting Your Tees: Closing the Deal

When you attend a closing, the title company's closing agent hands out a bunch of forms and contracts, and tells you to read everything, make sure that you understand it, and sign and initial the documents as directed. Except for a handful of control freaks, nobody reads through all those forms, but you really should. People can hide all sorts of zingers in a legally binding contract.

To be safe, you or your attorney should read, understand, and agree to everything stated on a document before you sign it. To keep closings from taking much more than an hour, I recommend that you ask the title company for the closing packet in advance, and read everything or have your attorney or your agent look at the paperwork before the scheduled time. (You may have only 24 hours before closing to review the paperwork.) Write up a list of questions along with any errors you find, and have them addressed before closing. If you wait until closing, some serious delays are likely to occur.

Don't sign anything unless you have read it and understand it! Pay close attention to the following items:

- ✔ **Your name:** Make sure that the documents include your legal name and not your nickname.

- ✔ **Your social security number:** These documents are official records and are likely to show up on your credit report, so make sure that your social security number is correct.

- ✔ **Information on the 1003:** If you're taking out a loan to purchase the property, you receive a 1003 (commonly referred to as a ten-oh-three) at closing. This is your loan application, and it includes your name, social security number, annual salary, and other details about your finances. The loan officer presents this information to the mortgage company. Giving false information is mortgage fraud, so make sure that all the information is correct before you sign the form. You can't leave this one up to your attorney to verify; read it yourself and correct any errors before you sign.

✔ **Mortgage and interest rate:** If you're taking out a loan to purchase the property, make sure that the mortgage amount and interest rate recorded on the form is the same as what the lender or loan officer quoted you. Have any necessary corrections made before you sign the form.

If you're a flipper and you're taking out a loan, make sure that it has no early-payment or prepayment penalty. Nothing is more shocking than reselling the house and finding out at the closing that the $200,000 loan you took out to purchase the house has an extra $6,000 added to it as a 3 percent penalty for paying off the loan in fewer than three years. Double-check for any prepayment penalties before closing.

Chapter 12

Closing In on Foreclosure Properties

*F*oreclosure is an unfortunate necessity that often wipes out any equity built up in the home, injures the homeowner's credit rating, and forces the homeowner and perhaps the person's entire family out of their home. The upside, if there is an upside, is that foreclosure provides an opportunity for the lender to recover the unpaid debt (or at least a portion of it), for homeowners to relieve themselves of their financial burdens and perhaps salvage some of the equity in their homes, and for you to purchase properties below market value.

As a real estate investor, you should know the basics of the foreclosure process so you can survive a foreclosure, if it ever happens to you, and profit from flipping foreclosure properties, if you choose to explore this area. And why should you explore it? Because foreclosures can be some of the best real estate deals in town.

This chapter introduces you to the foreclosure process, outlines the local rules you need to understand, and leads you step by step through the course of locating and purchasing foreclosure properties.

When dealing in foreclosure properties, you may or may not purchase the property through your agent, depending on the point in the foreclosure process at which you decide to make your offer. You may purchase the property at an auction. However, an agent who knows the foreclosure process in your area can be a valuable mentor and even steer you to opportunities for purchasing pre-foreclosure properties.

Getting Up to Speed on the Foreclosure Process

 A common misconception of foreclosure is that after the homeowner misses a payment or two, the bank immediately takes possession of the home and then turns around and auctions it off at a foreclosure sale. Actually, the process is more drawn out than that, typically falling in line with the following scenario:

> Homeowner stops making mortgage payments.
>
> After about 15 to 30 days, bank sends a gentle reminder.
>
> Homeowner still doesn't make payments.
>
> Bank continues to send notices.
>
> Homeowner still isn't making payments.
>
> Bank turns the matter over to its collectors, who continue to harass the homeowner with letters and phone calls.
>
> After about three missed monthly payments, the bank gets pretty steamed and sends an official notice, typically written and signed by an attorney, warning that foreclosure proceedings are about to begin.
>
> Homeowner doesn't reply or presents a solution that the bank deems unsatisfactory.
>
> Bank posts a foreclosure notice in the local newspaper.
>
> Property goes on the auction block for sale to the highest bidder.
>
> Highest bidder pays for property and becomes official owner, or the bank buys the property and transfers it to its REO (Real Estate Owned) department, which prepares it for sale.
>
> In some states, the high bidder takes immediate possession of the property. Other states have a *redemption period,* during which time the homeowner can buy back the property by paying the full amount of the loan along with interest and penalties. This period can last up to a year.
>
> Previous owner moves out or is evicted.

Lenders generally don't like to foreclose on properties. They prefer that homeowners pay their bills. At any point before the foreclosure sale, the lender may, if the homeowner cooperates, set up an alternative payment plan commonly called a *forbearance.* This is a private deal; as an investor, you won't hear about it.

If you or a loved one is ever facing a foreclosure, contact the lender immediately to explore your options. Seek help sooner rather than later. Shame, anger, and denial may discourage you from seeking assistance, but the longer you wait, the fewer your options. As with any relationship, communication is key. Educate yourself and communicate with your lender.

Boning Up on Local Rules and Regulations

Although the foreclosure process is similar in all states, laws and other details vary, as I explain in the following sections. Before you join in the game, know the rules and find out where to go for additional information and assistance. You can gather most of the information you need by visiting your county's Register of Deeds office or by talking to a real estate agent or other professional who's familiar with the foreclosure process in your area.

Don't rely on information from foreclosure gurus who appear on late-night TV infomercials for insight. They make buying and flipping foreclosure properties seem easy so they can sell their books and tapes. If it were as easy as they lead you to believe, everyone would be doing it. You can profit from foreclosures, but you have to invest some time in learning the ropes and establishing the right connections, as I recommend throughout this chapter.

Procedural stuff

Because the foreclosure process varies from one state to another and from one locale to another, I can't offer any hard and fast information on what to expect, but I can tell you the things you need to know:

- ✔ **Where to find foreclosure notices.** You may have to register to have your name added to the mailing list (or e-mailing list).

- ✔ **The number of times a foreclosure notice is published before the property actually goes up for sale.** This number differs from state to state; Michigan, for example, follows a five-week process in which the foreclosure notice must be posted at least four times in a qualified legal publication.

- ✔ **Where, when, and by whom the foreclosure sales are held.** Foreclosure sales are always held at the courthouse, by either the local sheriff or someone the sheriff hires. Get the location of the courthouse and the dates and times of foreclosure sales.

✔ **Terms of sale at the foreclosure sale, such as acceptable forms of payment and the amount of time you have to come up with the money.**

✔ **Whether the state has a mandatory redemption period, and if it does, how long it is.** Redemption periods can be as long as 365 days.

✔ **How *liens* (claims against property as security for repayment) are handled.** Senior liens wipe out junior liens. For example, a house may have three liens — the mortgage (the senior lien), a home equity line of credit (the first junior lien), and another junior lien from a contractor. After the foreclosure and redemption period, the second two junior liens are wiped out. (The holders of the junior liens have a right to redeem the senior lien to protect themselves. This redemption consists of buying out the senior lien holder, so that their liens aren't wiped out by the foreclosure.)

✔ **How evictions are handled and how long they typically take.**

Be very careful not to bid on a junior lien. Sometimes, a junior lien holder can foreclose on a property before the senior lien holder forecloses. A foreclosure ad announces the foreclosure (looking no different than a foreclosure notice for a senior lien), and you can bid on the junior lien just as if it were a senior lien. If your bid wins, you end up the loser in many cases, because when the senior lien holder forecloses on the property, your junior lien is wiped out, and you end up with a worthless piece of paper. I've seen unwary investors lose over $100,000 buying junior liens based on the advice of real estate investment "gurus."

Different types of foreclosures

The foreclosure process varies depending on whether your state performs judicial or nonjudicial foreclosures:

✔ **Judicial foreclosure:** This type of foreclosure passes through the justice system — the state or district court. The bank or lender files a claim to recover the unpaid balance of the loan from the borrower. The courts decide the case, and, as you may guess, typically take a long time to resolve the issue — usually 4 to 6 months, but sometimes up to a year.

✔ **Nonjudicial foreclosure:** In so-called *deed of trust* states, a third-party trustee (typically a bank or trust company) holds the first lien position on the mortgage until the loan is paid in full. If the borrower defaults on the loan, the lender works through the trustee to foreclose on the property, and the entire process is typically wrapped up in the course of two to four months.

Taxes

Before purchasing a foreclosure property, you should also be aware of any taxes that the property owner owes and how those taxes are paid. Note the following:

- ✔ Property taxes follow the property. If you purchase a property on which taxes are owed, you owe them.

- ✔ IRS income taxes may be wiped off the records by the foreclosure. Attorneys for the lenders put the IRS on notice that the property is going through foreclosure. The IRS has a certain number of days to respond and has the right to pay off the senior lien, but it rarely happens. In most cases, the IRS releases its lien.

- ✔ State tax liens pretty much follow suit with the IRS. Attorneys notify the state, and the foreclosure wipes any taxes owed off the books.

If you owe a lot of back taxes, you may think that you can sell your home and then buy it back with a clean slate to avoid paying the taxes altogether. Not so fast. No matter how long you wait between the time you lose the house and the time you buy it back, the liens reattach themselves to the property as soon as you finalize the deal. If you don't want the debt, don't buy back the house.

Picking Your Point of Entry into the Foreclosure Process

Foreclosures are drawn-out ordeals that typically span a period of several months to over a year. As an investor, you're free to choose your point of entry. You can deal with homeowners directly before the foreclosure proceedings begin, wait around for the foreclosure auction to place your bid, or acquire the property from the bank's REO department or from the new owner after the messiness of the foreclosure has passed. The following sections explore the pros and cons of the available entry points.

Understand all phases of the foreclosure process before trying to carve out your niche. Flexibility and creativity are often key ingredients in working out a deal that's beneficial for all parties involved, and until you understand all phases, you can't put together an effective strategy.

Flipping with integrity

If you're an honest, hardworking individual, you can make a good living by flipping foreclosure properties and doing it with integrity. You may not turn every prospect into a transaction, but the more people you help, the more leads you receive. In many cases, the best solution for homeowners who are facing foreclosure is to sell their homes to an investor like you, but present the facts accurately and let the homeowners decide what's best for them. Your reputation depends on it.

Unfortunately, several investors who deal in foreclosure properties are nothing more than con artists, misrepresenting the facts to pounce on naïve and gullible homeowners. I know of one fellow in the Metro Detroit area who shows up at houses in pre-foreclosure, befriends the homeowners, takes them to the grocery store, buys them a vacuum cleaner, prays with them, and then preys on them.

He may find a house worth $125,000 that has a debt of $9,000 and offer a payoff of $22,000, convincing the distressed, unsophisticated homeowner that she has the right to live in the house forever. After he gets the deed signed over to him, he turns around and sells the house to another investor for a huge profit, never disclosing the fact that he has a "tenant" living in the property.

In this particular example, the homeowner could have sold the property and walked away with about $100,000 or even refinanced to cover the bills and retained ownership of the property. However, the con artist swooped in, scammed the homeowner out of more than $100,000, left the owner without a place to live, and passed the headache along to the unsuspecting investor. Don't con people out of their homes to make a quick buck. You can make a fair profit and still retain your integrity.

Pre-foreclosure

Inserting yourself early in the foreclosure process, before it begins in earnest, is the most effective way to eliminate your competition and acquire the property for a decent price. After the foreclosure notice is posted, the competition begins to swarm, and other investors attempt to strike a deal with the homeowners, which can drive up the price. Of course, you have to be able to approach homeowners tactfully and be prepared to deal with heated emotions and plenty of complications. It's not for everyone.

In the following sections, I show you how to search for pre-foreclosure properties and work with homeowners tactfully.

Finding pre-foreclosure properties

When a lender initiates the foreclosure process, the foreclosure goes public. To get a jump on the competition, try these heads-up strategies:

✔ **Interact with friends and neighbors.** You often obtain your best leads by talking with friends, neighbors, fellow church members, and others. Let them know that you buy homes. Let everybody know who you are and what you do, and let them come to you. (See Chapter 8 for more advice on networking your way to leads.)

✔ **Talk with lawyers.** The first person a homeowner contacts when the foreclosure process begins is often a lawyer. The lawyer may recommend that her client sell the property and can steer the client in your direction.

✔ **Talk with real estate professionals.** Real estate agents and other real estate professionals often know about foreclosures before they're made public.

✔ **Contact condo or homeowner associations.** Condo and homeowner associations frequently hear about a homeowner's financial woes long before the news becomes a matter of public record.

✔ **Advertise in the paper.** A small ad with your phone number and a statement such as "I pay cash for homes" or "We buy ugly homes" can steer distressed homeowners in your direction.

Advertise only after you're well established, have access to plenty of cash, and have a solid plan and team assembled to handle the calls and transactions.

Approaching the homeowners gingerly

Attaining success at the pre-foreclosure stage hinges on your ability to establish trust with the homeowner. If you swoop down like a ravenous vulture, the homeowner is likely to hang up, slam the door in your face, and fling a few choice words in your direction. You have to build credibility. Ninety percent of the people who go into foreclosure lose less and benefit most by selling the house. It's the best option they have. Let them know this fact and help them decide whether their situation falls into that 90 percent category.

Stepping in at the pre-foreclosure stage isn't for everyone. The homeowners are often embarrassed, bitter, and reluctant to trust anyone . . . especially someone offering to help by buying their house out from under them. Approach gently and follow these guidelines:

✔ **Be honest.** If the homeowner has gobs of equity built up in the home and can refinance his way out of the problem, say so. You may not get this property, but you make a friend who can steer others to your door. Steering distressed homeowners into making a decision that's in your best interest and not in their best interest is wrong. The deal is good only if it's good for both of you.

✔ **Add a personal touch.** If you have the person's address, pay him a visit or hand-deliver a letter introducing yourself and explaining how you can help. A brief phone call to introduce yourself and settle on a time to meet in person is often a good idea, assuming the person has a phone and is answering it.

✔ **Take notes and pictures.** Getting past the front door to inspect the property is perhaps the biggest challenge you face. If the homeowner invites you in, ask to look at the property. Take notes and photographs, unless you get the feeling that it would upset the homeowner too much. In that case, take good mental notes. You need all the information you can get to determine the right price to offer.

✔ **Verify the facts.** A homeowner may tell you something, but that doesn't make it true. Inspect the property as closely as possible, determine its true market value, and research the title closely, as you would before purchasing any property. (I give details on researching the title and inspecting the property later in this chapter.)

✔ **Make a decision.** The longer you waffle, the more time another investor has to make her move. Decide quickly whether or not you want the property, and if you want it, make your offer . . . after checking the title and inspecting the property, of course.

Pitching your offer for a pre-foreclosure property is very similar to making an offer on any home that's for sale. If the homeowner listed the property for sale, your agent should present your offer in the form of a written purchase agreement to the listing agent. If the property is not yet listed, have your agent present the purchase agreement to the homeowner for consideration.

The more you assist homeowners through a difficult situation, the better your chance of acquiring the property and establishing yourself as an investor with integrity. When people hear that you helped so-and-so out of a tough jam, they're more likely to seek your assistance when they run into similar problems.

To keep yourself honest, take off your investor shoes and put yourself in the homeowner's shoes. Ask yourself whether what you say, suggest, and propose is in the homeowner's best interest. If it's not, don't do the deed.

Foreclosure

The foreclosure process begins with the posting of the Notice of Default (NOD) in the county's legal newspaper, proceeds through the sale (typically at auction), and ends with the transfer of property from the previous owner to the new owner. At any step along this journey, you have the opportunity to acquire the property. The following sections show you how to acquire properties after the NOD is posted or at a foreclosure sale.

Perusing foreclosure notices

When a lender initiates foreclosure proceedings, the lender posts a foreclosure notice or Notice of Default (NOD) in the county's legal newspaper. (See Figure 12-1 for a sample foreclosure notice.) Contact your county's Register of Deeds office and ask where they post foreclosure notices. You may be able to subscribe to the paper or register to receive the postings via e-mail.

The posting of the foreclosure notice provides you with another entry point into the process. With the foreclosure notice in hand, you now have more information at your fingertips, including the following useful tidbits:

- **Mortgagors' names (who owes the money):** This bit of information can help you track down the property owners and perhaps approach them before the property ends up on the auction block.

- **Lender's name (bank or mortgage company):** You may not need this information right away, but it could come in handy in the future if the lender ends up with the property after the auction and needs to sell it.

- **The amount that remains to be paid on the loan:** By knowing the amount remaining to be paid on the loan, you have a clear idea of what may be considered a reasonable opening bid.

- **The interest rate:** This is another tidbit of information that probably won't help you, but file it away just in case.

- **Legal description of the property:** The notice doesn't provide you with a mailing address, but through the Register of Deeds office or your agent, you can figure out the mailing address from the legal description. After you know where the property is located, you can drive by or possibly even get inside to inspect it.

- **Length of the redemption period, if any:** This tells you how long the current owners have to buy back the house after the sale . . . and how long you'll probably have to wait before you can place the house back on the market.

If you live in a county that sees a fair share of foreclosures, the foreclosure listings can seem overwhelming at first. The trick to making the listings less cumbersome is to know what you're looking for and then weed out any listings that raise red flags. For example, if you find a property on Main Street with a mortgage of $200,000, and you know of no property on Main Street that you'd pay more than $150,000 for, you know that property isn't for you. If the same property is listed for $75,000, it may be worth investigating.

The foreclosure notice doesn't provide the property owner's phone number or even the mailing address — only a legal description of the property and the mortgagors' names. To find the missing pieces of information, try looking up the mortgage owner's name in the phone book or taking a trip down to your county's Register of Deeds office to search the records for the property's address.

ROBERTS & KRAYNAK, P.C.
Attorneys and Counselors
123 Your Street, Ste. 200
Somewhere, MI 01234

THIS FIRM IS A DEBT COLLECTOR ATTEMPTING TO COLLECT A DEBT. ANY INFORMATION WE OBTAIN WILL BE USED FOR THAT PURPOSE. PLEASE CONTACT OUR OFFICE AT THE NUMBER BELOW IF YOU ARE IN ACTIVE MILITARY DUTY.

ATTN PURCHASERS: This sale may be rescinded by the foreclosing mortgagee. In that event, your damages, if any, shall be limited solely to the return of the bid amount tendered at sale, plus interest.

MORTGAGE SALE - Default has been made in the conditions of a mortgage made by **JOHN Q PUBLIC** and **JANE Q PUBLIC**, husband and wife, original mortgagor(s), to Walnut City Mortgage Co D/B/A Filberts United Mortgage Company, Mortgagee, dated March 4, 2002, and recorded on April 10, 2002 in Liber XXXXX on Page 617, in Cashew County Records, Michigan, on which mortgage there is claimed to be due at the date hereof the sum of Four Hundred Seventy-Two Thousand Seven Hundred Fifty-Eight And 23/100 Dollars ($472,758.23), including interest at 5.625% per annum.

Under the power of sale contained in said mortgage and the statute in such case made and provided, notice is

hereby given that said mortgage will be foreclosed by a sale of the mortgaged premises, or some part of them, at public venue, at the Main entrance to the Court House in Brazil, MI at 10:00 AM, on **JANUARY 31, 2007**. Said premises are situated in Pistachio Township of West Chestnut, Cashew County, Michigan, and are described as:

Homesite No. XX, Hazelnut Condominium, according to the Master Deed recorded in Liber XXXXX, Pages 665 through 730, Cashew County Records, as amended, and designated as Cashew County Subdivision Plan No. XXXX together with rights in the general common elements and the limited common elements as shown on the Master Deed and as described in Act 59 of the Public Acts of 1978, as amended.

The redemption period shall be 6 months from the date of such sale, unless determined abandoned in accordance with MCLA 600.3241a, in which case the redemption period shall be 30 days from the date of such sale.

Dated: December 30, 2006
For more information, please call:
FC F 555.555.5555
Roberts & Kraynak, P.C.
Attorneys and Counselors
123 Your Street, Ste. 200
Somewhere, MI 01234
File #055000F05

Figure 12-1: A foreclosure notice contains a lot of useful information for a flipper.

After you find a property in which you're interested, double-check to make sure that it's going to be sold. Sometimes, the foreclosure notice is posted, and then the homeowner files for bankruptcy or takes some other action to cancel or postpone the sale. Call the attorney listed in the foreclosure notice before you waste a lot of time researching the property (see "Step 2: Following the paper trail," later in this chapter, for more about research). You may be able to obtain additional information from the attorney, such as the exact price, but don't count on it — the attorney is acting as a debt collector on behalf of the lender.

Hurry. The clock's ticking. You have about 30 to 90 days from the time the foreclosure notice appears in the paper before the property goes on the auction block. You also have more competition now that the foreclosure is public knowledge.

Taking part in the foreclosure sale

Many real estate investors choose to wait until the foreclosure sale to make their move, trusting that they can successfully outbid the competition. Before you choose to make your entrance at the foreclosure sale, sit in on a few auctions to get a feel for how they work. Talk to one or two veterans who actually purchase properties at auctions, and place your bid only after taking the following precautions:

- Research the title thoroughly to check for any liens on the property. (I cover researching the title later in this chapter.)

- Make sure that you're bidding on a first mortgage or senior lien, not a second mortgage or junior lien. (This information also is on the title.)

- Accurately estimate the value of the property by researching recent sales of comparable properties. (See Chapter 9 for details.)

- Inspect the property as thoroughly as possible with your own two eyes (as I explain later in this chapter and in Chapter 10).

- Settle on the maximum amount to bid and don't exceed this amount no matter how keyed up you get over the property. (I show you how to rein in your impulses later in this chapter.)

I give you the nitty-gritty on placing bids at an auction in the section "Step 4: Bidding on a property," later in this chapter.

Don't assume you're getting a good deal just because you're acquiring the property at an auction. Research a property and its title work thoroughly before placing a bid. You can really get burned by not doing your homework.

Post-foreclosure

You may think that your chances of purchasing a property end when the auctioneer hollers "Sold!" but the property can still exchange hands. Jumping in this late in the process may mean that you have to pay a little more for the property than you could have gotten it for by acting more aggressively early on, but after the property is sold or passed back to the lender, you can deal directly with the new owner . . . and without a lot of emotional baggage. In the following sections, I show you how to contact the new owner: the lender or the investor who purchased the property.

Buying an REO property

In most cases, the lender buys back the property and, after the redemption period, transfers the property to its REO (Real Estate Owned) department, which prepares the property for resale. The lender may be willing to sell you the property before or after transferring it to its REO department. From the foreclosure notice (discussed earlier in this chapter), you can obtain the lender's name and the amount owed on the mortgage.

When you're ready to make an offer, have your agent draw up a purchase agreement to submit to the lender. Many times, the lender stipulates that you must add some standard addendums to the purchase agreement, such as a statement that you agree to purchase the property as is, subject to inspections. Your agent can help you determine which addendums you need to add.

You may have better luck purchasing a property from the REO department at the end of a month or quarter. In an attempt to make its numbers for a particular month or quarter, the REO department may be under a little pressure to clear out some properties. They may accept an offer on June 25 that they rejected on June 3.

Contacting another investor

If another real estate investor won the bid, she may be willing to sell the property after she takes possession of it or even during the redemption period. If you purchase the property before the redemption period expires, keep in mind that the property owner can buy back the home at any time during the redemption period by paying the loan balance and any accrued interest.

In all purchases in real estate, presenting an offer in writing (as a purchase agreement) is best. Sometimes an investor has a property already tied up with the seller through a purchase agreement, but the investor doesn't have the funds to close and wants to pass it off to another investor. This is called a *pass through transaction,* typically accompanied by a *bird dog fee* (a finder's fee), which can range from $5,000 to $10,000.

Paying a bird dog fee isn't something I recommend. You're better off putting that $5,000 to $10,000 to work on another property that you can buy directly from a homeowner or at auction.

Purchasing Foreclosure Properties Step by Step

Profiting from foreclosures isn't the slam-dunk proposition that many conceive it to be. For every story of someone buying a property and selling it at a 500 percent profit, I can tell three stories of rank beginners who lost their shirts making ill-informed decisions. The truth is that investing in foreclosure properties is risky.

Although you can't eliminate the risk, you can whittle it down to the point at which success becomes more probable than failure. The following sections present a step by step process of finding, researching, and purchasing foreclosure properties that reduces the risk.

Step 1: Finding a property

The method for finding foreclosure properties depends on where in the foreclosure process you decide to look (I cover these stages in more detail earlier in this chapter):

- ✔ **Pre-foreclosure:** A homeowner may contact you directly, knowing that you're an investor who buys houses, or you may obtain leads from lawyers, real estate agents, friends, or acquaintances.
- ✔ **Foreclosure:** Search through the foreclosure notices in your county's legal newspaper or register to get on the mailing list.
- ✔ **Post-foreclosure:** Contact the lender's REO department or the investor who purchased the property at the foreclosure sale.

Step 2: Following the paper trail

After you locate a property that looks promising, it's time to do your homework. Begin by researching the title to make sure that it doesn't contain any hidden surprises, and then dig a little deeper, especially if you're purchasing the property in a pre-foreclosure deal, to uncover additional details that can help you during negotiations.

Researching the title

The title is like the property's diary, revealing a history of all the former owners. The title marks the major events in the life of the property, including when an owner sold the property, died or divorced, added a son or daughter to the title to avoid probate, failed to pay property taxes, or had a judgment against him. It also indicates the names of any lenders who have liens on the property.

You can hire a title company to research the title and determine whether the property owner has title insurance (see Chapter 4 for details on finding a title company), or you can hop down to the Register of Deeds office and ask for assistance in researching the title on your own.

On your way to the Register of Deeds office, turn on your charm. The office workers can choose to help or hinder your efforts, and their choice often hinges on your demeanor. A polite, unassuming approach is more effective than one of demanding arrogance.

When you get your hands on the title, examine it carefully:

- ✔ Follow the chain of ownership back to the time when the property was first built or back to at least the last two or three owners. Any breaks in the chain raise a warning flag — a possible indication that the current owner doesn't fully own the property.

- ✔ Note any stray deeds that don't jibe with the names of the current owners. Look for strange last names or names on the deed that don't share the obligation of paying the mortgage.

- ✔ Check for any liens on the property, as I discuss earlier in this chapter in the section "Procedural stuff."

A break in the title chain can mean nothing or signal serious trouble. For example, say you do your search and find that Mr. and Mrs. Smith took title in 1989. But then in 2006, you see Jim Jones gives a deed to Mr. and Mrs. Rogers. How can Jim Jones deed something he doesn't own? You didn't see a deed from the Smiths to Jim Jones, so what gives? Perhaps it's no big deal — maybe the deed just wasn't recorded, and the title company can track it down. However, the problem can be more serious. Jim Jones may have pulled a scam and sold that property not only to Mr. and Mrs. Rogers, but also to the Howards and the Thompsons. Illegal? Yes, but it happens, and you don't want to get yourself or your money involved in it.

If you do notice discrepancies on the title, work with the title company to address any concerns you have and correct any errors. Ask the title company to provide you with a marked-up policy or a letter (or both) that addresses your concerns. In most purchases, you can put the seller on notice to have the items corrected — this is cause for cancelling your purchase agreement with a full refund of your earnest money deposit.

Investigating more closely

If you're planning on purchasing the property directly from the homeowner prior to the foreclosure sale (see the section "Pre-foreclosure," earlier in this chapter), ask the homeowner for additional information about the first mortgage and any junior liens. As the foreclosure sale nears, the homeowner and junior lien holders stand to lose their interest in the property. You may be able to negotiate a deal with the homeowner and junior lien holders that enables you to acquire the property before the sale. Sometimes lenders, especially junior lien holders, are willing to discount the payoff amount that's due. They often feel that 70 cents on a dollar is better than nothing. By negotiating with all involved parties, you may be able to work a deal that's good for everyone.

When dealing directly with the property owner, seek the advice of a qualified real estate attorney to watch your back, especially if you're planning on negotiating a deal in which you assume the loan. (I explain how to find an attorney in Chapter 4.) Some mortgage agreements prohibit the property owner from transferring the mortgage to a buyer, no matter who it is. Others require that the loan be paid in full in the event that the property changes hands.

Step 3: Inspecting the property

The first rule in flipping houses is to never buy a property without looking at it first, but that can be a bit tricky. In a foreclosure situation, the property owner may be less than enthusiastic about showing his home to someone who's ultimately going to take possession of it and evict him.

The least you should do is drive past the property, get a look at it from all sides, and snap some photos. The care and handling of the house's exterior and landscaping are often pretty good indications of how well the owner cared for the inside of the house. A house with a perfectly manicured lawn, trimmed hedges, and freshly painted garage reflects a pride of ownership that generally permeates the house.

If you can establish a good rapport with the homeowners, they may invite you in to look around, especially if you need to meet with them to go over some paperwork or explain their options to them. Do what you can to get inside the house, short of breaking in or appearing too pushy. After you're inside, follow the guidelines for inspecting a property, as I suggest in Chapter 10, to whatever degree possible.

Stamp the following rule on your forehead: *Your eyes or no buys.* Never buy a property that you don't inspect yourself. If you decide to have someone else inspect the property, don't blame them if they miss something.

Step 4: Bidding on a property

You performed your due diligence. The price is right, the house looks great, and the title is clear. You're one bid away from financial freedom. Now it's time to place that winning bid, right? Not so fast. Assuming that you're entering the process at the foreclosure stage, read through the following sections to prepare for auction day.

Settling on a maximum bid

The single most important step in bidding on foreclosure properties is to establish your maximum bid — an amount you're not to exceed no matter what happens.

To determine your maximum bid, use the same system I present in Chapter 5 to ensure that you stand to earn at least 20 percent.

If you're unable to get inside the house to inspect it, estimating the costs of repairs and renovations can be tricky. Use the following techniques to come up with some rough estimates:

- Assume the house needs painting inside and out and new carpet from wall to wall.

- Estimate high for older homes, because they generally have more costly surprises, such as substandard plumbing and electrical.

- Remain cautious of brand new homes that may not be finished on the inside.

- When in doubt, overestimate expenses.

Always commit to a maximum bid before the auction begins. Otherwise, you may find yourself in a bidding war and spend all your profits before you even get the house.

Testing the waters

Sit in on a few auctions before placing your first bid. Observe other bidders to size up your future competition and discover their techniques and strategies. Bring your list of properties along with your maximum high bids and compare your bids with the winning bids. If your bids are way out of line, you may want to tweak the process you use to arrive at your estimates before you do any serious bidding. Don't bend your estimated resale price in an attempt to bring your profit in line with what you *want* to bid.

Surveying bidding strategies

Foreclosure auctions are like poker tournaments. Every bidder has a unique strategy and various techniques for psyching out the competition. Here are some common strategies you may want to try:

- ✔ **Bore 'em into submission:** Keep outbidding the highest bidder by the minimum bid. If the minimum increment is $10, whenever someone makes a bid, bid $10 more. Just don't exceed your maximum.

- ✔ **Speak softly and carry a big wad of cash:** Quiet bidding often conveys confidence and can undercut the high-energy, emotional tone of the auction. It forces other bidders to ask, "What did he bid?" which can be a little unsettling and give you the edge you need.

- ✔ **Crank the volume:** Bark your bids as if you're a mad dog in control of the room. If you've ever had your parents yell at you, you know the effect this technique can have. It can rattle your opponent just enough to make him back off or make him think that you've lost your mind. Either way, you're in control.

- ✔ **Mix it up:** Go erratic, random. Don't follow a pattern. As long as your bids make sense to you without exceeding your cap, experiment and see what works best.

Many auctions require buyers to submit their bids in writing in sealed envelopes. When all the bids are in, they're opened, and the property goes to the highest bidder. If you're flipping in an area that uses sealed bids, you won't be able to use the clever techniques I describe here.

Step 5: Surviving the redemption period

If you win the bid in some states, you pay off the mortgage and any taxes due on the property, and immediately take possession of the property. In other states, you have to sit on the property until the redemption period passes, which can last up to 365 days.

While you're waiting, you may be tempted to start working on the house. Don't. You may invest $10,000 in renovations only to have the property owner decide to redeem the property just before you wrap up the project.

During the redemption period, the deed holder (homeowner) still has control of the real estate. You can, however, gain a sense of security by offering the seller cash for keys and having them execute a *non-redemption certificate*. A non-redemption certificate is an agreement by the homeowner to not redeem the property. It's not a deed. Because you purchased the first lien at auction, and the only one entitled to redeem has agreed not to, the process continues through redemption. After the redemption period expires, you can acquire the deed, and all junior liens are wiped away.

Be very cautious when working with the homeowner. You don't want to be accused later of taking advantage of the homeowner while he was under duress.

Never spend money on a house you don't own or that doesn't have a clear title. You can pay taxes and insurance and file an affidavit to add that amount to the balance required to redeem the property, but don't spend money on renovations until you take possession.

Part IV
Fixing Up Your Fixer-Upper

The 5th Wave   By Rich Tennant

"You did an excellent job, Dave. But two months seems a long time to paint the bathroom."

In this part . . .

Houses lose value when nobody — including the owner — wants them. Maybe the house looks bad. Maybe it smells bad. Maybe the last time the kitchen was updated was in the early 1960s. Whatever the reason, the owner doesn't want it, and people aren't exactly standing in line to look inside. It's a fixer-upper, and it needs some fixer-upping.

In this part, I steer you toward the repairs and renovations that can add appeal and real value to a property, and I steer you clear of repairs and renovations that merely chip away at your bottom line. In the process, you can expect to pick up some basic skills that no respectable house flipper should lack.

Chapter 13

Prioritizing and Planning Your Renovations

Prioritizing and planning renovations is like planning for a vacation. You have a limited amount of time to complete the trip, a list of activities you want to accomplish during that time, and a certain amount of money set aside to pay for it. With a vacation, you need to schedule flights and car rentals well in advance, plot your journey from point A to point B, and pack sufficient clothing, necessities, and accessories for a comfortable journey. Repairing and renovating a property requires the same foresight and attention to detail. You need to prioritize your list of projects, order materials well in advance, schedule the work, hire workers, and make sure that everything gets done on time and on budget.

In this chapter, I steer you toward valuable resources that can help you train your tastes and choose the renovations that are most appealing to the majority of house hunters in your area. Then, I lead you through the process of prioritizing and planning your renovations to complete your projects in a reasonable amount of time without spending too much money.

Before you even buy a property, you should carefully inspect it and have a solid idea of the work you need to do. For more details, check out Chapter 10.

Spotting Trends in Home Renovations

A flipper is like a talent scout. She can gauge a home's potential instantly and envision it as a final, finished product on her first walk-through. She can picture the kitchen with new cabinets, countertop, sink, tile, and appliances. She can imagine the barely functional restroom converted into a luxurious new bathroom. She can close her eyes and visualize the outside of the home completely revamped to seduce passersby into taking a look inside.

Some people have it, and some people don't. But if you're one who doesn't have it, don't despair — you can develop the required sensibilities by (among other things) visiting open houses, attending home shows, and talking with lots of homeowners and prospective buyers about their likes and dislikes. It's never too early to start training your tastes. Knowing your renovation options (and their costs) before you even start looking at properties is key to buying a property you're sure can turn a profit. The following sections explore resources you can tap to develop a taste for home renovations.

All home buyers want a nice, clean house in the price range they can afford, in the best neighborhood possible, with good schools for their children, and with as few mechanical problems (plumbing, gas, electric, and heating) as possible. When you buy and renovate houses, let these factors guide your decisions as you choose which renovations make sense.

Visiting open houses with an open eye

Attending an open house is like going on a reconnaissance mission. It provides you with a free border pass to gather valuable intelligence. You can find out the asking price, view the condition of the home, talk with actual home buyers about what they like and dislike about the house, meet a real estate agent or two face-to-face, discover the types of improvements the owners made to the property, and perhaps even meet the owners.

Search the classifieds for open house dates and times — they're often held on Sunday afternoons — and plan to attend two or three this weekend. Try to find open houses in your target neighborhood and in your desired price range to get a better idea of the types and styles of renovations optimum for your market. While visiting each home, do your homework:

> ✔ **Note the curb appeal.** When you pull up to the curb, don't scramble out of the car and sprint to the front door. Linger for a few moments, observe the outside of the house, and note the features that make you want to go inside (or stay in your car). Compare the house to neighboring houses. What features make it look more (or less) inviting?

✔ **Grade the entryway.** When you step through the front door, do you feel as though you entered an oasis or do you feel as though someone shoved you into a closet? Note the features that make an entryway more attractive. You may be able to use these design elements in your flip.

✔ **Adjust your eyes to the lighting.** Note whether the house allows outside light to penetrate. Which light fixtures seem to illuminate a room most effectively? Look at the windows and window dressings, the colors of the rooms, landscaping that may shade one or more rooms, and sky-lights designed to let in more light. Noting these details gives you a clear idea of the items you want to purchase when renovating your property.

✔ **Imagine yourself living in the house.** Picture your friends and family hanging out in the kitchen or living room. Does the floor plan make it easy to move from one room to another? Do you feel crowded? Does the house have enough space for you to store your stuff? Jot down any cool design features that improve the livability of the house, so you can follow the same design principles when you decide to do major rehabs.

✔ **Observe crowd reactions.** If other people are touring the house, listen to what they say and watch their reactions. These people are the same people who are going to be looking at your renovated home, so their reactions give you a good sense of what your future customers consider most appealing.

Although you're certainly free to jot down notes at an open house, onlookers may gawk and ask what you're doing. Consider keeping a notepad or digital recorder in your car and logging ideas as soon as you leave . . . but not while you're driving, of course.

Attend several open houses and do a comparative analysis in order to gauge the hottest home fashions in your market. They vary depending on your geographical location, price range, and current styles. Become a trend spotter.

Doing a little home show surveillance

In the dead of winter or early spring, you can shake off your cabin fever while honing your tastes in home construction and décor by spending a day or two at a local home and garden show. These shows typically feature model homes, the latest in building supplies and gadgetry, and renovation ideas and demonstrations, along with plenty of catalogues and brochures you can tote home for reference.

Home shows typically tour in late winter and early spring. Two or three weeks before the show, you can usually spot an ad for it in your local newspaper (typically in the Sunday edition's Lifestyle or Home & Garden section) or on the local TV news.

Perusing periodicals and other home renovation resources

Books, magazines, Web sites, and other publications on paper and online can further sharpen your insight into trends in the housing market. Check out the following resources:

Books

- ✔ *Bathroom Remodeling For Dummies* by Gene Hamilton and Katie Hamilton (Wiley)

- ✔ *Home Decorating For Dummies,* 2nd Edition, by Katharine Kaye McMillan and Patricia Hart McMillan (Wiley)

- ✔ *Home Improvement For Dummies* by Gene Hamilton and Katie Hamilton (Wiley)

- ✔ *Kitchen Remodeling For Dummies* by Donald R. Prestly (Wiley)

Magazines, TV Shows, and Web sites

- ✔ Better Homes & Gardens at www.bhg.com

- ✔ HGTV at www.hgtv.com

- ✔ DIY Network at www.diynet.com

- ✔ Hometime at www.hometime.com

- ✔ This Old House at www.thisoldhouse.com

A house hunter's taste buds are trained not only by what he sees at open houses (as explained in the previous section), but also by what he sees in the media. He settles for what he can afford, but he dreams of the possibilities. By attending home shows, you experience the leading, bleeding edge of what's available for the modern home. Occasionally, these newfangled options are even more cost effective than the old stuff.

Developing an eye for attractive landscaping

Jewelers showcase diamonds in settings or at least nestle them in a bed of deep blue velvet. Without an attractive background to set it off, the diamond would look about as pretty as a polished block of salt. Houses are the same way. On a barren lot, even a mansion can look dreary. On a lush, manicured lot, a modest house can look magnificent.

Whether you're out for a morning drive, visiting open houses, or simply taking a stroll around the neighborhood, examine the landscaping and try to identify the current trends.

Note the features of the landscape and try to imagine how you could landscape the front of the house to improve its curbside appeal. You may not want to chop down any 50-year-old trees, but a careful trim can freshen up a house, much as a new hairstyle can make you look years younger.

Landscaping books, magazines, and Web sites are about as plentiful as plants, and most are packed with copious collections of color photos. When you need some landscaping ideas and advice, check out the following offerings:

- *Landscaping For Dummies* by Phillip Giroux, Bob Beckstrom, Lance Walheim, and the editors of the National Gardening Association (Wiley)
- LandscapeOnline.com at www.landscapeonline.com
- LandscapeUSA.com at www.landscapeusa.com

Gleaning advice from a renovation mentor

Not everyone is equipped to acquire an instinct for the types of improvements that make prospective buyers gape in admiration rather than in shock. If you don't have a knack for it, that's perfectly okay. What's important is that you can admit it and network your way to someone who's skilled in this area.

The world is full of artistic types who have a gift for seeing the potential in a home and knowing exactly what it needs to achieve full bloom. Find such a person in your circle of family and friends and then ask her to accompany you on your walk-throughs and offer her advice. The final decisions are still up to you, but a gifted pair of eyes can help you make superior choices.

Prioritizing Your Projects

Unless you have a bottomless bank account and an infinite amount of time to flip your house, you have to prioritize your renovation projects. The overall strategy for prioritizing projects is as follows:

1. **Underlying structural problems and *mechanicals* (plumbing, electric, heating, and air conditioning) are the top priorities.**

   In other words, don't build a house on a shaky foundation with substandard mechanicals.

2. **Essential repairs that aren't structural or mechanical, such as dangling gutters, cracked windows, and rickety doors, are your next concern.**

   If something is broken, repair, replace, or remove it. If it ain't broke and it doesn't look bad, don't fix it.

3. **Next, concentrate on renovations that promise to deliver the highest return on your investment, such as laying new carpeting, replacing the bathroom vanity, or installing a new kitchen countertop.**

   Renovate only if it makes financial sense to do so.

4. **If time allows, do anything you can do yourself for little or no money that makes the house more attractive, such as adding decorative shutters and replacing blinds.**

   Save items that won't sink your sale for last.

In the following sections, I guide you through the process of prioritizing your renovation projects. When you're done, you should have a list of projects ranked by importance along with projects that promise the most bang for your buck. Check out "Coming Up with a Game Plan," later in this chapter, for the full scoop on making sure that you complete your projects with minimal fuss.

Start planning renovations and lining up contractors as soon as you're pretty sure you're going to buy the property, especially for larger projects including roofing, heating and cooling, and foundation repairs. Don't spend any money before you close, but be prepared to start your renovations the next day. If you wait until closing, you may find that all the contractors in your area are already backed up with projects. Get things moving right away. (Check out Chapter 4 for details on hiring contractors to work for you.)

Tackling essential repairs

Making a condemned home look pretty is like putting lipstick on a pig — and that's not something I recommend. You want a good, solid home void of any problems that may crop up later during your buyer's home inspection. The best way to purge a house of problems is to go through your home inspection report and address every item on the list. (I cover home inspections in detail in Chapter 11.) Focus on the big stuff first:

- Foundation problems
- Worn or damaged roof
- Furnace that needs to be repaired or replaced
- Electrical system that's not up to code or doesn't work
- Plumbing that's not up to code or doesn't work
- Air conditioning that's nonexistent or inoperable
- Insulation that's absent, insufficient, or ugly

After listing the major repairs required, you can address any minor problems that cropped up during the inspection and are essential to fix, such as light fixtures that don't work, leaky faucets, broken doors, or peeling paint.

Gauging renovations to get the most bang for the buck

When you're planning renovations, you always want your ROI (return on investment) to exceed 100 percent. Otherwise, you become a real estate philanthropist — giving the buyer something for nothing. So when you see articles claiming that you can expect an 80 percent return on a new kitchen or a 75 percent return on a bathroom remodel, you may wonder why any flipper in his right mind would consider rehabbing the kitchen or bath. Three reasons:

- ✔ As a flipper, you already covered the cost of the renovation by purchasing the property below market value (see Part III for more details). In other words, the renovation is already paid for.

- ✔ When you look at those ROI numbers of 75 or 80 percent return, keep in mind that the person punching numbers into the calculator is usually assuming that you're having a professional do all the work. By doing some or all of the work yourself, you may be able to boost the ROI well over 100 percent.

- ✔ Few buyers can afford to renovate the kitchen or bathroom after paying a boatload of money for a house. They'd rather borrow a little more and pay for a house that's finished. To avoid excluding these first-time home buyers from your market, some renovations are essential, even though on their surface they may not appear to be cost effective.

The fact that renovations boost your ROI doesn't mean that you should redo every room in the house. When you have a limited budget and timeframe, you may find that you need to make some tradeoffs. When debating which tradeoffs to make, keep your eye on the bottom line (see "Drawing Up a Tentative Budget," later in this chapter, for more about money matters) and let the following considerations guide your decisions:

- ✔ **Enhance curb appeal.** In flipping, curb appeal rules, and you usually get more bang for your buck from landscaping and exterior renovations. A fresh coat of paint coupled with some basic landscaping is often a lot less expensive than the cost of remodeling a kitchen or bath. Chapters 14 and 15 have tips for enhancing the curb appeal of your house.

- ✔ **Add fresh paint and carpeting.** For a few thousand dollars, you can carpet most houses and add a fresh coat of paint. It's a quick, inexpensive way to make the house look new-ish. For additional ideas on quick, affordable repairs and renovations, see Chapter 14.

- ✔ **Consider the competition.** After touring comparable homes in the neighborhood, you know what your house needs to make it slightly more attractive than comparable homes. As attractive or slightly more attractive is good enough. See "Visiting open houses with an open eye," earlier in this chapter, for tips on checking out the competition.

✔ **Weigh the expense.** Don't invest any more than it takes to bring your house up to neighborhood standards. If the kitchen is good enough for the neighbors, it should be good enough for you.

✔ **Target popular demand.** By knowing what most house hunters in your target area find attractive (see "Spotting Trends in Home Renovations," earlier in this chapter, for details), you can more effectively base your renovation decisions on what sells rather than on what you prefer.

Adding inexpensive, last-minute touches

After you've done your major remodeling and checked your bank account to see how much money remains, take a step back and see whether any final touches can further enhance the property's appearance. You may want to add decorative shutters to the windows, light up the landscaping with exterior lamps, or spring for some new throw rugs. Look for cheap, easy stuff that won't blow your budget or take more than a few hours.

Delegating Duties

After you have a detailed to-do list, it's time to delegate — to determine which jobs you can do yourself, which jobs you can rope your friends into doing, and which jobs you need to hire a professional to complete. In the following sections, I provide some guidance on how to pick the people on your team who are best qualified for various jobs.

The first rule in house flipping is to do the job right, so as you assign duties, be honest about your abilities and inabilities. If you don't know a screwdriver from a scuba diver, maybe you should stick to real estate investing and leave the repairs to someone who's more qualified. You may save a little money by doing it yourself, but you pay later for any shoddy workmanship.

Identifying do-it-yourself projects

The most obvious way to cut costs is to do the work yourself. You may not be able to install a new furnace or hot water heater, but most people can push a broom, mow the lawn, scrub a toilet, or tear out old carpeting. The following list points out the chores that most house flippers who are just starting out choose to do themselves:

✔ Scheduling

✔ Basic cleaning

✔ Yard work

✔ Tearing out old stuff

✔ Odd jobs for the weekend warrior

When considering whether to do a job yourself or hire a professional, ask yourself this question: "Can I do the job as well and as quickly as a professional?" If doing it yourself jeopardizes the quality of work or the schedule, then hire a professional. The $100 per day rule (see Chapter 5) applies here. If a project takes you seven days to complete, it costs you $700. If you can hire someone to do the same project in two days for $500, you save $200 and cut five days off the schedule.

Getting a little help from your friends

Consider asking friends, family members, and neighbors to help with the cleanup and renovation and assign tasks based on your helpers' skills and experience. Of course, this means you have to pitch in when they need a hand, but you can pick up additional skills and knowledge by working alongside people with expertise in a variety of areas. You can work as a group on landscaping renovations, work alone, or team up with one other person to perform a task such as drywalling or wallpapering that's a little easier to do with four hands.

When bartering with friends, family, and neighbors, the value of what you're trading may be subject to taxes. Consult your accountant (I help you find a good one in Chapter 4).

Flagging jobs that require professional expertise

Licensed, insured contractors and subcontractors have four things that many do-it-yourselfers don't have: time, tools, know-how, and good insurance. When faced with the decision of whether to do the job yourself or hire a professional, consider these four factors:

✔ **Time:** Do you personally have the time to complete the job yourself, or would your time be better invested in other pursuits, such as your day job? Can you complete the job on schedule?

✔ **Tools:** Do you own the tools required to do the job? How much do the required tools cost to buy or rent? Do you have the means to haul large, heavy materials, such as rolls of carpet or sheets of drywall to the work-site? How much would it cost to have materials delivered?

✔ **Know-how:** Do you have the expertise to do the job well? Be honest. Materials can cost a lot of dough. If you tear up fancy wood paneling in the process of installing it or if you ruin a roll of vinyl flooring by making the wrong cuts, these missteps add to the cost of the job.

✔ **Insurance:** Is the job dangerous? If you or someone who's helping you is injured in the process, will your insurance cover the doctor bills and any income lost from missed work?

Unless you have the basic qualifications to do the job right, consider hiring a professional to do the following work:

✔ Structural repairs, including the foundation

✔ Major renovations that require knocking down or building walls

✔ Roof replacement or repairs

✔ Siding or tuck pointing

✔ Window replacement

✔ Furnace and air conditioning installation or repairs

✔ Upgrading the electrical system

✔ Major plumbing repairs, including septic system

✔ Removal or treatment of toxic substances

✔ Laying new carpet, tile, or vinyl flooring

For major projects, such as remodeling a kitchen or bathroom, tell the contractor, in writing, exactly what you want done, the deadline, and the budget. If you leave decisions to the contractor, you're likely to experience cost overruns, both in time and money. Chapter 4 has more information on finding and contracting contractors, subcontractors, and handymen.

Drawing Up a Tentative Budget

How much you profit from the sale of the house often hinges on the cost of repairs and renovations. Overzealous flippers get burned when their visions for improving a house exceed their ability to pay for them. Whether you have $10,000 or $100,000 budgeted for repairs and renovations, decide early on, preferably before closing, how much of that money to set aside for each project.

To establish a budget, follow these steps:

1. **List the projects you plan on hiring a professional to complete (covered earlier in this chapter).**

2. **Obtain estimates for these jobs.**

   Estimates should break out the cost of materials and labor.

3. **Jot down the projects you plan on doing yourself (covered earlier in this chapter).**

4. **For each of these projects, list the required materials.**

   If you're remodeling a bathroom, for example, you may need a new toilet, sink, cabinet, tile (for the walls), flooring, paint, and caulk. Visit your local hardware store to research the cost of materials.

   Many hardware stores display two prices for materials — an uninstalled and an installed price. Use these comparisons to determine how much you're saving by doing the work yourself.

5. **Tally all the estimated costs and add 20 percent to cover sales tax and unexpected expenses.**

   The cost of most projects exceeds estimates.

Use the renovation planner shown in Figure 13-1 to estimate costs and keep all your notes in one place. It features space for listing each project, its start and completion dates, and its costs for materials and labor. To estimate your renovation costs while keeping your profit in mind, before you even buy a house, head to Chapter 5. If costs are running over budget, skip to Chapter 23 for some cost-cutting strategies.

Don't let some sweet-talking investor charm you into taking on a project in which you assume most of the risk and the investor stands to gain most of the profit. When budgeting, make sure that you're the one making the decisions on how to spend your money.

Renovation Planner					
Project	**Start Date**	**Completion Date**	**Materials Cost**	**Labor Cost**	**Total Cost**

Figure 13-1:
A renovation planner is a handy tool for estimating costs.

Total Materials Costs	$_____
Total Labor Costs	+ $_____
Total Materials and Labor Costs	$_____
20 Percent for Sales Tax and Unexpected Costs	x 1.2
Grand Total	$_____

Coming Up with a Game Plan

Without proper planning, you can literally paint yourself into a corner when you're renovating a house. If you refinish the hardwood floors first, subsequent construction traffic ruins the finish. If you install new drywall before the plumbers show up, you may find them hacking chunks out of it later to

Working from the outside in, or vice versa

Weather permitting, work on the outside of the house first to generate some neighborhood buzz. By working on the outside of the house first, you immediately put the wheels of your marketing machine in motion, and have a much better chance of selling the house when you put it on the market.

Plan ahead to take advantage of the weather and keep in mind that house-hunting season generally starts to heat up in early spring and cool off in the late fall. You don't want to get stuck with a house over the long winter months when heating bills peak.

If the weather is super cold or super hot or you plan on spending a year or more renovating the inside, you may want to reverse your strategy. Begin inside and then complete the outside renovations when you're closer to the date on which you plan on planting the For Sale sign on the front lawn.

If you have to kick it up a notch to meet deadlines or get the house ready for closing, work inside and outside at the same time, and consider scheduling crews in shifts, but keep in mind that the neighbors may not welcome the graveyard shift. Check with your neighbors first, invite them over to witness your progress, and ask them whether multiple shifts for a limited period of time would be acceptable. Becoming friendly with the neighbors is always (well . . . usually) a good idea.

Allotting sufficient time for your projects

At this point, you may be wondering just how long it's going to take to renovate your house and put it back on the market. The best answer I can offer is this: It depends. It depends on the shape of the house; how extensive the planned renovations are; how much work you're planning to do yourself; the number of waking hours you can reasonably commit to the project; how well you plan the renovations; how much help you have; and how long you plan on holding the house, especially if you're living in the house you flip.

If you're doing a cosmetic job (as described in Chapter 14), you hire out the work, and you have plenty of hired hands working in unison, you can expect to complete your renovations in one to two weeks and place the house right back on the market. On the other hand, if you're completely gutting the house and doing most of the work yourself on nights and weekends, the project can easily stretch out over months and years rather than weeks.

Consult with your contractors to set reasonable dates for completing the work, and, based on the information you gather, plan on placing the house on the market the day after work and the final cleanup are scheduled to be completed. Then, let everyone know the date. You can bump it out later, if needed, but having a date in place is a great motivator.

Chapter 14

Giving Your Property a Quick Makeover

*Y*ou stumble upon a great house at a great price that's just plain ugly. The foundation is solid, the roof is only a few years old, the floor plan works, and all the big-ticket items appear to be in working condition. Fortunately for you, the previous owners trashed the place. Perhaps they were too busy to maintain the property themselves and too financially strapped to hire out the maintenance. Maybe they just didn't care. They paid the price of their neglect by having to sell the property to you at a discount.

You now have a house that looks worse than it really is. It requires few or no major repairs and its features cater to the demands of most house hunters in the area. The house just needs a good scrubbing, a proper grooming, and a little makeup to improve its appearance and draw prospective buyers inside.

In this chapter, I show you how to do a quick flip, a *cosmetic job,* or a *makeup job,* as seasoned house flippers call it. You discover how to transform an ill-kempt home into a crowd pleaser for the cost of a few thousand dollars and several weekends. You can then quickly place the property back on the market and sell it for several thousands more than you invested in it . . . assuming that you purchased it at the right price. (If you followed my advice on negotiating a price in Chapter 11, then you did!) *Home Improvement For Dummies,* by Gene Hamilton and Katie Hamilton (Wiley), provides illustrated instructions on performing most of the more complicated tasks in this chapter.

Sprucing Up the Yard

The front, back, and side yards provide two ways to improve your property's curb appeal — the appearance of the yard itself and how the yard contributes to the appearance of the house. Some houses are so overgrown with trees and shrubs that you can barely see the house from the street. If the house is gut-retching ugly, that could be a good thing, but in most cases, you want the landscape to accent the house, not hide it.

Start from the top and work down, focusing on the following:

✔ **Trim tree limbs and brambles away from the house.** Overhanging limbs drop leaves and twigs in the gutters, damage the roof, and prevent light from penetrating into the house. Nicely trimmed trees and shrubs shade and accent the house without obscuring it.

✔ **Pull weeds.** A weedy driveway, walkway, or curb is an eyesore. Pull the weeds or spray them with weed killer and then sweep up afterward.

✔ **Dig up any dead plants.** Dried up gnarly shrubs and dead flowers can make a yard look more like a cemetery. Extract the dead stuff.

✔ **Plant fresh shrubs and flowers.** If the weather's nice, plant fresh shrubs, decorative grasses, and flowers, especially along the front of the house and any sides that are visible from the curb. (You can save a little money by purchasing less-mature plants.) If the front yard doesn't have a place for flowers, you may be able to place a planter on or near the front porch or hang a basket of flowers near the front door to add color.

✔ **Remove clutter and eyesores.** Remove the rusty carcasses of old cars or bikes, storage sheds that have outlived their usefulness, ugly lawn ornaments, old fences, piles of bricks or stones, and anything else that catches your eye . . . and not in a good way.

✔ **Lay down a fresh layer of mulch.** Roll out a layer of landscaping fabric to keep the weeds down, and then add a layer of mulch. Fresh cedar mulch or decorative stones make the greenery and other colors pop out and provide a nice trim at the base of the house.

✔ **Mow and edge the lawn.** Mow the lawn nice and high so it looks lush and green and chokes out the weeds. Edging improves the appearance of the walkways, giving the whole house a more manicured look. Pull any weeds that are poking up through the walkways and along the curb, and sweep up when you're done.

✔ **Fill driveway and walkway cracks.** Your local hardware store has the materials you need to patch asphalt and concrete. For asphalt drives, reseal the drive after the patch has cured.

Before you start digging or pulling shrubs out from around the house, call the utility companies and have them mark the locations of gas and water lines and buried electrical cables. If you don't know where the utilities are buried, you may turn up something that's quite shocking and leads to costly repairs. Hacking into a gas line or buried electrical cable can also be dangerous.

Figures 14-1 and 14-2 illustrate the selling power of a quality landscaping job. Notice the difference that adding just a few new plants and flowers can make! The homeowner also placed bricks around the planting area to create a lovely trim and removed clutter such as the garden hose near the front door.

Figure 14-1: Before landscaping, this property looks a little boring.

Jeremy Goodell

Don't forget the backyard! Even though it's not visible from the street, the backyard is still an important selling point of your house and can be cleaned up in a snap. Now that you have the front yard looking like a gardener's paradise, you want the backyard to match; otherwise, the shock could sink a potential sale. Figures 14-3 and 14-4 demonstrate the difference that a little TLC can make in a backyard. Among other tasks, the homeowner removed all the ivy from the back fence and replaced it with a variety of beautiful plants.

For great tips on sprucing up any yard, check out *Landscaping For Dummies* by Phillip Giroux, Bob Beckstrom, Lance Walheim, and the editors of the National Gardening Association (Wiley).

Figure 14-2:
After land-
scaping, this
house pops
out from
the street.

Jeremy Goodell

Figure 14-3:
Before land-
scaping, this
backyard
was
crawling
with ivy.

Jeremy Goodell

Figure 14-4:
New plants
make this
backyard
look brand-
new.

Jeremy Goodell

Freshening the Façade

When you purchase a quick-flip property, the shell of the house should be in good repair. The shell includes the roof; gutters; and brick, vinyl siding, or wood siding that covers the house. "Good repair," however, doesn't always mean "pretty." Even a house that's in good shape can use a quick power wash and some touching up. Here are some tips for shining the shell:

- ✔ **Trim the ivy . . . or not.** If the ivy is growing on brick, isn't causing damage, and looks nice, leave it be. It can add character to the house and make it more appealing. If it looks bad or is tearing away the gutters or siding, trim it back.

- ✔ **Remove the window air conditioners.** A house with air conditioners hanging out of the windows makes the house look like it belongs in a trailer court. Get rid of them.

- ✔ **Power wash the siding.** You can rent a power washer at your hardware store or a tool rental service (or buy one if you plan on flipping several houses), and do it yourself, or hire someone to do it for you. For a few hundred bucks, a power wash can make the outside shell look like new.

- ✔ **Repair or replace windows and screens.** Nothing is a better indicator of an unkempt house than broken windows and tattered screens. If the window is totaled, install a replacement window that matches the other windows in the house. See Chapter 17 for more on replacement windows.

- ✔ **Add or replace shutters.** Decorative shutters are fairly inexpensive, easy to hang, and add dimension to an otherwise boxy, flat house.

- ✔ **Apply a fresh coat of paint.** If a power wash isn't sufficient for brightening the exterior, a fresh coat of paint can do the trick. Check out Chapter 15 for more about painting your property's exterior.

- ✔ **Paint the front door and threshold.** The first thing a buyer sees when she walks up to the house is the front door. Even if you don't paint the entire house, paint the front door or clean the stain and apply a fresh coat of shellac. Paint the trim around the door as well as the threshold.

- ✔ **Paint the garage to match.** Your house and garage should be the same color to make your property look like a complete package.

- ✔ **Replace the gutters.** Seamless gutters are relatively inexpensive to have installed and instantly add curb appeal. You can purchase gutters and hang them yourself, but they usually don't look as good as a professional, seamless gutter replacement or save you enough money to make the project worth doing yourself. If the gutters are in good shape, a quick cleaning and a fresh coat of paint should be sufficient.

- ✔ **Replace the front and rear storm doors.** Storm doors often take a beating and generally look worse than the rest of the house. Chapter 17 has details on replacing doors, including entry and sliding glass doors.

- ✔ **Replace exterior light fixtures.** Even if the exterior lights still function, if they look bad next to that fresh coat of paint, replace them with new fixtures that are inline with the neighborhood décor.

- ✔ **Paint the curbs.** Painting the curbs white or yellow is a nice touch, unless it makes the curbs clash with neighboring properties. You can also paint the address on the curb. Use stencils; don't try to freehand it unless you're an artist. Use a high-quality enamel paint designed for concrete.

- ✔ **Replace the mailbox.** A new black or white mailbox with gold lettering for the address is a nice touch.

Figures 14-5 and 14-6 reveal the dramatic effects that a little tender loving care can have on the exterior of a house. The homeowner added new windows, repainted the house white, and painted the trim black. (Notice the new plants, too; see the previous section for details on updating landscaping.)

Take a photo of your house and the neighboring houses to your local paint store and ask for recommendations on which colors to use. You want your house to stand out without clashing with neighboring homes. A medium-grade paint should be good enough. Paint the garage and fence while you're at it.

For more on making extensive repairs to a house's outside shell, see Chapter 15.

Figure 14-5:
No house hunter would want to stop at this house for a closer look.

Jeremy Goodell

Figure 14-6:
After a few affordable touch-ups, the house is a real attention getter.

Jeremy Goodell

Touching Up the Interior

A home's exterior draws buyers in, but the appearance of the interior ultimately sells the home. For a quick flip, you're not doing any major remodeling. The goal here is to make the interior appear clean and properly maintained. In the following sections, I walk you through the process of preparing the interior of the house for prospective buyers. I begin with repairs and renovations that apply throughout the house and then lead you from room to room to ensure that you don't overlook any important areas.

Renovating from room to room

Some repairs and renovations apply exclusively to certain rooms in the house. When you're looking at the countertops, for instance, you're in the kitchen or the bathroom. Other repairs and renovations apply to just about all the rooms in a house. In the following sections, I show you what my crew and I typically do on a quick flip to every room in the house. Figures 14-7 and 14-8 demonstrate how some of these techniques can completely transform a room. In this room, the homeowner replaced the carpeting; sanded, patched, and retextured the walls; added a fresh coat of paint (from green to a neutral shade); and replaced the registers, switches, and faceplates. (The window also was replaced; see Chapter 17 for details on replacement windows.)

Figure 14-7:
This room
can use
a little
updating.

Jeremy Goodell

Jeremy Goodell

Figure 14-8:
New carpet, paint, faceplates, and registers breathe new life into a room.

De-junk and scrub the house

Every house I've flipped is like a storage shed full of junk and debris. Call a rubbish company, ask the company to deliver a roll-off container, and pitch the debris. Tear out the carpet, clean out the garage and attic, and toss any trash that stands in the way of your work. You can also pitch your landscaping trimmings leftover from earlier in this chapter.

After you eliminate the junk, gather your vacuum cleaner and cleaning supplies and scrub the house from top to bottom. Perform the following tasks:

✔ Wash the windows.

✔ Vacuum or sweep away any cobwebs, especially near the ceiling.

✔ Wash the drapes, have them professionally cleaned, or replace them.

✔ Scrub the sinks, toilets, baths, and showers.

✔ Vacuum out the closets and cabinets.

✔ Apply fresh contact paper to any shelves inside the closets and cabinets.

Inspect the house and make sure that it's immaculate before every showing. Everyday cleaning is okay to keep the house from appearing pitted out, but your final cleaning before a showing should pass the white-glove test. If you don't have a passion for cleaning, hire someone who does. Check out Chapter 20 for more tips on staging a successful showing.

Apply a fresh coat of paint

The best way to make the interior house look like new is to apply a fresh coat of paint. When painting, adhere to the following guidelines:

- ✔ Remove any hooks or nails and patch holes before painting. Walls should be smooth.

- ✔ Treat any stains with Kilz to prevent grease or mold from bleeding through the paint.

- ✔ Use water-based paint rather than oil-based paint for the interior.

- ✔ Paint the walls a neutral color using a flat paint — no deep purples, fire engine reds, or lemon yellows. Flat paint hides imperfections in the walls better than semi-gloss or gloss.

- ✔ Use white ceiling paint for the ceilings.

- ✔ Use semi-gloss white paint for the trim. If the trim is stained wood, don't paint it. Clean the stain and then apply a fresh coat of shellac, if needed.

Install new window blinds

In a high-end market, shop for quality window blinds. In a low-end market, paper blinds will do. Again, don't go wild with color — white or cream is best. If necessary, trim the blinds to fit. Keep the blinds closed about a quarter of the way to let in plenty of sunlight but prevent the house from appearing vacant.

Check and repair all doors and doorknobs

If a prospective buyer or agent has to wrestle with a sliding glass door, fiddle with a lock, or yank on a door to shut it, his frustration becomes the focus of attention. Make sure that the doors look good and open and close effortlessly:

- ✔ Clean and lubricate the tracks on sliding glass doors.

- ✔ Tighten any loose hinges and lubricate them if they're creaky.

- ✔ If locks are sticky, lubricate them with powdered graphite or WD-40.

- ✔ If locks don't work, change them. A locksmith can common-key all locks so that the same key unlocks the front and back doors.

- ✔ If doorknobs look crusty, polish them or swap them out.

- ✔ If a wooden door is warped to the extent that it won't close, sand it down before painting it or have the door replaced (see Chapter 17 for more about replacing doors).

Update or add lighting

Properties you buy on the cheap often have one or both of the following lighting problems: insufficient lighting or dated light fixtures. In either case, replace the old light fixtures with newer models designed to better illuminate the rooms. For example, if a room has a fixture that takes a single bulb, install a new fixture that has room for two or three bulbs. Follow these three guiding principles: Make it new, make it bright, and make them match.

Just because you love ceiling fans doesn't mean that everyone does. I once had a very tall man walk through a house I owned. He bumped his head on the ceiling fan, and his toupee flew off. When replacing light fixtures, play it safe and choose the standard, ceiling-hugging fixtures.

Install new light switch and outlet faceplates

Old light switch and outlet faceplates look nasty against a freshly painted wall. Replace them with white or cream colored faceplates. If the switches or outlets themselves look bad or don't work properly, replace them as well.

Swap out the register covers

Heat registers gather dust, dirt, grime, and usually several layers of paint when the owners simply paint over the registers instead of removing them during the painting. Identify all register covers in the house, measure them, and then head out to your local hardware store to purchase new ones. Some register covers, especially those that sit in the floor, lift right out. Others simply require the removal of a few screws.

While you have the register covers off, use a Shop-Vac to vacuum as far into the ductwork as the hose can reach. The dust nearest the register cover is most likely to be spewed throughout the house when the furnace kicks in.

Clean exhaust fan covers and replace the fans (if necessary)

Many kitchens and baths have exhaust fans that draw the dirty, greasy, often damp air out of the room. Build-up on the fan covers and on the fans them-selves is often difficult to remove and may eventually affect the operation of the fan. At the very least, clean the fan cover and fan blades thoroughly by spraying them with a strong grease-cutter and wiping off the grease and dirt. If a fan isn't working, replace it.

Before you start messing with a fan, make sure that the power is turned off. Some fans are automatic and may turn on when they sense humidity.

Install new smoke detectors

Buyers, agents, and inspectors often look at and test the smoke detectors, so you can avoid problems by installing new ones. At the very least, change the batteries and test every detector to make sure it works.

Replace the thermostat and doorbell

An old thermostat or doorbell can make even a new house look old. Replace them. You can pick up a wireless doorbell at your local hardware store and install it without having to mess with any wiring, and it sounds nice, too. Replacing a thermostat can be a little tricky, so consider hiring a heating and air conditioning specialist to do the job.

Re-carpet, refinish, or replace damaged or worn flooring

When you're done with the rest of your repairs, turn your focus to the floors. In almost every house I flip, I tear out the old carpeting and install new carpeting in its place (assuming those rooms don't have hardwood floors that I can refinish). In low- to mid-range housing, you can usually get by with lower-grade carpeting and a higher-grade or top-grade pad. In a mid- to upper-end market, upgrade the carpet and use a top-grade pad.

Install the same carpeting throughout the house. Carpet salespeople often try to talk you into putting different colors in the bedroom, so they can unload their remnants. Insist on using the same design and colors in every room. Remember to use a neutral color (don't fall for the current trend).

If you plan on flipping several houses, consider buying carpet in bulk — by the roll — to save money. My carpet company allows me to buy in bulk and then stores the carpet for me in its warehouse.

Don't cover those hardwood floors! For years, people looked down on hardwood floors — and not because the floors were under their feet. They tended to make a house look dated. Nowadays, they add class and value to a home. Unless the wood is severely damaged, have the floors professionally sanded and refinished. If you don't know what you're doing, you can seriously damage a wood floor.

Unlike wood floors, old vinyl or tiled flooring can make a house look dated and generally shows the wear of several years of traffic. If a good scrubbing doesn't make the floors look like new, then install new vinyl or tile flooring. Your choice depends on your market and your pocketbook.

See Chapter 17 for details about redoing hardwood, vinyl, or tile flooring.

Updating the kitchen

You don't have to remodel a kitchen to make it look new. For pocket change and a moderate amount of labor, you can accessorize the kitchen to give it a whole new look. Consider the following affordable updates:

- Install a new stainless steel sink.

- Install a new faucet. Nothing makes a kitchen look more dated than the faucet.

- If the countertop looks old or crusty, have it replaced.

- Short of replacing the cabinets, you can refinish them or add new hardware — knobs and handles.

New kitchen appliances can enhance the appearance of the kitchen, but now you're talking big bucks. In most cases, if your profit margin is strong enough and the house is without major kitchen appliances (dishwasher, refrigerator, and range) or the existing appliances are ugly or in disrepair, you should buy new ones. First time home buyers often don't have enough cash to purchase these appliances after purchasing the house and need a house that comes fully equipped. If the house has ugly, smelly appliances or the appliances don't work, and you don't have the profit margin to cover the expense, then do without — no appliances are better than broken down appliances.

For a more extensive discussion of kitchen renovations, see Chapter 16.

Spending quality time in the bathrooms

A bathroom can be the scene of some pretty nasty business, yet everyone expects the bathroom to look sparkling new. Fortunately, as long as the sink, tub, shower, and flooring are in pretty good shape, you can rejuvenate a bathroom with a reasonable amount of cash and in a reasonable amount of time. Following are some bathroom essentials:

- Install all new fixtures, including a faucet for the sink, a new shower head, a new handle on the toilet, and new drain covers and plugs.

- Replace the toilet seat. For a little over twenty bucks, this small update makes the toilet look brand-new.

- Replace old towel hangers.

- If the bath or shower has a curtain, at the very least, replace the curtain. If you're a little more ambitious, install glass shower doors.

- Apply a fresh bead of caulk around the edges and base of the tub or shower, around the sink, and around the base of the toilet.

- You may need to replace wall tile, but if it's in fairly good shape, spraying the grout with a soap scum and mildew remover and then scrubbing it down may do the trick.

- If the bathtub looks like a breeding ground for bacteria and vermin, get it re-glazed for a few hundred dollars.

In a tiled bathroom, the grout between the tiles can begin to crack or wear away. Using a grout saw, you can grind the grout out between the tiles. You can then apply new grout and seal it when it sets to make the tile look new. Better yet, call a grout doctor in your area to do it. An affordable grout doctor can save you enough on tools and manicures to pay for the service.

See Chapter 16 for full details on redoing the bathrooms in your flip.

Modernizing the bedrooms

A bedroom is a box with lights and outlets, so if you already painted, installed new light fixtures, replaced the faceplates, cleaned or replaced the window dressings, and re-carpeted, you're pretty much done. (See the earlier section "Renovating from room to room" for details on these tasks.)

The only item you may have missed is the closet. Check out the closet to make sure that it looks clean inside. If it has sliding doors, make sure that they stay on the tracks. Check the hanger bar to see whether it's sturdy, and if it's not, fix it. If the closet doors have removable handles or other hardware, you can often make them look like new by swapping out the hardware.

Now, if you want to boost the storage space in the closet without knocking out any walls, install a closet organizer. A closet organizer can nearly double the amount of clothing and shoes you can shove in a standard closet.

I don't recommend spending much more than $100 per closet. Don't shell out the big bucks for designer closets; your local hardware store has more affordable options. In this price range, you can buy a kit that contains everything you need for a closet organizer, along with complete instructions. With a hacksaw, screwdriver, measuring tape, and the all-important hammer, you should be able to handle the job yourself in two to three hours.

Making the basement look livable

A finished basement can be anything from a simple, open, multi-use area to an entirely separate flat complete with a bedroom, living room, bath, and kitchen. To quickly update it, follow the instructions earlier in this chapter.

If the house has an unfinished basement, on the other hand, it can be anything from a clean, dry storage area to a dank, mud floor cave. However, an unfinished basement doesn't have to look like a dungeon. With some deep cleaning, a little paint, and fresh insulation, it can look more like a very sanitary morgue. Consider the following affordable basement enhancements:

✔ Sweep the cobwebs out of the rafters. (You can paint the rafters black, as I explain in Chapter 18, to open up the ceiling.)

✔ Dust off any ductwork, pipes, or wiring.

✔ Tack up any dangling cables, but be careful if they're electrical wires.

✔ Seal all cracks in the walls.

✔ Whitewash concrete or cement-block walls with a sealing paint. Not only does this effect look clean, but it also provides a moisture barrier.

✔ Paint the floor using a gray or beige (depending on the color scheme of the house) enamel paint. Indoor/outdoor carpeting is another option.

✔ Install new glass block windows.

✔ Buy a roll of insulation and stuff pieces of it between the joists where the joists meet the outside wall. If these areas are already insulated, tear out the old insulation and install new.

Painting the basement not only makes it look neat and clean, but also adds a fresh-painted smell to a room that may otherwise smell a little musty. Another great way to keep the basement smelling fresh is to run a de-humidifier around the clock. (Be sure to eliminate the source of the moisture first and remove the de-humidifier before showing the house.)

Attending to the furnace and hot water heater

You can't do much to make pipes or electrical wiring look more attractive, but you can enhance the appearance of two mechanicals in the home — the furnace and the hot water heater:

✔ **Change the furnace filters.** New filters decrease the amount of dust floating around, and if the buyer, an agent, or an inspector happens to peek inside the furnace, she sees that the house is being properly maintained. If you had the furnace recently repaired or inspected, attach the paperwork to the outside of the furnace.

✔ **Clean or replace the hot water tank.** If the hot water tank is relatively new and still works, clean it up so it looks like a freshly waxed car. Vacuum any dust or rust first, and then wipe the hot water tank down with a household cleaning solution and dry it thoroughly. If the water tank is ugly, damaged, or more than ten years old, have it replaced; hot water heaters are relatively inexpensive both to buy and install.

Chapter 15

Perking Up the Curb Appeal

. . . .

In This Chapter

▶ Pruning and preening your way to an eye-popping landscape

▶ Sprucing up the driveway and walkways

▶ Rejuvenating the entryway

▶ Refreshing the roof, gutters, and siding

▶ Sprucing up the garage

. . . .

*W*hen you shop for a used car, you don't pop the hood and look at the engine first. You browse for an affordable car that looks pretty clean and well-maintained. You immediately rule out any vehicles whose bodies are rusty, dented, or caked with dirt, because if they look bad on the outside, they're probably worse on the inside.

When prospective buyers look at homes, they follow a similar shopping pattern. They drive up to the curb and take a quick glance at the outside of the house. If the exterior looks run-down, they conclude that the interior is probably in no better shape. Many buyers simply drive away, unwilling to waste their time on a house that the owner didn't care enough about to properly maintain.

In this chapter, I show you how to enhance a property's exterior through landscaping, painting, siding, roofing, and other improvements to stimulate the interest and enthusiasm required to pack your house with prospective buyers.

Landscaping 101

Most houses start out with attractive landscaping — a lush lawn, a few shrubs near the house, and maybe a couple of flower beds. After years of neglect, the landscape becomes unruly and faded. Grass and weeds creep across the borders. Shrubs obscure the house. Flowers get buried in their beds. And the surrounding lawn begins to appear a sickly green.

Because landscaping improvements often require several weeks or months to take hold, one of the first steps you should take in renovating the property is landscaping. In the following sections, I walk you through the most important tasks and provide a few tips along the way.

Doing the bare minimum

Even if you choose not to do any heavy-duty landscaping, don't overlook the following bare essentials in landscaping:

- De-junk the yard by removing any broken-down jalopies, ugly lawn ornaments, and errant bricks and stones.

- Trim all trees and shrubs, and cut them back, away from the house.

- Wipe out the weeds, especially in the driveway and walkways and along the curbs and fences. Use a weed killer in these areas.

- Mow and edge the lawn, and trim the grass around everything — walls, fences, poles, swimming pools, and so on. Manicure the lawn.

- Remove any dead or dying shrubs and replace them with new shrubs, grasses, or other plants that are currently in style.

- Keep everything watered, especially during the hot, dry summer months. Consider hiring a neighborhood kid to water the plants every couple of days.

In most cases, you plan to sell a property in the spring or summer, so landscaping makes sense. If you're selling the house in the winter, though, your activities may change. If you live in an area where it snows, keep the walks shoveled and the driveways plowed. Consider hiring a kid from the neighborhood to shovel the walks whenever it snows, and check to make sure he does it.

Revitalizing a tired lawn

A scorched, grub-infested, or mole-infested lawn is a big turnoff in areas where lush, green lawns are the norm. Following are several tips that can help you affordably rejuvenate a lawn in about 30 to 60 days:

- Spring and fall are the two best times to revitalize a lawn, because the ground remains cool and moist. Don't even try to revitalize a lawn in the middle of summer.

- Have the lawn aerated. You can hire a lawn care company to do this task or you can rent an aerator and plug the lawn yourself. Early spring is the best time to aerate, but fall is okay, too.

✔ After aerating the lawn, fertilize it with a slow-release fertilizer. A quick-release fertilizer is okay, but if you apply too much, you can fry the lawn or leave brown spots where you spilled the fertilizer.

✔ If the lawn looks bad due to weeds, hire a lawn care company to inspect and treat the lawn on a regular basis. After you sell the house, the new owner may appreciate the service and choose to continue it.

✔ Mow regularly at the highest setting to allow the grass to choke out the weeds.

✔ Sod the front yard if you're on a tight schedule (that is, if you plan on putting the house back on the market in fewer than 30 days).

✔ Seed takes better than sod if you have 30 or more days for the seeds to germinate and grow into a decent looking lawn. If the lawn is in terrible shape (bare dirt), consider having it hydro-seeded. *Hydro-seeding* consists of spraying a slurry of seed and nutrients on the ground. The slurry keeps the seeds moist, so more seeds germinate more quickly.

✔ A relatively inexpensive way to refresh a severely damaged lawn is to have it *over-seeded.* With over-seeding, a machine cuts grooves into the ground and plants grass seed in the grooves, which makes more of the seeds sprout and take root. You can rent a machine to do this job, but after wrestling with the machine for three hours and wasting about 20 pounds of seed, I recommend hiring an expert. Keep the ground moist until the new grass takes hold.

✔ Bare spots smaller than a coffee saucer generally fill in on their own. You can patch larger bare spots with a mixture of topsoil and seed — about 2 cups of seed per 40 pounds of topsoil. Keep the mixture moist and don't mow these spots until the grass is at least three inches tall.

Designing an adequate landscape

Avid gardeners may be tempted to sculpt a landscape that looks like something out of *Better Homes and Gardens,* but when you're flipping a house, an adequate, affordable landscape is perfectly suitable. When designing a landscape to accent a home, you have some very simple goals:

✔ **Direct water away from the foundation.** Rain should flow away from the foundation of the house to keep the foundation as dry as possible. So, when you're landscaping around the house, slope the ground down away from the house.

✔ **Create a smooth transition from the natural surroundings to the house.** The natural surroundings must lead up to the house and anchor it without obscuring it. In other words, frame the house without hiding it. Instead of planting a tree front and center, for example, plant it off to the side and plant shrubs and other shorter plants in front.

✔ **Add color and variation.** A house typically has only a few color variations — the roof, siding, and trim. With landscaping, you can introduce additional variation in dimension and color. Choose complementary colors and plants of differing heights, but don't go overboard — two or three complementary colors are sufficient.

Watch your wallet. Do enough landscaping to properly accent the house, but no more than that. You're not living here; you're simply trying to sell the property.

Creating the proper setting for your plants

Think of trees, shrubs, and flowers as the jewels that bedeck your landscape. The dirt and mulch create the setting for these jewels, and like any good setting, this one must hold the jewels firmly in place and provide a background against which the jewels stand out. How do you prepare a stellar setting for your plants? Start by putting up edging and getting the soil set, as I describe in the following sections.

Installing edging

To prepare a setting for your plants, thoroughly rake the area you want to landscape, plot the perimeter of that area, and install edging along the perimeter. You can purchase affordable plastic or aluminum edging in rolls or use something more expensive, such as paving stones, bricks, or landscaping timber. Edging creates a clear division between the garden and adjacent landscaping and prevents grass and weeds from creeping into the flowerbeds.

Before digging around your house, call the utility companies to have them mark the locations of buried power, gas, and water lines. Dig slowly and carefully to avoid hacking into any power or gas lines that a previous owner may have buried.

Readying the soil

If the soil is too hard or sandy for the plants, loosen it and mix in some high-quality top soil. You can use a shovel, but a smaller tiller simplifies the task. Using a rake, level the ground, or if you're landscaping near the house, gently slope the earth down and away from the foundation. Apply a layer of landscaping fabric over the soil to prevent weeds from popping up in the flowerbeds.

Use landscaping fabric rather than plastic sheeting. The fabric is a tightly woven mesh that blocks sunlight from reaching the weeds but allows moisture to pass through. Plastic sheeting traps water, so if you don't lay it down just right, the mulch washes off it during heavy rains or pools of water form, which can make a flower bed look like a cesspool.

Strategically positioning and planting your greenery

In most cases, you want to plant at least a few new plants — perhaps replacement shrubs or colorful flowers. After laying the landscaping fabric (see the previous section), set the potted plants where you think you want them planted. Take a step back to envision your new garden, and then rearrange the plants until you achieve the desired look.

When you're ready to plant, cut an X through the landscaping fabric at the location of each planter, just about the size of the planter. Follow the instructions that came with the plant to plant it at the proper depth, and then tamp down the soil around the plant and water it.

To trim costs, landscape with small shrubs and trees, but throw in a few more mature plants, as well. Older, mature plants cost more, but they make the entire landscape appear well-established. If you have two or more properties, you may be able to dig up a plant that looks terrible next to one property and replant it at another property that needs a larger, mature plant. What may be too large for one property can be just the right size for another.

Adding the final touch: Fresh mulch

Whether you plant new trees, shrubs, and flowers, or simply trim back the old landscaping, you should always lay down a 3 to 4 inch layer of fresh mulch on top of the landscaping fabric. I recommend using natural cedar mulch, because it's insect- and disease-resistant, it adds a nice color to the landscape, it's biodegradable, and it's easy to replace if you need to freshen it up later.

Don't be stingy with the mulch. You can have a truck full of topsoil and a truck full of mulch delivered to the house and dumped on the driveway. That should be sufficient to rejuvenate the entire landscape. If you have leftover topsoil, simply spread it over the lawn. You can place any extra mulch around trees and bushes or offer it to the neighbors.

After you mulch, you're done with your landscaping. Congratulations! Figures 15-1 and 15-2 reveal the power of proper landscaping. The homeowner removed old pines and shrubbery from the front of the house and then planted a variety of new trees and flowers. Notice the clear edging around the plants, the careful spacing between the plants, and the fresh mulch pulling everything together.

Figure 15-1:
Before land-
scaping, this
property
looks
dreary.

Figure 15-2:
Proper
landscaping
makes the
house
appear
more
inviting.

Maintaining the landscape

After all your hard work getting the landscape into shape, you may be tempted to forget all about it and move on to the interior renovations. Don't fall into this trap! To maintain your landscaping from the time you complete it until the time the house sells, water it regularly. Read the instructions that came with the plants or ask the manager of the nursery where you purchased the plants for guidance. You can kill a plant just as easily by over-watering it as you can by not watering it at all.

Tidying Up the Driveway and Walkways

Driveways and walkways, by their nature, get pretty beat up. They carry all the traffic into and out of the house; they're exposed to sun, rain, snow, and ice; and they're the favored location of the most stubborn weeds.

To spruce up the driveway and walkways, trim the edges, pull any weeds or trees growing through the cracks, and then mend the pavement, as I explain in the following sections.

To significantly improve the curb appeal of a home with a rough gravel driveway, consider paving it, especially if neighboring homes have paved driveways.

Asphalt driveways

Patching and sealing an asphalt driveway is a perfect job for a do-it-your-selfer. It requires no skill or special knowledge, and the materials are cheap. You can complete the entire process in three steps:

1. **Spray off the driveway with a hose, thoroughly spraying dirt out of the cracks, and let it dry.**

   Power washers are great for cleaning out cracks and weeds. If you don't have a power washer, use a screwdriver to get inside the cracks, and then a Shop-Vac to remove all residue. This trick prolongs the life of any patches.

2. **Squirt asphalt patch in the cracks and holes and let it dry for about a day.**

3. **Apply sealant with a brush or mop and let it dry for about a day.**

Check the weather before performing steps 2 and 3. A good downpour washes driveway sealant right down the drain. Seal the driveway at a time when you're not expecting rain for at least 24 hours. Keep an eye on the driveway until it dries. Rope off the area with buckets (that the sealant came in) and plastic "crime scene" tape (available at most hardware stores) to remind yourself and others to stay off the area.

Concrete driveways and walkways

If your driveway or walkway looks like Stonehenge, you may want to have it professionally repaved. Any deep cracks or changes in elevation that make you trip as you walk across the pavement are safety hazards that you must repair. Depending on how serious the problem is, you have several options for dealing with it:

- **Patch cracks.** You can fill in small cracks with concrete patch. If the cracks are wider than a quarter inch, stuff a rope in the crack, pour some sand over the rope, and then add a layer of flexible concrete patch. For larger cracks, or areas where the pavement meets at different levels, you may need to fill the gap with concrete mix.

- **Level concrete slabs.** If portions of a sidewalk or driveway have settled, you can have entire slabs leveled off without replacing them. A contractor can drill holes through the concrete and then inject a liquid sand mixture or other substance below the slab to raise it to its original level. The service costs about half as much as having the concrete replaced, and the slab can handle traffic immediately.

- **Resurface the walkway or driveway.** If the surface of a driveway or walkway is crumbling but otherwise in good repair, you may be able to resurface it for a fraction of the cost of replacing it. Most building supply stores have epoxy materials that are perfect for resurfacing concrete.

- **Replace concrete.** Tearing out the old and pouring new concrete is the priciest option, but for walkways or driveways that are a lost cause, this choice may be your only viable solution.

Laying asphalt over a cracked and crumbling concrete driveway may seem like a brilliant, quick, and affordable repair, but it's more like a big mistake. I've tried it myself, as have many investors I know, and it never works. By the second year, the cracks show through exactly where they were before the repair. By the third year, the driveway looks like a gravel road.

Sidewalks may be the responsibility of the town or city in which you live, so call the streets department before taking on any expensive repairs. The city may pay all or a portion of the costs. If you notice a red or yellow paint mark on your sidewalk or driveway, the city may be planning to assess you for repairs. Notify the city immediately and complete your own repairs as soon as possible. If you don't have it done by the time the crew is on the street, they'll do the repairs and bill you!

Stone or brick walkways

Stone and brick walkways can pose a problem, especially if the previous homeowner was a do-it-yourselfer and not a do-it-righter. Improperly laid bricks or stones typically settle in odd formations and turn into weed patches.

First decide whether the walkway is necessary. If it's in good shape and just needs a little TLC (weeding and maybe repositioning or replacing a stone or brick), give it the tender loving care it needs. If it's merely a decorative piece and it looks bad, it no longer serves its purpose. Remove it, lay down some new topsoil, and plant grass seed or sod (see "Revitalizing a tired lawn," earlier in this chapter, for more about sod and seeding).

Another option is to remove all the stones or bricks and redo the walkway the right way. *Landscaping For Dummies,* by Phillip Giroux, Bob Beckstrom, Lance Walheim, and the editors of the National Gardening Association (Wiley), has complete instructions on how to properly build attractive stone, brick, and concrete walkways.

Making Entryways More Inviting

Some entryways beckon visitors to step inside. Some inspire yawns. And others send visitors fleeing in disgust. An entryway should project a sense of security along with a warm greeting. In the following sections, I suggest various ways to achieve the desired look.

Refinishing the front door

As a prospective buyer approaches the house, the front door becomes the focal point. If the door is solid, you can alter its appearance through a few minor modifications, including the following:

- ✔ Paint or refinish the door in a bold color that complements the house.

- ✔ Install new hinges, doorknob, and locks.

- ✔ Install a new door knocker or doorbell, especially if the doorbell isn't working. (If the doorbell isn't working, you have three options — repair, remove, or replace.)

If the door is broken or it looks old or cheap, consider replacing the door. Most home improvement stores have a wide selection of gorgeous, secure front doors in the range of $300 to $500.

If you install a new front door, don't hide it behind an old storm door. Replace the storm door, as well. Check out Chapter 17 for more about replacing doors.

Refurbishing the front porch

Inspect the front porch for any damage, and repair it in one of the following ways:

- ✔ If you're flipping on the cheap, you can resurface concrete steps and a porch with an epoxy material designed specifically for that purpose.

- ✔ Another option is to resurface the steps and porch with ceramic or slate tile to give the porch a whole new look.

- ✔ Damaged wood is fairly easy to replace. You can patch small cracks or gaps and apply a fresh coat of paint to all the woodwork to make it match, or pry up old boards and install new ones.

If the house is in an area where people often sit out in front, you may be able to significantly increase the value of the house by expanding the porch or replacing the existing porch with something larger. If you have to pay someone to perform the work, you probably won't recoup your investment, but if you can handle the job yourself in a day or two, you can install a porch or deck for about $1,000, increasing the sales price by a few thousand dollars. Recycled decking material that lasts a lifetime is now very affordable. For additional tips, see Chapter 18.

Adding some finishing touches

When you're done with the major repairs and renovations to the entryways, focus on a few final touches to pull the outside of the house all together. Following are a few improvements I do on all my investment properties:

- ✔ Install new brass light fixtures for the coach (porch) lights.

- ✔ Install a brass kick plate at the base of the door.

- ✔ Replace the mailbox. I use brass if the mailbox is on the porch.

- ✔ Replace the address posted on the house. I use white wood with over-sized brass numbers.

- ✔ Polish the front door handle.

- ✔ Yank out any nails or hooks that the previous owners used to hang Christmas lights.

- ✔ Add a planter or hanging plant.

- ✔ Accent the flowerbeds with a few affordable solar lights.
- ✔ Remove the pink flamingo lawn ornaments.

Refreshing the Outside Shell of the House

The shell of a house consists of its roof, gutters, siding, doors, and windows — everything that keeps the elements out and the heat or air conditioning in. In the following sections, I show you how to refresh the exterior with improvements to the roof, gutters, and siding. Chapter 17 shows you how to improve the outside shell with some moderate makeovers, including replacement windows and new sliding glass doors, which also enhance the appearance of the home's interior.

If the house has any window air conditioners, remove them immediately. Check out *Home Improvement For Dummies* by Gene Hamilton and Katie Hamilton (Wiley) for additional tips on upgrading the exterior of your house.

Laying a new roof

If the roof appears worn or stained or if the shingles are curling up at the edges, I strongly recommend that you tear off the old roofing material and install a new roof. A new roof gives the house a whole new head of hair. Inspect the roof, keeping the following important points in mind:

- ✔ The steeper the pitch, the more visible the roof is from the street, and the more important it is to make sure the roof looks great.
- ✔ If the roof has two or more layers, tear off the old roof before installing the new. This is usually required by local building codes.
- ✔ If the roof has only one layer of roofing and your budget allows for it, tear it off before installing the new roof. If the budget's tight, you can install the new shingles over one layer of old shingles.
- ✔ Don't just patch damaged areas. Blending the new shingles in with the old ones is nearly impossible.
- ✔ If the roof has any soft, spongy areas, tear off the old layers of roofing, so you can inspect and repair the sub-roofing before installing the new roof.
- ✔ Unless you're a roofer, hire an insured roofing contractor to do the work.

To estimate the cost of a new roof, use the roofing estimator at www. improvenet.com. When you get to the home page, find the project calculator resources and select the roofing calculator.

Dimensional roofing shingles cost more than standard shingles, but they enhance the appearance of the home in excess of the added costs. Opt for a lower-quality dimensional shingle over a higher-quality standard shingle.

 If the roof was damaged by strong winds or hail, the previous owner's insurance company may be willing to pay for repairs, as long as you bring up the issue before closing. If you can get the insurance company to pay, the previous owner is only out the cost of the deductible, and you can offer to split the cost or pay the deductible in full, saving on the cost of a whole new roof.

Repairing or replacing gutters

If the gutters are in great shape, you may be able to clean them out and add some gutter brackets or nails to pull the gutters flush against the house. Otherwise, call a contractor to install new, seamless gutters around the entire house and garage. This upgrade is a fairly inexpensive and quick fix, and it significantly improves the exterior appearance of the house. Pick a color (usually white or brown) that matches the trim.

Retooling the siding

When talking siding, you're in three little pigs territory. Is the house made of straw, sticks, or bricks? In the case of human homes, siding can consist of wood, vinyl, aluminum, brick, or stucco. Each requires its own unique upkeep, as I reveal in the following sections.

Figures 15-3 and 15-4 show the dazzling effects of a few moderate improvements to the siding of a home. The homeowner repainted the siding a slightly brighter color (with white trim as a complement) and retooled some of the brickwork.

Freshening wood siding

A house with wood siding typically requires a thorough cleaning with a power washer at the very least. If the wood siding is damaged, you may be able to patch or replace damaged boards, but if the damage is extensive, siding over the old wood siding with vinyl, as discussed in the following section, is probably more cost effective.

Figure 15-3:
This house, in its original state, appears ho-hum.

Jeremy Goodell

Figure 15-4:
A few enhancements to the outer shell make the house perky.

Jeremy Goodell

If the paint is chipping or faded or the colors make you physically ill, repaint the house. To choose appropriate colors for your neighborhood, snap photos of a few houses in the neighborhood that have color schemes you like, and take the photos to the paint store. Also, snap a photo of your house and the houses neighboring your house, so you can choose a color scheme that makes your house stand out a little more (but not so much that the neighbors decide to sell).

If you're flipping a house in an addition that has a homeowner's association, be sure to contact the homeowner's association to have your colors approved. Otherwise, you may find yourself having to repaint the house.

Several interactive tools on the Web help you choose color combinations for the outside of your house. Visit Behr at www.behr.com or Sherwin-Williams at www.sherwin-williams.com. Color combinations you may never imagine can really perk up the curb appeal.

If you can't stay inside the lines when you're coloring pictures in a coloring book, hire a professional painter. Although painting seems like something everyone can do, there's a lot more to it than you may think. Proper preparation is the key. You also need to maintain a consistent brushstroke with an equal amount of paint. A professional also knows how to paint so that he doesn't spend too much of your investment capital cleaning up or repairing items ruined because of a bad paint job.

Installing vinyl siding

When wood-sided homes are too ugly to paint or existing aluminum or vinyl siding is peeling away from the home's outer shell, consider re-siding the house with vinyl siding. (Vinyl siding costs less than aluminum and is more durable and popular.) The cost to have an average home (1,200 square feet or so) completely re-sided is about $7,000, so don't take on this job unless the existing siding is in terrible shape or you can do it yourself for much less. Otherwise, you probably won't recoup your investment.

If you live in or near a major metropolitan area, locate distributors who carry seconds to see whether they have rejected materials. Sometimes a company rejects perfectly good siding from a production run simply because the color is a shade off. The siding looks great, but you can often pick it up at less than half price, and nobody can tell the difference.

Renewing the beauty of brick

Brick homes require the least amount of upkeep, but if the mortar between the bricks is wearing away or if settling has caused cracks in the mortar, tuck point the brick. *Tuck pointing* consists of spreading new mortar between the bricks; it's a fairly easy job, but it requires the patience of a saint. If you're not patient, and you're not a saint, hire a professional. Otherwise, you end up dribbling mortar all over the brick and making it look even worse.

Personally, I'm not a big fan of painting over brick, because I like the way most brick looks, and the paint commonly peels off later, but some brick can make the house look dark and dreary. A bright colored paint can give some homes just the pop they need.

Patching and re-coating stucco

Stucco is like plaster for the outside of the house, and, like plaster, it often cracks and peels over time. You can patch small cracks and holes yourself and even paint the stucco if the house is in an area with a fairly warm climate. Otherwise, hire a professional to patch and re-coat the stucco. A contractor who has the necessary equipment can spray a new layer of colored stucco over the old stuff and give the house a whole new look.

In a cold climate, painting stucco is a bad idea, because moisture gets behind the paint and causes it to bubble and peel.

Glamming Up the Garage

When you're focused on fixing up a house, overlooking the garage is easy, but when prospective buyers show up, I guarantee that they won't overlook it. Here are a few tasks you can do to breathe new life into a garage:

- ✔ Paint or re-side the garage to match the house.
- ✔ Replace the roof, if needed, to match the house.
- ✔ Replace the windows, especially if you replaced them in the house.
- ✔ Install a new automatic loft door with decorative glass.
- ✔ Install a new garage access door or repaint the existing door, if it's in good shape.

Prettying up the garage improves the overall appearance of the entire property, as Figures 15-5 and 15-6 demonstrate. On this project, my flipping team gave the garage a new overhead door and a new loft door on top, fixed the trim, and freshened the paint.

Figure 15-5:
This garage looks disheveled.

Figure 15-6:
With some improvements, this garage is a place where you really want to park your car.

Chapter 16

Dazzling the Crowds with Updated Kitchens and Baths

Kitchens and baths are about more than just space and functionality. People build emotional attachments to these rooms. The bathroom is a personal place where you look yourself in the mirror every day, prepare yourself for the outside world, and pamper yourself at the end of a grueling day. The kitchen is the community center where you keep the calendar and phone; where families gather to talk about their day and plan activities; where friends and family celebrate every single holiday, birthday, and anniversary together.

As everyone in sales knows, emotional reactions trump necessities. If you can redesign or redecorate a bath or kitchen in a way that evokes a positive emotional reaction from prospective buyers, you have them hooked. In this chapter, I show you how to renovate kitchens and baths in various ways that are sure to make them more appealing to buyers.

Material and labor costs vary depending on where you're flipping and on the quality of the materials and craftsmanship. For current, accurate prices, obtain quotes from local stores and installers. You may be able to save money by doing some tasks yourself, but, as always, you benefit only if you have the time, interest, and skill to do the job right.

Giving Kitchen Cabinets, Countertops, and Sinks a Facelift

Homeowners often overcook when they renovate their kitchens. They're tired of looking at the same old cabinets and appliances, so they go with their gut, rip everything out, and install all new cabinets, a new countertop and sink, and sparkling new appliances. Thirty thousand dollars later, they have a gorgeous kitchen that adds about $10,000 to the value of the house.

Assuming the homeowner loves the kitchen and plans on staying in the house and using the kitchen for several decades, the choice may be a good one. When you're flipping houses, however, you can significantly improve the appearance of a kitchen for just a few thousand dollars. Figures 16-1 and 16-2 illustrate the dramatic effect that a moderate renovation can have on a kitchen. Among other updates, the homeowner:

- Removed some old cabinets, added some new cabinets, and replaced the doors on existing cabinets
- Added new drawer knobs and cabinet handles
- Installed new countertops, a new sink, and a new faucet

Figure 16-1: This kitchen is well-suited to curbing your appetite.

Jeremy Goodell

Figure 16-2:
The remodeled version is ready for dinner guests.

The homeowner also installed several new appliances and new flooring (see Chapter 17 for more about flooring options).

In the following sections, I reveal affordable options for cabinets, counter-tops, and sinks that can transform a dull, dreary kitchen into one of the main selling features of the house. For more about redoing a kitchen, check out *Kitchen Remodeling For Dummies* by Donald R. Prestly (Wiley).

Refinishing or replacing cabinets

I've seen investors completely gut a kitchen with solid plywood cabinets and install all new cabinets made of particle board. Sure, the new cabinets looked great, but the old ones were perfectly fine. The moral of the story is don't gut the kitchen if it doesn't need to be gutted. Not only do you risk ending up with lower-grade cabinets, but you also take on the added expense and mess of tearing out the old ones and disposing of them.

Consider the following options before replacing the cabinets:

✔ **Paint the cabinets white.** The safest, cheapest option is to paint the cabinets white with a high-gloss enamel. For about $50 total and a day's work, you get cabinets that are immaculately clean and shiny, which is what most buyers are looking for.

✔ **Strip and stain.** If the wood is good — oak, maple, hickory, cherry, mahogany — show it off. Take the doors off the cabinets, strip the stain, and re-stain everything for a fresh, new look. This option is cheap in terms of money, but expensive in terms of time and mess.

Refinishing cabinets is like sanding and refinishing hardwood floors; it seems easier than it is. Hire a pro. (See Chapter 4 for details on hiring contractors to do some work for you.)

✔ **Reface doors and drawers.** Some companies specialize in re-facing cabinets, which consists of removing the doors and the fronts of the drawers and then applying a wood or plastic laminate to all exterior surfaces. This re-facing is much more expensive than a standard paint job, but it's about a third less than the cost of installing new cabinets.

If the kitchen has rusting metal cabinets or wood cabinets that are falling apart or if the kitchen layout is poorly designed, refinishing the doors and drawers won't do the trick. In such cases, new cabinets are the only choice. Affordable prefab cabinets are fine for most houses priced in the low- to mid-range. In high-end markets, consider upgrading to custom-built cabinets.

Updating hardware for a quick cosmetic job

Most cabinets and drawers have hardware attached to them that's both functional and decorative. You can often improve the appearance of the cabinets simply by replacing the hardware — door and drawer handles, knobs, hinges, and latches. This improvement can cost as little as $5 per door and drawer, and you can expect to get every penny of that back when you sell the house.

Before you run out and purchase new cabinet hardware, make a list of everything you need and then take measurements so that you purchase new hardware with holes that match up with the holes already drilled in the doors and drawers. The less re-drilling you have to do, the better.

Resurfacing or replacing countertops

To gain a deeper understanding of the emotional reactions that homeowners have to kitchens, wander around the kitchen displays at the local building supply store and watch the reactions of customers to various cabinet and countertop displays. The right countertop can make homeowners swoon.

Before you jump to the conclusion that you need a new countertop to make buyers swoon, consider these more affordable solutions:

✔ **Polish the existing countertop.** If the countertop is made of a solid material, such as granite or a composite, you may be able to have it professionally polished for much less than the cost of a new countertop.

✔ **Resurface the countertop.** You can strip off the existing veneer and glue on new veneer, but when you add up the cost in terms of money, time, mess, and the dangers of using volatile solvents, you're probably better off installing a completely new countertop.

✔ **Replace a damaged section of the countertop.** If a section of the countertop is badly damaged, cut it out and install an attractive cutting board in its place. You can also use glass or Corian.

✔ **Add molding.** You can glue a molding to the leading edge of some countertops to cover damage and give the countertop a new look.

A new countertop can brighten and modernize a kitchen. Combine it with a new sink and faucet, and even the cabinets start to look new. Countertops range in quality, material, and price. If you're going to install a new countertop, choose a material that's suitable for your market. In low- to mid-range markets, that means laminate. In high-end markets, look for granite, Corian, stainless steel, or other custom products.

You're not buying the countertop for yourself, so tame your personal tastes and choose colors and patterns that are conservative and neutral.

Installing a new sink and faucet

Cleaning and polishing a sink is often sufficient, but if a thorough scrubbing doesn't do the trick, install a new sink and faucet. In the low- to mid-range market, stick with stainless steel. In high-end markets, consider cast iron with a porcelain or acrylic finish or a customized sink.

The problem with old kitchens

Old kitchens were designed for the days when mom stayed in the kitchen and cooked and people didn't have so many modern appliances cluttering the countertops. In other words, kitchens were designed to accommodate one cook, an oven/stove, and a refrigerator.

Nowadays, an entire family of four can be found doing the bump in the kitchen, and we have dozens of countertop appliances — microwave ovens, cappuccino machines, electric can openers, blenders, toasters, and sometimes even a TV or radio. Modern designs factor in all this new stuff and attempt to maximize the use of available space.

While you're swapping out the sink, consider adding a garbage disposer (often called a *garbage disposal*) if the kitchen doesn't have one, or replacing the disposer if the current one looks old. A new ½ or ⅝ horsepower garbage disposer ranges in price from $50 to $100, and when the homeowner or inspector takes a peek under the sink, you've already earned that money back.

Modernizing Kitchen Appliances

When you purchased the property, the generous owner bequeathed you her 1970s refrigerator with the avocado finish. Now that you've completed your kitchen remodel with a tasteful display of muted tones, the fridge just doesn't fit. It works fine, but it doesn't work with the décor. What should you do?

You have several options. If you have rental property in a low-rent district, move the refrigerator to one of your rental units. Otherwise, donate it to charity or call a used appliance dealer to haul it off. Whatever you do, don't keep it. The house is more valuable without a particular appliance than with one that clashes with the surrounding décor.

When you're trying to make your kitchen look its best, update any appliances you include with the property, as discussed in the following sections.

Deciding whether to install appliances

Appliances can jack up the cost of your kitchen remodel in a hurry. You can drop anywhere from $250 to $3,500 on an electric range, $400 to $6,000 on a refrigerator, $150 to $2,000 on a microwave oven, and another $200 to $1,500 on a dishwasher. Go top of the line on every appliance, and you add over $10,000 to your kitchen remodeling budget.

Before you splurge, take a deep breath and a look around at the housing market in your area. Do most homes for sale include all those appliances? If they do, are the appliances in the low-end, medium, or nosebleed price range? Just as you assess your renovations to meet the demands of the market (see Chapter 13), gauge the amount you spend on kitchen appliances to meet the demands of most home buyers in your area without exceeding those demands:

✔ In low- to mid-range housing, supply the bare essentials — a dishwasher, garbage disposer, refrigerator/freezer, and freestanding range. (You can replace the disposer when you put in a new sink; see "Installing a new sink and faucet," earlier in this chapter.)

✔ In mid- to upper-end housing, consider supplying the higher-end essentials along with a cabinet with warming drawers and a built-in wine cooler. Upgrade to a built-in refrigerator with an ice maker and water dispenser, and consider upgrading the oven and cooking surfaces, as I describe in "Roaming the range, oven, and cooktop" later in this chapter.

You can trim the cost of kitchen appliances by purchasing gently used or returned merchandise at outlet stores. If you buy used or returned appliances, inspect them carefully for any damage and make sure that the doors open and close without a hitch.

Adding or replacing the dishwasher

In the not so distant past, a dishwasher was a luxury. Now it's a necessity. Not only does a dishwasher automate the task of washing the dishes, but it also frees up valuable counter space that may otherwise be consumed by an ugly dish drainer.

If the kitchen already has a dishwasher, inspect it inside and out. If you wouldn't take a bath in it, replace it.

If you purchased a house without a dishwasher, add one, even if it involves losing a little cabinet space. Expect a first-time installation (for a kitchen that doesn't have a dishwasher) to cost another hundred bucks or more for the plumbing installation.

One of the main features of a dishwasher is how quiet it is. Most brand-name dishwashers, including Kitchen Aid, Whirlpool, Maytag, Amana, and Bosch are pretty quiet. Cheaper models can make washing dishes sound like a Harley Davidson convention. Of course, nobody looking at your house is likely to run the dishwasher, but you don't want to install a unit that makes the buyers blame you for the racket later.

Install the dishwasher as close to the sink as possible. This proximity makes loading the dishwasher more convenient, places the washer close to the hot water pipe, and prevents you from having to snake the water and drainage hoses through several cabinets. If you're installing new flooring (see Chapter 17 for details on flooring), lay the flooring before installing the dishwasher.

Roaming the range, oven, and cooktop

No kitchen surface gathers as much dirt, grease, and grime as the oven, cooktop, or range. If the kitchen's cooking equipment is old, cheap-looking, or crusty beyond cleaning, look into replacing it with a new unit that's appropriate for your area's housing market. Your options are limited only by your imagination, budget, and market demands:

- ✔ **Freestanding range:** This most common cooking unit combines an oven with a cooktop and has finished sides, so the range looks good no matter where you position it.

- ✔ **Slide-in range:** Like a freestanding range, a slide-in range combines the oven and cooktop, but its sides are unfinished, so you must install it between cabinets to hide the sides.

- ✔ **Drop-in range:** Like the slide-in range, a drop-in unit has unfinished sides, but the top rests on the tops of the adjacent cabinets.

- ✔ **Wall ovens:** Unlike a range, a wall oven has no cooktop. The oven is built into a wall or the surrounding cabinets, placing it about chest high, so you don't have to bend over to check your pizza.

- ✔ **Combination ovens:** A combination oven typically consists of two stacked ovens, which is great if you need to bake a pork roast and an apple pie at the same time. Some units combine microwave, conventional, and convection (hot, swirling air) energy to cook faster and more evenly.

- ✔ **Dual Fuel units:** Can't decide whether you want to cook with gas or electric? Then get a dual-fuel unit that uses both!

- ✔ **Cooktops:** A cooktop consists of burners (gas or electric) with no oven below them; they mount level with the countertop. Cooktops are great for kitchens that have wall ovens or an island on which you want to add another cooking surface.

- ✔ **Downdraft cooktops:** Downdraft cooktops are essential for those homeowners who want to grill steaks all year. A fan pulls the smoke down below the cooktop and vents it out of the house. Some downdraft cooktops include grills, griddles, rotisseries, and even woks.

You may be able to get a builder discount for ranges, cooktops, and other kitchen appliances. Tell the retailer that you flip houses on a regular basis and ask whether you qualify for the discount.

Don't forget the hood. Most kitchens have a ventilation fan to pull smoke, grease, and humidity from the air and vent it outside. That's the least you should have. For a high-end kitchen, an exhaust hood over the range is a must, and an attractive hood can really jazz up a kitchen. Houses in the low- to mid-range market commonly have hoods that circulate the air through a charcoal filter, so they don't require an external vent. You can easily replace the hood without going to the trouble of venting.

Installing a space-saving microwave

The microwave oven has revolutionized the way we cook, but it also adds to the countertop clutter, unless you can move it elsewhere. One option is to go with a combination oven that has built-in microwave capabilities, as I discuss in the previous section. Another, more affordable option is to mount the microwave over the range. Some microwave ovens double as a cooktop hood, providing ventilation for the range.

When mounting a microwave/hood combination over the range, allow sufficient space between the bottom of the microwave oven and the top of the range. If you're mounting the microwave oven under an existing cabinet, you may need to install a shorter cabinet before installing the oven.

Choosing to keep or replace the refrigerator

I can almost guarantee that anyone looking at the house is going to open the refrigerator, so the inside of it shouldn't look like a high school science project or smell like roadkill. The refrigerator must be immaculate, inside and out, from top to bottom, and from back to front. If you have to use a bungee cord to tie the door shut, if it's beyond cleaning, if it's loud, or if it just doesn't work right, it's time for a new fridge.

Your approach to providing a new refrigerator depends on the market in which you're flipping. In the low-end market, in which you plan on selling to first-time buyers, supply an affordable *top mount* model (freezer on top and refrigerator on the bottom). First-time buyers are usually moving from a furnished apartment and don't want to have to spring for appliances after purchasing a house. In the mid-range market, a house without a refrigerator is the norm, because most home buyers bring their old refrigerator with them. In the upper-end market, buyers expect a built-in refrigerator.

Clear all the refrigerator magnets, calendars, sticky notes, and photos off the outside of the refrigerator. All that stuff contributes to the sense that the kitchen — and the owner's life — is cluttered.

Bringing Bathrooms into the 21st Century

Modern and shiny-clean — that's what most buyers want in a bathroom. Examine the bathrooms first, to see what you have to work with, and then head to your local home improvement store to check out what's currently available. The latest offerings are mesmerizing — free-standing sinks, elegant fixtures, one-piece shower stalls, prefab vanities with single or double sinks, lighted medicine cabinets, and numerous collections of floor and wall tile — and they're all pretty affordable.

Don't let a substandard bathroom sink your flip. The following sections lead you through the process of exploring your many options. Figures 16-3 and 16-4 illustrate the possibilities. Among other tasks, the homeowner replaced the old linoleum floor; the shower/tub; the countertop, sink, and faucet; and the mirror and medicine cabinet.

Want more information on bathrooms? Chapter 14 has a list of affordable bathroom touch-ups; Chapter 18 has the scoop on adding a bathroom (only if necessary); and *Bathroom Remodeling For Dummies,* by Gene Hamilton and Katie Hamilton (Wiley), is full of bathroom renovation ideas.

Modern isn't always better, especially in bathrooms. People spend thousands of dollars to get their hands on antique claw-footed bathtubs, so know what you have before you toss it in the roll-off container. Sometimes, redesigning the bathroom around a precious antique showpiece makes more sense than trying to shoe-horn in a modern bathroom.

Checking and repairing bathroom walls and floors

Unless you're renovating a houseboat, the house you purchased probably wasn't constructed to come into contact with a lot of water, but that's exactly what happens in a bathroom. Before you get into any heavy-duty bathroom remodeling, inspect the walls and floor for any water damage. Rock the toilet to make sure that the floor below it is solid, and press on the walls, especially around the sink and the tub or shower to determine whether they're spongy. If you detect any water damage, replace the walls and flooring before you do anything else. Other things to keep in mind:

- ✔ When replacing walls around a tub or shower, use cement board rather than standard drywall. Cement board is designed to repel water. Install cement board to the top of the shower stall or at least three feet above the bathtub.

- ✔ Even if the floor requires no repairs to the sub-flooring, most bathrooms can use new vinyl or tile, and I recommend that you hire a professional for the job. After a quick look around, the eyes of most buyers immediately travel to the floor and check the edges around the bathtub, toilet, and baseboards. If you install the flooring yourself and don't get the edges just right, the floor looks terrible. See Chapter 17 for details about flooring.

If the bathroom floor feels a little spongy, don't succumb to the temptation of jumping up and down on it to see how bad it is. I made that mistake. My foot went clear through the sub-flooring and crawl space and landed right in the mud below the house. It ended well, though. I knocked a few dollars off my offer and still purchased the property.

Figure 16-3:
This bathroom was a little drab.

Jeremy Goodell

Figure 16-4:
A remodeled bathroom is a sanitary sanctuary.

Jeremy Goodell

Refinishing or replacing tubs and showers

Bathtubs and showers are prone to becoming matted with soap scum, mildew, and other colorful collections of slime and microscopic organisms. In addition, the surfaces get scratched up and eroded away by years of scrubbing. When a bathtub or shower is beyond cleaning, even with that foul-smelling mildew and soap scum remover, you have a choice to make — you can replace or refinish. In the following sections, I show you how to make the best decision for tubs, shower stalls, and tile.

Evaluating bathtubs

Bathtubs are pretty sturdy, so you rarely need to replace them unless one has severe cracks and chips. If the color is hideous or the finish is rough, you can have it professionally refinished. *Refinishing* consists of treating the old finish with a caustic substance, such as a strong acid, to roughen the surface and then applying a glaze that makes the bathtub look like new. After refinishing, replace all the old fixtures and the drain cover, and you have a whole new bathtub.

Resurfacing a bathtub is something I don't recommend for do-it-yourselfers, even though you can buy a kit at your local hardware store to do the job yourself. The chemicals are harsh, and applying the glaze properly requires the right tools and skills. If you wouldn't think of painting your own car, don't consider resurfacing a bathtub by yourself.

Replacing a tub is usually a two-person job, especially if the old tub is a heavy-duty steel model, but most weekend warriors can handle the job with a little help. When choosing a tub color, you can't go wrong with classic white.

Surveying shower stalls

In bathrooms that have just a shower (no tub), and the old shower stall is damaged or too filthy to clean, consider ripping out the shower stall and installing a brand-new one. You can purchase a new shower stall complete with a floor, walls, and glass or plastic doors. Of course, if the old shower stall is in good shape, a thorough cleaning and some fresh caulking around the edges may be enough to salvage it.

Assuming you can measure properly and cut or drill the necessary holes in the right places, installing a shower stall is within the realm of a do-it-yourselfer. Keep in mind, however, that if you're off an inch, you're going to be buying a new shower stall for a lot more than it costs to pay a qualified installer.

Taking a look at the tile

If your bath or shower walls are tiled, chances are good that they look like the inside of a Petri dish. To make them look sparkling new, you have two options — strip the tile and retile the walls or call a grout doctor. Other tips:

✔ Always re-tile the walls if the walls behind the tile are damaged. Don't simply try to patch the wall. Chances are good that if one section of the wall is damaged, surrounding sections are soon to follow. You should also re-tile if the existing tiles are out of style or if tiles are missing or damaged.

✔ If the tiles look good and are securely in place, don't waste money replacing them. Hire a grout doctor to make them look like new. A grout doctor leaves the existing tile in place and re-grouts it, typically restoring it to mint condition for a lot less than you'd have to pay to have new tile installed and your fingernails redone.

Dealing with la toilette

Toilets are built to take a lot of abuse, so a good scrubbing, a new seat, and a new handle is all that most toilets need. If the bowl or tank is cracked, however, you may need to replace it. The following sections reveal your options.

Replacing the seat and handle

The fastest, cheapest way to restore a toilet to mint condition is to replace the toilet seat and the handle to the tune of about $25 and 15 minutes of your time. Two bolts hold the seat in place, making it a simple out-with-the-old-in-with-the-new operation. The handle is a little more complicated, because you have to pop the hood on the tank, disconnect the chain, and work inside to remove the nut that secures the handle in place. Still, these fixes are easy.

When shopping for seats, make sure that you buy a round seat for a round toilet or an elongated seat for an elongated toilet. Otherwise, the new seat is going to look worse than the old one. For a little extra, you can purchase a soft-closing seat and lid that doesn't slam down when a kid drops it. Solid wood seats are an added bonus, but cheap particle board seats don't last.

Replacing the toilet

Shopping for a toilet can be more complicated than actually installing it. You can buy a basic model for less than $100, but if you're looking to upgrade in both function and appearance, check out the following features:

✔ **Elevated height:** 2 to 4 inches higher than a standard toilet, elevated-height models make it easier for tall people to do their dismounts.

✔ **Elongated bowl:** An elongated bowl provides a little more room to relax on the throne.

✔ **Power flush:** To avoid having to flush twice, a power-flush toilet puts some oomph behind the water to shove it down the drain. These models can be a little on the noisy side.

✔ **Quiet flush:** If the bathroom is near the kitchen, hearing the toilet flush may help curb your appetite, but people generally prefer a more muted tone. A quiet-flush toilet muffles the sound.

✔ **One piece:** One-piece toilets combine the bowl and the tank in a single unit. Although they cost extra, they give a nice, streamlined look to the bathroom, and they're easier to clean. As an added bonus, most of the one-piece units include the seat.

✔ **Insulated tank:** Condensation often builds up on the outside of the water tank, because it's colder than the surrounding air. An insulated tank reduces the condensation.

✔ **Two-level flush:** When a little water will suffice, pull one lever. When you need a little extra power, pull the other lever.

Here are a few tips for selecting and installing a new toilet:

✔ If you have a two-piece toilet (tank and bowl), you don't need to replace the entire toilet if the tank is bad. You can purchase the tank separately for about half the price of a whole new toilet.

✔ Match the size of the toilet to the size of the bathroom. You shouldn't have a small bathroom with a large toilet. An oversized toilet consumes precious maneuvering space, and people may mistake it for the bathtub.

✔ If you're a weekend warrior, a toilet should be no challenge to install, although you may need a little help lifting it.

Updating the sink and medicine cabinet

The first thing you see when you step into a bathroom is the sink or vanity (cabinet with a sink) and the medicine cabinet or mirror, so these items should all be in tip-top condition. If they're not in showcase condition after a good scrubbing or if they're out of sync with the rest of your renovations, you have several options for replacements. Begin by choosing a sink:

✔ **Wall sink:** A low-cost wall sink is an option for a second bathroom in the basement or attic, but the pipes under the sink are visible, and this option offers no under-sink storage.

✔ **Pedestal sink:** Stylish pedestal sinks can add a touch of class to a bathroom and are great for small bathrooms and half baths, but again, they offer no storage below.

✔ **Countertop sink with vanity:** More expensive than a wall or pedestal sink, a vanity with a countertop sink features two benefits: it hides the pipes and provides additional storage.

If it ain't broke, don't fix it. You can often refinish a vanity and resurface a sink without replacing either one. You save money on both materials and labor and cut your renovation time in half.

Even if the existing sink is in excellent condition or you choose to have it resurfaced instead of replacing it, you should install a new faucet and drain. Bathroom faucets tend to corrode at the base. A new double- or single-handle faucet with a matching drain is a nice, final touch.

You also need a mirror above the sink, and in some bathrooms, that's all you have — a mirror glued or screwed to the wall. If that's what you're working with, upgrade the bathroom with a lighted medicine cabinet.

For smaller bathrooms, you can often save space by installing a corner vanity and medicine cabinet.

Adding or improving ventilation

If the bathroom you're renovating has a lot of mold and mildew, chances are good that the ventilation is insufficient. Fix the problem by adding sufficient ventilation either through a window or a ceiling or wall fan. Window ventilation isn't the best. When you're paying to heat or cool your house, the last thing you want to do is open a window in the middle of winter or summer to air out the bathroom each time you use it. A $50 exhaust fan provides a more economical solution.

If the bathroom isn't infested with mold and mildew, it probably has sufficient ventilation, in which case you don't need to worry about adding or improving the ventilation.

Make sure that you have the right size fan for the room. Fans sizes are expressed in CFM (cubic feet per minute). Multiply the area of the ceiling by 1.1 to calculate a good ballpark estimate.

You want to vent the warm, humid bathroom air to the outside of the house, not to the inside of a wall or ceiling or even into the attic. Venting the air the right way requires installing a pipe that extends through an outside wall or through the roof of the house, and that's certainly not a job for the average do-it-yourselfer.

Chapter 17

Sweating Through Some Moderate Makeovers

As a quick-flip artist, you look for properties that look worse than they really are with the hope that a quick makeup job is all the house really needs. But sometimes, even a great property needs a more intensive facelift — maybe all new windows, a fancy new front door, or great new flooring — to bring it to life.

In this chapter, I show you how to tackle some moderate makeovers that can improve the quality of the home, increase its value and marketability, and attract buyers.

Giving Your Home Some New Glasses with Updated Windows

When you're flipping a house with worn, aging windows in a neighborhood where most homes have updated windows, giving your house new glasses becomes a necessity. New windows not only look nice, but they also conserve energy and make window washing a lot easier. Figures 17-1 and 17-2 demonstrate the added appeal of new windows. The bedroom looks plain with old windows, but new windows make a beautiful, stylish difference.

Figure 17-1:
Old
windows
give a room
a droopy-
eyed
appearance.

Jeremy Goodell

Figure 17-2:
New
windows
make the
room more
perky.

Jeremy Goodell

In the following sections, I discuss different window options and provide a few tips on cutting the costs of new windows.

Tossing your money out the replacement window

I recently called around for some estimates on having replacement windows installed on a house that had 17 windows — 16 standard windows and a picture window. I asked each contractor to supply me with a price to cover both the windows and installation, and I chose the least expensive window each supplier had to offer. In terms of quality and energy savings, all the windows were comparable. Prices ranged from $5,000 to $12,000. That's about $300 to $700 per window. Quite a range.

I went down to the local building supply store to price comparable windows. They sold for about $160 apiece, not installed. The low estimate I had received from the replacement window company wasn't bad, but a couple of the high ones were astronomical. It made me think that maybe I was in the wrong business.

The moral of the story is to shop around. For realistic prices on windows, visit your local hardware store before making any final decisions.

When you design your marketing flyers (covered in Chapter 19), highlight the fact that the house has all new windows, and make sure that the MLS listing includes information about the new windows (see Chapter 9 for more about MLS). This tactic not only advertises the new windows to potential buyers, but it also passes the word along to the appraiser.

Knowing your window options

When shopping for new windows, call around for estimates. Every town and city in the country has plenty of window installers and building supply stores with a wide selection of windows. Building supply stores typically carry a selection of standard size windows, or you can order custom windows if the window openings aren't standard sizes.

Windows also vary based on how you install them:

- **New construction windows:** If you're going to re-side the house (see Chapter 15 for details), consider buying new construction windows and having your contractor install them before hanging the new siding. New construction windows attach to the studs on the outside of the house. If the house is stucco or brick, new construction windows aren't an option.

- **Replacement windows:** Replacement windows include a frame that fits in the old window opening. You remove the old sashes and any sliding mechanism that's in place and mount the new window in the opening. You usually have to remove some trim, but if you're careful, you can reuse the old trim. The best part of this job is that it doesn't require a ladder. Installation is an inside job.

If you're flipping a high-end house, stick with the top brands, including Andersen and Pella. For lower-end homes, middle-of-the line vinyl fiberglass replacement windows are sufficient.

You can add a nice touch to a kitchen or dining room window by replacing a standard window with a garden window. A garden window is like a small bay window that juts out from the house.

Trimming the cost of new windows

Most window companies make more money on the installation of new windows than on the windows themselves. Part of the reason for this fact is that installing windows doesn't require a great deal of expertise. The two critical tasks in window installation are measuring the existing opening and making sure that the window is square. You can significantly cut the costs of replacing windows by doing one of the following:

- ✔ **Buy locally:** The window companies that advertise on TV have the highest markups to pay for all the advertising. For more competitive prices, check your local phone book or hardware store.

- ✔ **Do it yourself:** If you're handy with a tape measure, square, and screwdriver, consider doing it yourself and saving the cost of labor.

- ✔ **Hire a subcontractor:** When the installers show up at the neighbor's house, pay them a visit. They're generally subcontractors working for a big window company. Ask them the best place to buy windows. If the installers are entrepreneurs, they usually offer to look at your house and provide an estimate. This enables you to cut out the middleman and directly hire professional installers for a lot less. Just be sure that the subcontractor has his own insurance or is insured under your homeowner's policy, as I explain in Chapter 4.

- ✔ **Hire a handyman:** Buy windows at your local building supply store and hire a handyman to install them. See Chapter 4 for full details on hiring subcontractors and handymen.

A good installer spends time measuring the existing window openings and ordering the right-sized windows. Measuring is the most critical step during the installation. Some installers cut corners by ordering windows that give them plenty of room for error, and then they shove a bunch of insulation around the frame and tack up the trim to hide the huge gaps.

Replacing Drab, Weathered Doors

Savvy buyers inspect every door in the house. When they walk through a doorway, they can't help but notice the door, and many buyers open and close the doors to make sure that they're working properly. Home inspectors follow the same routine, so you want your doors and doorways to look nice and function properly. If you have a sliding glass door that takes a gorilla to shove open, you have a problem.

In the following sections, I lead you through the process of ensuring that all the doors in your house meet market demands and steer you clear of the types of doors that can lead to problems.

Doing the quick fix with a new storm door

Storm doors are notorious problem areas. In a good strong wind, a storm door acts as a sail, catching the wind broadside and nearly being ripped off its hinges. Over time, the screens rip, the metal gets dented, and the rod on the door closer gets bent.

Because the storm door or screen door is on the outside of the house, it often contributes more to curb appeal than the main entry door itself. If it looks bad, replace it. You can purchase a quality storm door for around $100 and install it yourself in an hour or two. Standard white is typically the color of choice, but check out the neighborhood to see whether another color predominates.

Replacing an entry door

You may think that entry doors never go out of style, but some of the old designs look about as appealing as a leisure suit. Walk around the neighborhood and check out the entry doors. Chances are that one or two of your neighbors have already replaced their doors with something more appealing or more secure.

Your entry door should help your house blend with the neighborhood. Installing a $500 fiberglass entry door with leaded glass in a neighborhood where solid wood doors are prevalent may make the house look gaudy instead of adding a touch of class.

You can go a little crazy on the entry door, spending over $600 on a single door, especially if you're flipping in the high-rent district. Some entry doors come complete with decorative sidelights and a transom (sometimes called a three-panel unit) to brighten the entrance and reveal the warm glow of the interior lights. In most areas, however, a solid door with a nice stain or a fresh coat of paint that complements the exterior colors is sufficient for achieving the desired curb appeal.

Organizations like Habitat for Humanity often have their own stores where you can pick up scratch and dent doors and other building materials for much less than you can buy new ones. You can purchase a quality metal door that's dented, patch it with auto body filler, sand it down, and paint it, and have a beautiful entry door for less than $100.

If the entry door opens and closes easily but just looks bad, consider refinishing it rather than replacing it entirely. See Chapter 15 for more about jazzing up an entry door.

Repairing or replacing sliding glass doors

If you've ever seen a real estate agent or a buyer grapple with a stubborn sliding glass door, you know that these doors aren't the best when it comes to selling houses. The tracks gather dust and dirt, the rollers get gummed up, and over time, you wonder what the manufacturer meant by "sliding." In the following sections, I provide tips on improving the operation of sliding glass doors and recommend some more appropriate replacement doors.

Fixing a sliding door that's lost its slide

When your patio door loses its slide, it's time for a little cleaning and a lube job. Take the following steps to place the glide back in the slide:

1. **Use a toothbrush or a paintbrush with stiff bristles to loosen the dirt and grease that has gathered in the tracks, and then vacuum the debris out.**

   Clean the track both with the door open and with it closed, so you cover all your tracks. If you use a toothbrush, make sure to use your spouse's and not yours!

2. **Spray a lubricant on the tracks to keep the door sliding, at least for two or three house showings, and slide the door back and forth on the track to get it lubed up.**

3. **If you still have trouble opening and closing the door, play with the adjustment screws at the top and bottom of the door.**

   These screws raise or lower the wheels that ride on the tracks.

4. **If you can get to the wheels, spray some lubricant on them.**

5. **Lube the lock by removing it and spraying it with a lubricant.**

Replacing patio doors for a whole new look

When I install new patio doors on a house, I never install the sliding variety. Single or double French doors (the ones that open like normal doors) require much less maintenance, and you don't have to throw your back out opening them. Figures 17-3 and 17-4 demonstrate the improvement you can expect to see when you install a new patio door.

Figure 17-3:
This old patio door looks weathered.

Jeremy Goodell

Figure 17-4:
French doors improve both look and function.

Jeremy Goodell

In a house that has no clear exit to the back door, one of the best ways to improve the marketability of the house is to add a door where there is no door. See Chapter 18 for details about creating a new doorway and performing other more extensive renovations.

Installing new interior doors

In focusing on the high-profile entryway doors, don't overlook the interior doors on bedrooms, dens, and bathrooms. These doors can take a beating, especially if the previous owners were door slammers or had neurotic pets who liked to scratch and chew doors. Make sure that the interior doors open and close easily and completely and that they look good, too. Depending on the condition of the doors, you have several options here:

- ✔ **Change the hardware:** If you have trouble opening and closing a door, you may need to change the doorknobs and install new hinges, which are fairly easy do-it-yourself repairs.

- ✔ **Refinish the doors:** If the finish is dull or scratched, remove the doors, sand them down, and stain them, so all the doors in the house match and look fresh.

- ✔ **Replace the doors:** If someone punched a hole through the door or it has deep scratches, consider replacing the door. An average interior door unit, complete with trim, costs around $100 and is about as easy to install as a replacement window. If your carpentry skills aren't up to snuff, consider hiring an installer or handyman.

Putting on Your Own Floor Show

New flooring is a necessity in a house that has well-trafficked, old, or damaged floors. In most rooms, new wall-to-wall carpeting is the most cost-effective option and provides you with the biggest bang for your buck (see Chapter 14 for details). In kitchens and bathrooms, however, you almost always need to lay new vinyl, linoleum, or ceramic tile, and you should sand and refinish any hardwood floors.

You may not get all your money back on the cost of refinishing floors or installing new flooring, but it's still a good investment. After you paint the house and install new light fixtures, registers, and faceplates, old flooring can make the house look like a dirt-floor hut. In the following sections, I show you several options for new flooring. For complete steps on how to lay vinyl and how to repair and refinish hardwood floors, check out *Home Improvement For Dummies* by Gene Hamilton and Katie Hamilton (Wiley).

Laying down affordable vinyl or linoleum flooring

Next to carpeting, vinyl and linoleum are the most affordable flooring options, and because they resist water, they're perfect for kitchens, bathrooms, and laundry rooms. In addition, if the existing floor isn't warped or damaged, you can apply a new layer of vinyl or linoleum over the old. Costs are comparable for linoleum and vinyl, though linoleum tends to last about three times longer and is considered the "green" (environmentally friendly) option.

For bathrooms, laundry rooms, and other areas that get drenched, install sheet vinyl rather than the square tile vinyl or linoleum. Water tends to seep between the edges where the tiles meet and gets under the tile, completely ruining the floor. Whether you install vinyl or linoleum, consider hiring an experienced flooring installer; gluing down tiles may sound easy, but installers have the right technique for making sure the tile lies flat and meets the walls just right. If you botch the job, it'll cost you more.

Refinishing hardwood floors

In the 1970s and 1980s, sellers commonly hid their hardwood floors under a layer of cheap wall-to-wall carpeting, as if the hardwood was an ugly blemish. Now, when you stumble upon a house that has hardwood floors, it's almost like striking gold.

Many do-it-yourselfers choose to sand and refinish hardwood floors them-selves, but I discourage beginners from attempting it. Floor sanders have a nasty habit of taking off on you and digging deep gouges into the floor. If you don't know what you're doing, you can easily sand a hole clear through the flooring! And if you don't apply the stain just right, the finish appears splotchy. Hire a professional.

Laying new hardwood or laminate flooring

In a room that has damaged or severely worn hardwood floors and in rooms with carpeting or vinyl that are crying out for a touch of wood, consider having new hardwood or laminate flooring installed. As Figures 17-5 and 17-6 demonstrate, a new wood floor adds class and distinction to a home.

Figure 17-5:
A large
room with
carpeting
may not
have the
pop you're
looking for.

Jeremy Goodell

Figure 17-6:
A new wood
floor adds
character
and class.

Jeremy Goodell

After you decide to put down new wood flooring, you have a decision to make: hardwood or laminate flooring? That is the question! Most home buyers drool over hardwood floors, and they get pretty excited about laminate floors, which look like wood and cost about the same but clean up like tile. Personally, I prefer hardwood, because it looks classier and lasts longer, and you can refinish it when it starts to look bad, but let your market be your guide.

Both hardwood and laminate look great, assuming they're properly installed. Hire a craftsman, not a butcher. Ask for references and then visit the homes where the installer laid the floor.

Adding ceramic tile flooring for a touch of class

Homeowners love the look of ceramic tile flooring, but after they live in a house that has it in the kitchen or bathroom, they often change their minds. Drop a glass on a ceramic tile floor, and it shatters into a million pieces that fly everywhere. And if the tile gets a little grease and water on it, watch out! You'll be sliding right out of the kitchen.

However, you *can* install ceramic tile in the foyer — the area near the front door where visitors typically kick off their shoes. Tile not only looks nice, but it also makes this area easier to keep clean through your many house showings.

If the market demands ceramic tile floors, you need to meet those demands. If it doesn't, stick with vinyl or linoleum, which I cover earlier in this chapter.

At $10 to $15 per square foot, ceramic tile is the most expensive flooring option. Assuming the tiles don't crack or chip, they last forever, but even so, you probably won't see a big return on investment by choosing ceramic tile over vinyl. Some vinyl tile options look suspiciously like their ceramic equivalents.

Chapter 18

Reconfiguring Spaces and Other Structural Overhauls

Repairing and renovating a house is one thing. Restructuring it, converting storage space into living space, building room additions, and performing other structural overhauls is another beast entirely.

First, you need to decide whether a structural overhaul even makes sense. Misguided renovators often ruin a perfectly good floor plan by opening up too much space or chopping wide open spaces into tiny rooms. Then, you have to calculate the costs and benefits — major restructuring costs major moolah. Will you get enough money back when you sell to make the restructuring worth your time and effort?

After you decide to push your vision forward, the real fun begins, especially if your plans include the removal of a wall or a portion of the ceiling. You can study the original blueprints until you're blue in the face, but until you dig into a wall, you never know what's inside it.

I can, however, tell you what's inside this chapter. Here, I guide you through the process of deciding whether you really want to monkey around with the floor plan. I reveal some techniques for identifying load-bearing walls, and I offer some suggestions on restructuring and building projects that can add real value to a property.

Attending to Essential Structure and Infrastructure Repairs

Before you even think about performing major structural enhancements, attend to the structural and infrastructural repairs required to keep the house standing and keep the electricity and water flowing (without leaking). In most cases, these structural repairs require building permits and the intervention of licensed contractors to ensure that the repairs adhere to local building codes:

- **Foundation:** The foundation supports the house, so if the basement walls are bowing in, the house is settling unevenly, or the basement or crawlspace is damp, hire a company that specializes in foundations to shore it up. Foundation repairs are costly, sometimes creeping into the tens of thousands of dollars range, but you should already have budgeted for the repairs.

- **Electrical:** An electrical system that's not up to code can not only cause problems in the power grid, but it can also start fires. Have the electrical system checked and brought up to code by a licensed electrician.

- **Plumbing:** You may be able to perform minor plumbing repairs to faucets and drains on your own, but if the pipes are leaking inside the walls, water is backing up into the house, or you can't unclog the drains, call a licensed plumber. In some cases, such as with lead pipes, you may need to replace all the pipes, which may require tearing out some walls and tearing up some floors.

- **Furnace and Air Conditioning:** If you simply need a new furnace or air conditioning unit, you may be able to have that installed at any time. If you're planning on installing ductwork in a house to add central air, hire a licensed HVAC (Heating Ventilation and Air Conditioning) technician to install the ductwork. Again, this may require tearing up floors and walls.

Knowing When to Leave a Floor Plan Alone (and When to Change It)

When constructing a house, builders follow standard design principles and adhere to specific structural limitations. Older houses, for example, rely on load-bearing walls to support the roof and ceilings (see the next section for more about these types of walls). Within those limitations, architects designed floor plans that allowed fluid movement from one room to the next and enabled light to penetrate into the house as much as possible. If you begin fiddling with the floor plans, and you don't know what you're doing, you risk lowering the value of the property and causing costly structural damage.

Without seeing your property and knowing your market, I can't offer you hard and fast rules on when to restructure the floor plan. In Chapter 13, I encourage you to visit other homes in your market to check out the competition and get a feel for the possibilities.

Before you begin restructuring a house or converting unused areas into livable space, take the Hippocratic Oath and promise to "First, do no harm." The best way to follow that advice is to ask your agent to steer you clear of any big ideas you have for changing the floor plan that are sure to mess it up, and consult a licensed contractor for advice on how to properly support the structure when considering removing walls.

Then, plan your renovations carefully, as I explain in Chapter 13. Any changes you make during a project are confusing, time consuming, and costly. Plan the work carefully and follow through with the sticktoitism you need to remain on track.

If you're living in the house you're flipping, consider waiting a few weeks before you start renovating. Over time, problems in the floor plan tend to reveal themselves to you. The kitchen may seem cramped, or you may notice that you never use the breakfast nook. You can then make better decisions on how to restructure your living areas to improve flow and use.

Identifying Load-Bearing Walls

In the process of converting underutilized space into living quarters, you often have to deal with some major roadblocks — walls, beams, and other supporting structures. Before you take a sledgehammer to that nuisance of a wall, realize that it can store many surprises — electrical wiring, plumbing, and ductwork. In addition, that wall may be supporting the second story or the roof. Knock out that wall, and the whole house may cave in . . . with you in it. In the following sections, I define "load-bearing wall" and show you how to identify such walls in your flip.

Before tearing out a wall, strip the drywall or plaster off the studs to see what's behind it. If you find a costly surprise, and change your mind, you're out only the cost of hanging new drywall. If you knock out the wall with a sledgehammer, you may find yourself paying for new plumbing, new electrical lines, and new ductwork, as well.

What is a load-bearing wall?

Load-bearing walls are the pillars of your investment. They transfer the weight of whatever is above them — the upper floor or the roof — to the foundation. Houses have three types of load bearing walls:

- ✔ The outside walls of the house are always load-bearing walls, because they support the roof.
- ✔ In a house with a conventional roof frame, interior walls that run perpendicular to the rafters support the roof. A truss roof, as I explain in the following section, requires no support from interior walls; it rests entirely on the outside walls of the house.
- ✔ In a house with two or more stories, interior walls or beams that are perpendicular to an upper story's floor joists bear the load of the upper story.

You can remove a load-bearing wall, but never without replacing it with a support that's equal or stronger than what you're taking away.

What difference do conventional and truss roof frames make?

A conventional roof frame consists of joists that span the distance between the front and back or side walls of a house and the rafters that support the roof. A house with a conventional roof frame typically has an attic and requires an interior load-bearing wall to support the attic joists.

Truss roof frames consist of a web of sticks (typically 2 x 4s) that support the roof without the added support of an interior wall. Truss roof frames make removing interior walls much easier. The tradeoff is that truss roof frames provide little or no open space for an attic.

To figure out the type of roof your house has, check the attic. You can usually access the attic from inside the house. Search the ceilings, especially in hallways, closets, and the attached garage, for a pull-down staircase or access door. You may also be able to sneak a peek through a cubbyhole in the upper floor. If you have plenty of open space in the attic, chances are good that a load-bearing wall on the floor below is supporting the joists.

If you have a conventional roof with a lot of open space in the attic that you don't want to convert into a room (see "Creating a room in the attic," later in this chapter, for more info about converting the attic), consider using it to beef up the storage space. Add a pull-down staircase, lay sheets of plywood over the joists to create a floor, and add a couple of light sockets and a switch for turning the lights on and off.

Is this wall load-bearing?

You can't tell whether a wall is load-bearing just by looking at it. You need to know what's above the wall and what's below it:

- ✔ If the house has a basement, go downstairs and find out what's below the wall. If the wall above has a wall or beam below it, the wall above is probably the load-bearing variety.

- ✔ If the wall is below an attic, go to the attic and determine whether its floor joists are running perpendicular to the wall below. If they are, the wall is supporting the attic floor.

- ✔ If the floor joists are hidden by a floor above or a ceiling below, you may need to chip away some of the ceiling to determine whether the joists run perpendicular to the wall.

I've seen houses with floor joists that run one direction on part of the house and the opposite direction on another part, so don't assume that all the floor joists upstairs run in the same direction. You may have a situation in which two walls that meet at right angles are *both* supporting walls!

You can really open up the interior of a house by removing unnecessary walls, so I don't want to discourage you from knocking down walls, but the supporting structure of the house is nothing that a weekend do-it-yourselfer should mess with. If you decide to remove a load-bearing wall, an engineer can recommend options for replacing the wall with another structure that provides equal or superior support. And always obtain a building permit from your town's building inspector and ensure that your planned changes comply with building codes in your area.

Maximizing the Use of Existing Space

Dinky homes in the midst of mansions cry out for expansion. When buyers are touring the neighborhood in search of a home that can accommodate all family members comfortably, they may skip past a cramped crib. As a flipper, however, that scanty shanty may be just the bargain you've been looking for. By opening up existing space and transforming unused space into living space, you can often boost the house into a higher price bracket.

Every house has unique expansion opportunities, so I can't tell you the best solution for the property you're renovating, but the following sections provide some ideas to stimulate your creativity.

Gunning for more room by knocking out walls

Although I provide plenty of cautionary advice to make you think twice about knocking down walls, a little demolition can often add real value to a house. Here are some ideas you may want to consider:

- ✔ By knocking out walls and perhaps raising the ceiling (see the next section), you may be able to combine the kitchen, living room, and dining room to create an expansive living space, commonly called a *great room*.

- ✔ If combining the kitchen, living room, and dining room doesn't fit with the floor plan, but the house has a small eating area off the kitchen, consider combining the two areas to transform them into a *country kitchen* — a kitchen that encompasses a large eating area.

- ✔ If a house has four or five bedrooms, none of which qualifies as a master suite, combining two small neighboring bedrooms into a master bedroom can often make a house more attractive and comfortable for the king and queen.

- ✔ In some cases, the previous owners may have erected a wall to create a closet, laundry room, or pantry, compromising the original floor plan. In such cases, the wall is typically not a supporting wall, and you can easily remove it to restore the floor plan to its original condition.

Figures 18-1 and 18-2 demonstrate the appeal of knocking out a wall to increase room. In Figure 18-1, a wall awkwardly separated the kitchen and the laundry room.

The homeowner knocked out the wall to increase the space of the kitchen and moved the washer and dryer into a new closet-style laundry room. You can see the result — a lighter, brighter, roomier kitchen — in Figure 18-2.

Raising the ceiling

Expanding a room by moving walls may exceed your budget, but depending on the roof structure, you may be able to remove the existing ceiling to reveal the rafters. Although raising the ceiling to the rafters doesn't open up more living space, it makes the area *feel* roomier and adds a touch of character. If you're replacing the roof, as well, consider adding a skylight or two to really light up the room. (Chapter 15 has more information about laying a new roof.)

Figure 18-1:
This kitchen feels a little cramped.

Jeremy Goodell

Figure 18-2:
By knocking out a wall, the space becomes more airy and expansive.

Jeremy Goodell

I install skylights only if I'm redoing the roof. If you install them in an old roof, they never seem to seal properly, and you end up creating a rainforest in the living room.

Before attempting to raise the ceiling, explore the space above the ceiling to determine the type of roof structure in place. See "What difference do conventional and truss roof frames make?" earlier in this chapter. If the house has a truss roof frame, you probably won't be able to raise the ceiling at all.

Designing a whole new kitchen

Sometimes, no matter what you do to an existing kitchen, it's not enough. The layout of the kitchen was wrong from the day it was designed, and now you have to do something about it to open it up and make it more functional. In Chapters 1 and 10, I discuss the potential investment return on kitchen renovations.

Your first step is to pick up a copy of *Kitchen Remodeling For Dummies* by Donald R. Prestly (Wiley). That book introduces the four standard kitchen shapes — L-shaped, U-shaped, G-shaped, and I-shaped (single-wall kitchens). The book also explores the mysteries of the work triangle to illustrate basic kitchen design principles that make a kitchen usable.

Your next step is to read the book and remodel the kitchen yourself or head down to the local home improvement store or cabinet supplier and ask a kitchen designer for assistance. Most stores provide free consultations as long as you buy your building materials from them.

See Chapter 16 for general details on updating a kitchen.

Adding a bathroom

A great way to add real value to a home that has only one bathroom is to convert underutilized space into a second bathroom or a *powder room*. A powder room (commonly referred to as a *half bath*) consists of the bare essentials — a toilet, a sink, and a mirror. You can cram one of these puppies under a stairwell or into a medium-sized closet. For a *three-quarter bath* (with room enough for a sink, toilet, and shower) or larger, you need a room that's at least 8 x 8 feet.

Unless you're a licensed plumber and electrician, hire a pro to convert underutilized space into a bathroom. No matter where you decide to locate it, a new WC is a mini-construction project.

If you plan on designing the bathroom and doing most of the work yourself, check out *Bathroom Remodeling For Dummies* by Gene Hamilton and Katie Hamilton (Wiley). This handy guide leads you step by step through the tasks of designing the bathroom; installing bathtubs, showers, sinks, toilets, and vanities; and even roughing in the plumbing.

See Chapter 16 for additional information on redoing a bathroom.

Spreading out to an attached garage

In a small house with an attached garage, converting the garage into a living room, den, or additional bedroom often adds real value to a house. You can wall off the space left by the old garage door or install a patio door in its place. If the garage has an attic, it may offer additional opportunities for growth.

Because many attached garages aren't heated or air conditioned, your renovation may require you to install additional insulation and baseboard heat, but stop short of adding a window air conditioner — it makes the house look cheap. Don't convert a garage into living space unless you can make it comfortable living space.

If you decide to convert an attached garage into living space, you should also consider building a new garage. I've seen homeowners transform an existing garage into living space only to have a buyer come along and ask the homeowner to convert it back into a garage. You really need to know what most home buyers want before investing a lot of money in conversion projects. See Chapter 13 for details on taking the pulse of the real estate market in a neighborhood.

Transforming a porch into a room

Some older homes have enclosed porches that you can transform into a bedroom or home office. A porch conversion typically adds to the square footage of the house, thereby adding real value and increasing the property's salability.

Like attached garages, however, porches are poorly insulated and rarely heated. If you convert a porch into a room, insulate it well, install thermal windows, and add ductwork or baseboard heat to make the room livable year round. For a porch conversion to qualify as a bona fide bedroom, the room must have a closet and its own private access.

Creating a room in the attic

Unfinished attics are like overhead storage compartments on airplanes. Families cram them with useless stuff, boxes of photos they never intend to look at, and seasonal items they rarely use. If you purchase a house with an attic, chances are good that a lot of the stuff the previous owner stored in the attic is still there.

Builders of older homes often built spacious attics for additional storage or to enable the homeowner to add bedrooms later as the family grew. By running electricity up to the attic, installing a staircase, and finishing the walls, you may be able to add a bedroom or two. The most challenging part of the project may be finding a way to add a stairway up to the attic — that vintage pull-down staircase has to go.

If the house has plenty of bedrooms and few other storage areas (like a basement, for instance), think twice about converting the attic into living space. You may be able to clean it up, add lighting, and perhaps even add a floor, but most house hunters like the additional storage space that an attic offers. Base your renovation decisions on the specific property and on market demands.

Deciding whether to convert a basement into living space

A basement that's in pretty good condition may seem like the perfect prospect for a conversion job, and it may well be, as long as you're starting with a *walkout basement* — a basement that has a door directly to the outside world. With a walkout basement, you can expand usable living space by finishing the basement. Adding a couple of bedrooms and a bath or even a recreation room can significantly boost the home's value.

In basements that have no direct access to the outside, however, finishing the basement is often a waste of money. To an appraiser, no matter how fancy the basement, it's still a basement, and it doesn't count as living space or figure into the square footage of the house.

Converting a basement into living space is usually cost effective only if you do the work yourself. If you have to hire a professional, scrap the idea and do a little sprucing up instead, as I discuss in Chapter 14.

Building New Rooms from Scratch

Your options for converting unused areas into living spaces inside a house are limited by its four exterior walls, but that doesn't prohibit you from building up or out. Depending on your budget, the size of the yard, and building code restrictions (which you can find out about from your contractor), you may be able to add a dormer or even a second story atop the existing structure or build on to the front, back, or side of the house.

Older neighborhoods that are currently in the process of a generational shift (younger families moving in) are laboratories for studying ways to expand living quarters. Remain observant, and you can gather a host of ideas on how to build onto an existing structure.

When building onto a house, you have two options — you can build up or you can build out. If the yard is the size of a postage stamp, you have little room to build out. You need to allow sufficient space for the homeowners to walk their pet, hang out, and enjoy a bit of nature. Another option is to build up, either by expanding the attic space with a dormer or raising the roof and adding a second story.

If your budget allows it and your market demands it, adding a second story can add considerable value to a house. A small ranch house is the perfect candidate. By adding a second story, you essentially double the living space. You can even add a balcony.

Renovating outside the box

When building onto a house, most people build up or build out, but some creative renovators choose a third option that's outside the box — they build down.

A friend of mine, who's also a real estate agent, encountered some serious code restrictions when he decided to expand his lakefront property. He wanted to level the house and build a new three-story house on the property. Unfortunately, the building codes in the area prohibited

the building of any new structures above a certain height. To work around this limitation, my friend decided to keep his old house intact. He raised it up, built two floors below it, and succeeded in creating his three-story home.

By retaining the existing structure and building below it, he created a house that's three times the size than current code would allow. When the code was written, this scenario was never even considered.

Adding or Renovating a Back Deck or Patio

Builders often erect houses on beautiful, spacious lots and leave the back or side yard completely undeveloped. Without a deck or patio and a wide door to enable the dwellers easy access to the great outdoors, the yard becomes a wasteland begging for development.

Adding or updating a deck or patio is an affordable way to transform this unused space into an outdoor sanctuary — a place where families and friends can gather on evenings and weekends to grill out and chill out without having to make too much of a mess in the house. Installing a patio door for easy passage between the house and deck is a nice addition that can also let in more light, making the interior appear larger.

Figures 18-3 and 18-4 illustrate just how much a few affordable modifications can improve curb appeal while expanding living space. The homeowner replaced the old, cracked concrete patio with a larger, concrete/brick patio. He also built a new lattice-topped wooden patio cover.

Figure 18-3:
This under-utilized backyard has a lot of potential.

Jeremy Goodell

Figure 18-4:
Adding a
deck allows
the party to
spill out
from the
kitchen
to the
backyard.

Jeremy Goodell

Costs for patios and decks range from about $500 to $5,000 depending on the size of the project and the costs of materials and labor. A small team of weekend warriors can slap together an average deck in a day or two.

I'm not a big fan of building a patio with *pavers* (stone or concrete blocks). I had a beautiful patio with pavers, but I got tired of looking at the weeds growing through and watching the landscapers weed the pavers, so I replaced them with a concrete patio.

If you have some open back-wall space, consider installing a patio door where no doorway currently exists. You may also be able to replace a large window with a patio door that lets in more light in addition to giving the house another entryway. If the window is more narrow than a doorway, you may be able to widen the opening enough to fit a door.

You can add a patio door or *doorwall* out to the deck for anywhere from $250 to $1,500. (A doorwall is a sliding glass door with two or more panels.) You may be able to pick up a good quality doorwall for much less from a Habitat for Humanity distribution center or similar organization that sells scratch and dent building supplies.

Cutting a hole through the wall in the back of the house is no job for amateurs. Some walls support the roof. Others have electrical wiring, plumbing, or heat ducts inside them. Hack through an electrical cable with your circular saw, and you may be doing the electric slide down the hallway.

In some areas, sunrooms (often called *solariums*) are a popular feature. You can add a sunroom to just about any house. Most sunroom manufacturers offer kits for the do-it-yourselfer. However, unless most of the neighboring homes have sunrooms or enclosed porches, I don't recommend adding a sunroom to the house. Even if you do a classy job and the sunroom fits with the style of the existing structure, you probably won't recoup your investment.

Part V
Sold! Selling Your Rehabbed Home

The 5th Wave   By Rich Tennant

"Well, it always helps to put fresh flowers around, and simmer some potpourri on the stove. Oh, and let's get rid of those Alligator Motels."

In this part . . .

With flipping, the proof is in the profit, and the profit is assured only when the sale is final. The longer you hold the property, the higher your costs, so you want to sell your rehabbed home as quickly as possible at a reasonable price.

Although this part can't sell your house for you, it does provide you with solid advice on how to price your property at a level that's attractive for the current market, how to market and stage your home during showings to make it "worth" thousands of dollars more, and how to evaluate offers and negotiate effectively to avoid costly compromises while successfully closing the sale.

Chapter 19

Marketing Your Home

● ●

In This Chapter

▶ Collaborating with your agent

▶ Asking the right price for a quick and tidy profit

▶ Enticing buyers with attractive financing

▶ Designing and printing your own marketing publications

● ●

*W*hen most sellers think of marketing their properties, they envision classified ads, flyers, and maybe even an Internet listing on one of those For Sale By Owner Web sites, but marketing encompasses much more than that. It consists of calculating the right asking price — a price that's attractive to buyers, yet profitable for you. Marketing includes listing your house on the local MLS, so word gets out to all the buyers' agents in the area. And no marketing strategy beats the positive word-of-mouth advertising that only your quality craftsmanship and good reputation can generate.

In this chapter, I lead you through the process of effectively starting the selling process and marketing your home to spark as much interest as possible and perhaps even trigger a bidding war. Here you discover how to team up with a real estate agent who's well worth his commission, price your home to sell without pricing yourself out of a profit, produce marketing materials to dazzle prospective buyers, and provide other amenities that make the deal more attractive to first-time homeowners.

Harnessing the Power of a Real Estate Agent to Market and Sell Your House

In the following sections, I offer guidance on finding an agent who's qualified to sell your house, tell you how to increase the agent's motivation, and discuss how to take advantage of your agent's access to the MLS listings in your area. For general information about the qualities to look for when you hire any agent, whether you're selling or buying a house, head to Chapter 4.

My offer stands firm. No matter what market you're in, I can help you find the top agent in your area. E-mail me at ralphroberts@ralphroberts.com.

Knowing why you should hire a seller's agent

When the time comes to sell your investment property, the temptation to sell it yourself and pocket that 6 or 7 percent agent commission is enticing. When you're selling a property for $100,000 or more, 6 to 7 percent represents a pretty good chunk of your profit. However, after looking at what a seller's agent can do for you, you may want to reconsider. A seller's agent can

- ✔ **Price your property accurately for the current market.** See "Setting an Attractive Asking Price," later in this chapter, for more information.

- ✔ **Develop an effective marketing plan.**

- ✔ **List your property in one or more area MLS listings, advertising it to all buyers' agents in the area.** I cover your agent's access to MLS listings later in this chapter.

- ✔ **Show the house to prospective buyers while you work on finding other flipping opportunities.**

- ✔ **Sell your property in half the time it could take you to sell it on your own.**

- ✔ **Assist you in negotiating a higher price and picking the best offer.** (Chapter 21 has the full scoop on negotiating the sale of your rehabbed house.)

- ✔ **Offer the security of agent-accompanied showings to pre-qualified buyers, so you know you're showing the house only to serious prospects.**

- ✔ **Present competitive market analysis to convince a buyer that your asking price is right.** A prospective buyer is more apt to listen to an experienced agent than to a seller.

- ✔ **Ensure that all the necessary paperwork is completed and the process flows smoothly from offer to closing.**

Holding costs average about $100 per day. If an agent sells a house in 30 days that would take you 60 days to sell on your own, she's already earned back $3,000 of the commission you paid, and saved you a lot of time and trouble.

I recommend that you sell the property yourself only if you meet the following conditions:

✔ Someone walks through while you're rehabbing and is willing to sign a purchase agreement on the spot.

✔ You're in a seller's market — an area where you have significantly more buyers than sellers.

✔ The house is on a street that already has plenty of buyer traffic, and you have the best house with the best price. (Of course, if you follow my guidance throughout this book, you should always have the best house at the best price.)

✔ You have the time and desire to show the house at any time of day or night when a buyer calls to see it.

✔ You have the computer skills required to produce slick marketing materials and advertise on the Internet.

✔ You're able to show the house without tipping your hand.

✔ You intend to hire an attorney to approve all the documentation and attend the closing.

By listing your house with an agent and paying a fair commission, you strengthen your relationship with the agent and provide the necessary motivation — money. In the future, when your agent discovers a great investment opportunity, she's more likely to call you than some other investor who doesn't use an agent to sell his properties. In real estate, you must give to receive — the more you give, the more you get.

Negotiating with an agent during the selling process

Although agent commissions are negotiable, I discourage sellers from being too stingy on their commissions. An agent receives 6 or 7 percent only if he delivers a buyer who ultimately purchases your house. If the buyer's agent delivers the buyer, your agent has to split that commission with the buyer's agent — the split is typically 3 or 4 percent for the seller's agent and 3 percent for the buyer's agent. If you go much lower than the standard 6 or 7 percent, the agent is going to work harder selling other houses that offer a higher commission. In addition, agents talk, so low-balling an agent could hurt your reputation and harm future sales opportunities.

A more effective way to negotiate with an agent is to offer a higher seller's commission, especially if you're flipping in a slow market. Offer top of the scale — 4 percent. (That's the seller's cut. You pay the buyer's agent the standard 3 percent in addition to what you pay your agent.) When the agent sees that you're willing to reward performance, she's much more motivated to work for you and do an outstanding job.

Taking advantage of your agent's access to the MLS

When you hire a contractor, you indirectly hire his tools. The same is true with a real estate agent. When you hire an agent, you gain access to the most powerful tool for selling houses — the *Multiple Listing Service* (MLS). The MLS accounts for the sale of nearly 75 percent of all homes. Through the MLS, your listing goes out to virtually all the real estate agents in your area and eventually ends up in the hands of prospective buyers who are looking for homes comparable to yours. Make sure that your agent has access to all MLS listing services if your area has multiple services. Some MLS listings overlap, while others have county line borders.

You can find plenty of companies on the Internet or on TV who offer to list your home for a flat fee, usually ranging from $250 to $500. Avoid the temptation to list your home with them for the following reasons:

- ✔ As soon as the buyers' agents in your area see that you're listing your house with a discount broker, they don't show your property unless it's a last resort.

- ✔ Your reputation in your real estate market suffers, because you're undercutting the current system that butters everyone's bread.

- ✔ You lose all the benefits (discussed in the section "Knowing why you should hire a seller's agent," earlier in this chapter) of having a full-service agent working for you.

Setting an Attractive Asking Price

Asking price is the biggest factor in how quickly a property sells. Set the price right, and the house should sell within the first 10 to 15 showings. Aim too high, and the house languishes on the market for months or even years. Aim too low, and you risk either shortchanging yourself or spooking buyers who think that the house must have something seriously wrong with it.

In the following sections, I lead you through the process of exploring the main factors to consider in order to establish a realistic asking price that doesn't sell you short.

Whenever you try to sell *anything,* you have to make sure that your price is competitive with the price of comparable products on the market. Even if you choose to sell the house yourself, meet with several agents to pick their brains for an asking price based on comparable houses in the area. Compose a one-page defense of your asking price that proves your property is worth that price. Your one-page defense should include information about the sales prices of comparable properties, along with improvements you've made and how much they're worth.

Don't be greedy

In a sizzling housing market, you may get away with padding your asking price a few thousand dollars over comparable properties in the hopes that the market will eventually catch up. If, however, the house sits on the market for several months because you set the price too high, holding costs chip away at your profit, and you often have to lower the price anyway.

Price the house right the first time. Set a realistic asking price that's in line with or slightly below recent sales prices of comparable homes in your area. Set the price with your head, not with your heart. The amount you have invested and what the property actually sells for are two different things.

If you're debating between starting low and starting high, starting a little high is always better. List the house at the higher price for 15 days or so to test the market and see whether you get any bites. If the market shows little interest in the house at that price, then reduce the price.

Understand the current market

If you've ever invested in mutual funds, you've seen the standard disclaimer — past results do not predict future performance. What's true for the stock market applies to the housing market, as well. Housing prices fluctuate, so you need to keep your finger on the pulse of the market and set an asking price that's in line with recent sales prices of comparable homes in the same area. To assess current market prices, do the following:

- ✔ **Consult your agent.** A good agent keeps tabs on the area's housing market and can help you set an accurate asking price.

- ✔ **Visit comparable homes.** As part of your ongoing research, visit comparable homes for sale in the area to determine asking prices. See Chapter 13 for information on visiting homes in your market.

- ✔ **Research comparable sales.** Find out the prices that comparable homes have sold for within a 1- to 2-mile radius of your house in the last 6 to 12 months. The easiest way to obtain this information is to ask your agent, who can look it up in the MLS.

The entire time the house is on the market, keep a close watch on market conditions and be prepared to lower your asking price. The housing market can shift faster than you can say "flip."

Know the price you need to make the profit you want

One of the worst ways to establish an asking price is to base it on your desired profit, but you should know your bottom line before you put the house up for sale. Do the math to determine the lowest price you can afford to accept. You can then bump up your asking price based on the other information you gathered to bring it in line with prices of comparable properties. Chapter 5 provides guidance on how to project your profit.

If you can't sell the property for a profit, you have two options. You can sell at a loss (ugh!) and claim the loss against profits on other profitable flips (unfortunate, but it happens), or hold the property and lease it until market conditions improve. See Chapter 25 to gather some tips on how to survive in a slow market.

Offering to Help Secure Attractive Financing

Financing is a big issue with first-time buyers, and that demographic is usually a huge chunk of your market. First-time buyers often fall in love with a house and then talk themselves out of it, because they assume they can't afford it. If they really can't afford it, that's a good thing, but if they can afford it, you've just lost potential buyers simply because they made an ill-informed decision.

When marketing your home to first-time buyers, make sure that they know what their approximate monthly payment will be on a 30-year mortgage. You may also want to put together a spreadsheet that shows the average monthly utility bills. Enlist the aid of a top loan officer to help with marketing to first-time buyers, and include the loan officer's contact information on your flyers and other marketing materials (see the following section). Check out Chapter 6 for a quick primer on financing.

Helping interested buyers secure financing to buy your house doesn't mean encouraging them to lie on their loan applications or get involved in some cash-back-at-closing scam. It means pointing them in the direction of a loan officer who works aboveboard to help the buyers decide how much house they can afford and obtain a loan based on their accurate financial portrait.

Becoming a Real Estate Marketing Maven

Marketing begins as soon as you begin renovating a property and chatting with your new neighbors, but the official kickoff for your marketing campaign doesn't really start until a couple of weeks before you put the house on the market. Then it's time to execute a marketing blitz that's guaranteed to deliver an enthusiastic herd of house hunters to your newly renovated doorstep. The day you put the house up for sale, your marketing campaign should hit high gear and flood the market with advertising.

When selling a property through an agent, the agent takes on the role of marketing maven and consultant. He's a hired gun who handles the marketing and advertising for you and ensures that the buyers' agents in the area are in the know concerning your property.

By bypassing the agent, you assume the role of marketing maven. You set the asking price, build a marketing plan, and develop the advertising media that spreads the word. In the following sections, I guide you through the process of establishing and executing an effective marketing plan. Even if you use an agent, you can assist in the marketing by suggesting or implementing additional marketing tactics. Team up with your agent to execute an effective strategy.

To effectively market any product, determine who's likely to buy it — in this case by consulting with your agent and knowing your market. When marketing a house to a first-time homeowner, for example, you may highlight the affordability of the house and provide a lead on where to go for financing. When marketing to movin-on-up buyers, you may want to pitch the house as being spacious beyond belief. Empty-nester downsizers are often looking for something smaller that's in move-in condition. Modify your marketing materials to appeal to your target buyers.

Choosing a method of contact

Before you start printing your full-color flyers (which I cover later in this chapter), decide how you want interested buyers and agents to contact you. Do you want them calling you at work? At home? On your cell phone? Should they send you an e-mail message? Knock on your door at midnight?

To sell your house, you need to provide an easy and reliable way for interested buyers to contact you, but you also have to preserve your own sanity and the safety of your family. After you print your phone number on a flyer and post it around town, your number is available not only to interested buyers, but also to agents who want to list your house, prank callers, and telemarketers.

If you plan on flipping long-term, consider purchasing a cell phone exclusively for your flipping business, installing a separate phone line at home, or signing up for an answering service or voice mail system to field and screen your calls. If you use your home phone number, expect to receive calls at any time of day or night.

Remain available and responsive. When you choose to sell a house on your own, you make a commitment to customer service. If a prospective buyer calls and you don't answer or if you don't call back or send an e-mail reply within an hour a two, you risk losing a sale. The buyer may get frustrated, assume you're not interested, and move on to the next property on his list. By hiring an agent, you offload this sometimes onerous task to your agent, but some flippers like it.

Planting a For Sale sign on your lawn

The lowly For Sale sign is still the cornerstone of a solid marketing campaign. When you plant a For Sale sign on your front lawn, you automatically tap into what I like to call the Rule of 20. The five neighbors on either side of you and the ten neighbors across the street immediately notice the sign and start telling their friends, neighbors, coworkers, and acquaintances about the house that's for sale on their block. You now have your own personal sales force working for you.

Don't settle for one of those skimpy For Sale signs that blow over in the first spring storm. Invest in something solid with an attractive design. Following are some additional For Sale sign tips:

- ✔ **Check with the local government and the neighborhood association to find out whether they have any restrictions on For Sale signs.** Some uppity neighborhoods ban them altogether.

- ✔ **Order a sign from a professional sign maker.**

- ✔ **Use a sign that you can anchor soundly into the ground.** I prefer a sign with a metal or wooden post that you have to anchor in the lawn with a posthole digger.

- ✔ **Make sure that the sign is built in a way that enables you to add banners to it, like "Basement" or "Appliances Included."** A plastic box to hold copies of flyers is also a good idea. (I cover flyers later in this chapter.)

- ✔ **Include your phone number, not your name, on the sign.** Leaving your name off the sign isn't to protect your secret identity — it just keeps the information to a minimum so passersby can quickly jot down the phone number.

✔ **Omit the "By Owner" part to avoid getting low-ball offers from house investors and to screen out calls from agents who think that you may need a little professional assistance.** Some agents also may refuse to show FSBO properties to their buyers, because they're afraid you'll try to cut them out of their commission.

Listing your home online

Several companies list homes For Sale By Owner, where buyers can search for homes without going through an agent. Before you sign up with one of these services, make sure that it's legitimate, that it lists plenty of homes in your area, and that it's used by many buyers in your area.

The Internet makes it easy for con artists to create a phony company that looks perfectly legitimate. Do your homework, check references, and make sure that the company has a phone number and a real mailing address before you sign up and pass along your credit card number.

Many sellers list their homes on FSBO Web sites and completely miss other sale opportunities on the Information Superhighway. Consider beefing up your online marketing with some or all of the following techniques, whether or not you use an agent:

✔ **Post a notice on your own Web site or blog, if you have one.** Consider including links to neighborhood schools, parks, museums, clubs, organizations, local government agencies, and so on. You may even include a link to a loan officer who can supply information about financing (see "Offering to Help Secure Attractive Financing," earlier in this chapter).

✔ **E-mail notices to your friends and relatives telling them you have a home for sale.**

✔ **Post a classified ad on any Web site that provides free advertising space**.

✔ **Post a message in a newsgroup, assuming the newsgroup's rules and regulations allow for this.** Most newsgroups have a FAQ (Frequently Asked Questions) that states its rules.

Designing, printing, and distributing flashy flyers

If you have a digital camera, a computer, and a color inkjet printer, you have all the tools you need to design, lay out, and print professional-quality flyers to advertise your house. Your flyers need to include the following:

- ✔ Exterior and interior full-color photos of the house, showcasing its top features
- ✔ The address of the property
- ✔ Your asking price and terms
- ✔ Property description, preferably presented as a bulleted list
- ✔ Your name (It lends additional credibility to your flyer.)
- ✔ Your phone number and other preferred contact information

Figure 19-1 shows a sample marketing flyer.

If you're marketing the home to first-time buyers, you may also include the phone number of your loan officer, who can provide details about financing. A sample monthly payment schedule based on current interest rates can also be helpful in convincing interested buyers that they can afford the payments. See "Offering to Help Secure Attractive Financing," earlier in this chapter, for more information.

Some sellers invest hours in creating beautiful flyers and then proceed to print them on cheap paper. Buy some quality paper stock with a high brightness rating, so your flyers look good in print. Because color ink and toner is so expensive, you can usually save money by having your local copy shop run off a hundred copies or so.

So now that you have those good-looking flyers, where should you put them? Here are a few ideas, subject to your agent's approval, of course:

- ✔ Grocery stores
- ✔ Restaurants
- ✔ Churches
- ✔ Gas stations
- ✔ Area apartment complexes

Advertising your home in the classifieds

Taking out a classified ad in your local newspaper can generate additional buzz, but don't go overboard. A small ad that provides the address and phone number along with a teaser description of the property is sufficient — something like "lakefront property," "move-in condition," "affordable living," or "convenient shopping." Your main goal is to pique the buyer's interest enough to call you on the phone.

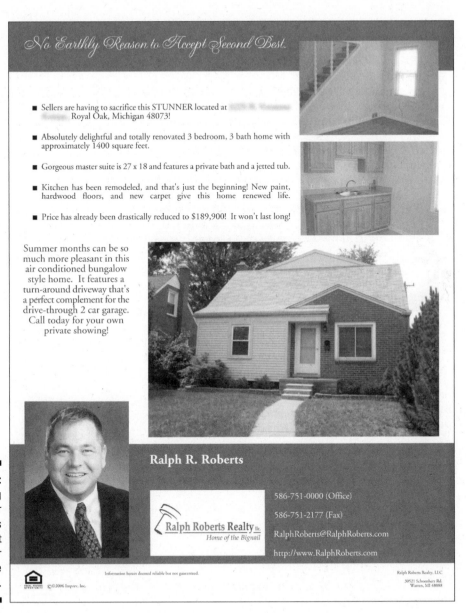

No Earthly Reason to Accept Second Best.

- Sellers are having to sacrifice this STUNNER located at ▓▓▓▓▓▓ ▓▓▓▓ Royal Oak, Michigan 48073!

- Absolutely delightful and totally renovated 3 bedroom, 3 bath home with approximately 1400 square feet.

- Gorgeous master suite is 27 x 18 and features a private bath and a jetted tub.

- Kitchen has been remodeled, and that's just the beginning! New paint, hardwood floors, and new carpet give this home renewed life.

- Price has already been drastically reduced to $189,900! It won't last long!

Summer months can be so much more pleasant in this air conditioned bungalow style home. It features a turn-around driveway that's a perfect complement for the drive-through 2 car garage. Call today for your own private showing!

Ralph R. Roberts

Ralph Roberts Realty llc.
Home of the Bignail

586-751-0000 (Office)
586-751-2177 (Fax)
RalphRoberts@RalphRoberts.com
http://www.RalphRoberts.com

Information herein deemed reliable but not guaranteed.

©2006 Imprev, Inc.

Ralph Roberts Realty, LLC
30521 Schoenherr Rd.
Warren, MI 48088

Figure 19-1: A marketing flyer contains important details for home buyers.

If you're selling By Owner and an agent brings someone to purchase the property, the agent will ask you to sign a one-time listing agreement, which lists the buyers by name. Remember that everything in real estate must be in writing.

Hosting an open house to build word-of-mouth buzz

Soon after you place your house on the market, host an open house and invite the neighbors. Sundays are the day of choice for open houses, because families are together and often looking for free food and entertainment. Pretty up the house, plant some Open House signs along the major thorough-fares, lay out some tasty hors d'oeuvres and drinks, and get ready for the after-church crowd. Be sure to distribute business cards, too. See Chapter 20 for guidance on how to properly stage your home for a showing.

In addition to the standard Sunday afternoon open houses, consider hosting an exclusive open house by invitation only for the neighbors. This prestigious event increases the neighborhood buzz and inspires your local word-of-mouth sales force to get to work. You may also do well with staging twilight open houses on a Tuesday or Thursday evening — after work but when a little sun-light still remains.

Chapter 20

Staging a Successful Showing

. . . .

. . . .

From the time interested buyers pull up in front of your house until the time they walk out that front door, they're asking themselves one question: "Do we want to live here?" Every buyer, no matter how much of a slob he is, wants to live in a house that's clean and shiny, spacious and uncluttered, and smells nice. Buyers need to envision themselves in the house, with their furniture, their family pictures hanging on the walls, their cars parked in the garage, and their stuff stored neatly in the closets.

At this point, you've completed your repairs and renovations and scrubbed the house from top to bottom. Now it's time to do some detailing, add the final touches, and knead the emotions of your buyers. In this chapter, I guide you through the tasks of properly staging your home for a successful showing by removing turnoffs and enhancing turn-ons. It's show time!

Jazzing Up the Front Entrance

During your renovations, you improve the appearance of the house so much that minor imperfections stick out. Twigs strewn across your manicured lawn catch your eye. A stray weed that pops up just before your showing takes on the appearance of an errant shrub. The old welcome mat looks like the hairball your cat coughed up.

Stand at the curb and look at your house from the front. Make a mental note of any imperfections and attend to them immediately. Then, walk up to and through the front door, taking the same path that your buyers are likely to follow. Put yourself in their shoes and imagine what they're seeing. The following sections hit on the most common problem areas you may face.

Primping the landscaping and walkways

You've already completed your major landscaping (see Chapter 15 for landscaping details), but you never know what can pop up or plop down on the ground in the course of the average day. The day before your showing, give your landscaping a final, close inspection. Attend to the following items:

- ✔ Give the lawn a fresh mowing.

- ✔ Edge and sweep the driveway and any walkways.

- ✔ Yank any errant weeds, especially the ones that pop up on walkways, driveways, and along the curbs.

- ✔ Pick up twigs and sticks.

- ✔ Remove any garden hoses or neatly roll them up.

- ✔ Get rid of any cutesy lawn ornaments — yep, the garden gnomes have to go.

- ✔ Scoop up any piles of doggy doo doo.

- ✔ Water the flowers if they need it.

- ✔ In the winter, plow or shovel any walkways and driveways.

Buying new welcome mats

A weathered welcome mat may have character, but not the kind of character you want hunkering down on your front stoop during a showing. Pitch the old welcome mat and replace it with a brand-spankin' new one. If you have a welcome mat at the back door, replace that one, too.

Don't chintz on the welcome mat. Spend a few extra bucks so it looks like an upgrade. Go with something generic, but classy rather than cutesy — choose the designer mat over the mat that advertises your favorite baseball team. Although the welcome mat may seem insignificant, buyers notice if it's ugly, and they can spot quality. A good welcome mat makes your guests feel that they're about to step into an upper-end property.

Adding a planter

A colorful planter outside the front door smoothes the transition from the great outdoors to the interior of the house, but you need to place it strategically. If the planter trips up your guests or makes opening the front door awkward, it defeats the purpose. Position the planter as close to the front entrance as possible without hindering movement into the house. You may even want to place a plant in a tall stand inside the front entrance, particularly if you're showing the house in winter.

Figures 20-1 and 20-2 demonstrate the difference that a planter and a few other last-minute improvements can make to the entryway of a house. In Figure 20-1, the entryway is bare and drab, and the welcome mat (see the previous section) has clearly seen better days.

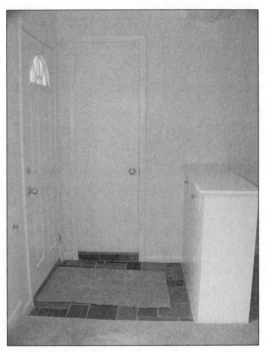

Figure 20-1:
A plain front entryway doesn't impress visitors.

Figure 20-2 shows a cleaner, more welcoming entryway. The welcome mat has been replaced, and a planter has been added for extra color.

Another option is to add a hanging plant near the entrance, especially if the entrance has a small roof or a deep overhang above it. Hang the plant high and out of the way of traffic, giving even your tallest visitor safe clearance. Get a hanging plant in a nice planter, not one of those cheap plastic pots that the nursery supplied.

Figure 20-2:
A few final
touches,
including a
bright plant,
make the
entryway
more
inviting.

Attending to the minor details

Even the smallest detail helps set a good impression for your showing. Smudges on the window, fingerprints on the doorknob, and muddy footprints on the porch can all distract from the impression you're trying to create. To eliminate any eyesores, check the following household areas:

- ✔ **Windows:** Clean any smudges on the outside of the windows, especially on the screen door and front door of the house.

- ✔ **Steps, porch, or patio:** Sweep the porch, stoop, or patio and any steps leading up to it. If you have a welcome mat, sweep that, too. Better yet, vacuum it.

- ✔ **Threshold:** Wipe any footprints or scuff marks off the doorstep.

- ✔ **Doorknob:** Polish the doorknob and door knocker.

- ✔ **Porch lights:** Flip the porch lights on and off to make sure that they work.

You can also place a neat stack of marketing flyers in the entryway that people can pick up on their way into the house. If you don't have a convenient place to stack the flyers, consider placing them on the kitchen counter or a small table in the kitchen, living room, or dining room.

Less Is More: Hiding All but the Bare Necessities

To witness a properly staged home, visit a builder's model home — the home they show buyers. Builders are masters of *minimalism* (less is more), and you can pick up a lot of tips just by observing a master's work. The most important point to note is what you don't see in a model home. You don't see a dish drainer on the kitchen counter, family photos hanging on the walls, religious icons on the shelves, or a Confederate flag waving above the couch in the living room. What you do see is wide-open spaces with a touch of tasteful décor.

In the following sections, I show you how to take a minimalist approach to staging your house. If the house is overly minimal in its décor (meaning vacant), head to the later section "Furnishing a Vacant Property."

Maximizing the minimal

When you live in a home, it becomes your nest, your pad, your sanctuary. You like to pack it with furniture that makes you feel comfortable, art that you appreciate, photos that stimulate your fondest memories, and knick-knacks that remind you of your travels and experiences.

All that stuff may seem cool to you, but when you're selling a house, even your most prized possessions can work against you. The following sections explain why.

Scantly furnished rooms appear larger

When homeowners move out of a house (frequently due to lack of space), they often do a final walk-through of their now-empty home for sentimental reasons. As they reminisce about their years spent in the house, it strikes them: "I never realized just how big this house really is."

As buyers tour your house, they're constantly wondering where they're going to put their stuff. Are we going to have enough room to spread out in the bedroom? Will our entertainment center fit in the living room? Will Junior have enough room to have sleepovers with his buddies?

When you sell a home, you're selling living *space*. To showcase just how much space you're offering, you need to open it up while keeping a few bare essentials in place to accent the space:

- A small kitchen or dining room table and chairs
- An attractive sofa and coffee table in the living room or den

> ✔ A standard-sized bed and small dresser in the master bedroom
> ✔ A few neutral paintings or other artwork on the walls

Visitors can more easily envision themselves in the house

That tiki bar motif you have through the house was inspired. It made your house a home and reminded the entire family of the great time you all had down in Cozumel. But when others look at your house, they don't necessarily want to buy a house that reflects your personality and tastes. Each buyer wants a house that he can imagine infused with his individual soul and spirit.

When showing a house, your goal is to create a blank canvas on which buyers can paint their dreams and visions. Less is more.

Decluttering the house

When you're residing in a house, your daily routines lull you into a sense of complacency. It's sort of like being married for 20 years. You and your mate are so comfortable with one another that you begin to think you look good in your frumpy sweats.

The same is true with a house. You add furniture to make it comfortable. You kick off your shoes wherever it's convenient. You store your coffee pot on the kitchen counter, so you don't have to pull it out of the cabinet every morning. You leave books and magazines strewn across the coffee table.

When you're showing a house, this stuff has to go into hiding. Just as you and your significant other have to primp a little to prepare for date night, you need to declutter and primp your house to prepare it for a showing. I break down how to do just that in the following sections.

Sell it, store it, dump it, or give it away

The first step in decluttering your house is to remove all nonessential items. If you don't need a particular item to live from day to day, do one of the following with it:

> ✔ **Sell it.** Auction the item on eBay, list it for sale in the classifieds, or have a garage sale.
>
> ✔ **Pack and store it.** Box whatever you decide to keep but don't need on a daily basis. Ideally, store your possessions offsite — at the house of a friend or family member or in a self-storage unit. If that's not an option, stack the boxes neatly in the garage. By the time most buyers see the garage, they've already decided whether they want the house.

If you have no nearby place to store your stuff, rent a storage unit or a PODS (Personal On Demand Storage) and pack away your superfluous belongings. For details about PODS, go to www.pods.com.

✔ **Give it.** If you haven't used something in 9 to 12 months, chances are good that you won't use it in the next 9 to 12 years. Give it away to a friend or a family member or donate it to charity or a local thrift store. Churches and other nonprofit organizations may even pick up items if you have a pretty good load. But before unloading your unwanted goods, call the organization or check its Web site for acceptable donations. If you have a garage sale, consider advertising a free day or the last few hours of the last day as a time when shoppers can pick up remaining items for free. You'd be surprised how much you can get rid of.

✔ **Dump it.** If you don't want something and you can't even give it away, dump it.

Before you kick your castoffs to the curb, check your local trash pickup guidelines, available from your local Department of Public Works. Curbside services don't usually accept *heavy items,* such as furniture, appliances, lawnmowers, and so on, on a daily basis, but set aside specific days or weeks to pick them up. Of course, you may get lucky and have someone who's passing by pick up your junk.

Clear the counters

Counter space is prime real estate, so you should show it off by ensuring it's in pristine condition. Work through the following checklist to make sure your kitchen and bathroom counters are immaculate:

✔ **Remove all nonessential items.** This clearing includes coffee pots, electric can openers, blenders, toasters, flour tins, and cookie jars. The biggest no-no of all is to leave a knife rack on the counter. Opening up counter space in the bathroom includes hiding the toothbrush holder, hairbrushes, lotions and creams, and anything else cluttering the vanity or sink. You can store this stuff temporarily in a cabinet.

✔ **Hide the rags, sponges, and soap.** In a pristine kitchen, these cleaning supplies are invisible. In the bathroom, however, you may want to leave out a new bar of soap or an attractive container of liquid soap and a hand towel.

✔ **Ditch the dish drainer.** It takes up counter space and reminds people of having to wash the dishes. And no one (well, almost no one) wants to think about that.

✔ **Scrub the bathroom.** Empty the trash, scrub the tub or shower (no mold around the base), and (guys) keep the toilet seat down and covered.

    ✔ **Do one last wipe-down.** Your kitchen should already be clean, but after you declutter the counter, wipe off the last remaining crumbs left behind by the toaster.

Figures 20-3 and 20-4 show just how much a little decluttering can improve the appearance of a kitchen.

Figure 20-3:
A cluttered kitchen is no place to cook a meal.

Tidy up the closets

Closets quickly become as cluttered as those overhead storage compartments on airplanes. You have to hold the stuff in with one hand while you jam the door shut.

When staging your home, empty your closets. If you can't entirely clear them out, then remove as much as possible and rearrange the rest to maximize the use of space. Closets should look like you can store more stuff in them.

Make your décor politically correct

A house showing is an emotional event. Any décor that may stir negative emotions in potential buyers has to go, including religious icons, political paraphernalia, zodiac signs, and that girlie poster you have hanging in the garage. You want your house to have a wide appeal, so don't narrow its charm by broadcasting your personal beliefs and preferences.

Figure 20-4:
Wide-open counter space is the way to go.

Furnishing a Vacant Property

Although you want to take a minimalist approach when staging a home, you don't want to create a soulless echo chamber, either. Buyers want to see a home that appears occupied, but that fact may create a problem when you don't live in the flip that you're trying to sell. Here's a room-by-room description of how to add some decorative furnishings:

- ✔ **Dining room:** A nice table with matching chairs and some dressing on the table — a tablecloth (not plastic), a bouquet of fresh-cut flowers, or some other attractive centerpiece.

- ✔ **Living room:** Couches and end tables with a few small lamps and a little greenery.

- ✔ **Master bedroom:** Good-sized bed that you don't have to stuff in the room and a small dresser.

Seasoned flippers often have some nice surplus furniture left behind in other homes they've flipped or purchased at garage sales. To help keep costs down, consider moving some furniture from your permanent residence to the house you're flipping or borrowing surplus furniture from friends or family.

If you don't have access to nice furnishings, you can rent furniture or hire a staging company to stage the house for you. A *staging company* attractively decorates and furnishes the house and can add thousands to the sales price. Here are a couple of helpful Web sites to check out:

- ✔ Home Stagers at `www.stagedhomes.com` provides facts and statistics about staging along with a referral service to help you track down accredited home stagers in your area.
- ✔ HomeStagers.com at `www.homestagers.com` features tips, before-and-after photos, and other resources to help you properly stage your home.

Contact furniture stores and furniture rental stores in your area to see whether they offer staging services and check their rates and terms on rental furniture.

If you frequently stage homes, go to moving sales and buy the furniture you need so you don't have to keep renting it. If you flip one house after another, you can move the furniture from one house to the next. When you're between houses, though, you may have a little trouble finding a place to store it.

Appealing to the Senses

When you dine out at a fine restaurant, dinner is about much more than the taste of the cuisine. The ambience of the restaurant transforms an ordinary meal into an extraordinary experience that engages your sense of smell, taste, sight, and hearing. It stirs your emotions, and by the time dessert arrives, you already know whether you'll come back in the future.

When you stage a house, your job is to create a comforting ambience that appeals to visitors. You want to stimulate a lasting sensory and emotional experience that makes prospective buyers want to move in. In the following sections, I highlight various ways that you can create an effective ambience for your next showing.

Lighting up the house

A dark house casts a pall on your showing. People begin to feel as though they're touring a funeral parlor rather than a house. Pretend your house is on center stage. You want to beam a spotlight on it to show off all the hard work you put into renovating it.

Just before your showing, light up your house by doing the following:

- ✔ Fling open the curtains and tie them back if possible.

- ✔ Open the miniblinds about three-quarters of the way. (Opening them all the way can make the house look vacant.)

- ✔ Turn on every light in the house, except those lights tied into annoying exhaust fans, such as those above the stove and in the bathroom.

- ✔ If you're showing the house at night, turn on every light outside the house.

Just before you place your house up for sale, change the light bulbs throughout the house. Use bulbs with the highest wattage and highest lumens (light production) rating recommended for each light fixture. For tubular fluorescent lights, you can also consider replacing the starters (the little silver cylinders that get the fluorescent gas glowing).

Keeping your house smelling fresh and looking pretty

With the glut of air fresheners, scented candles, and potpourri on the market, you may want to fill your house with odiferous splendor, but professional stagers advise against it. Scents that appeal to you may not appeal to someone else (especially people with severe allergies or sensitivity to smells).

Eliminate the potpourri and scented candles. Instead, bring the outside in. Open the windows to air out the house, bring in greenery from the trees, and tastefully decorate with fresh-cut flowers (which also add a touch of color to an otherwise sterile-looking room).

Playing soothing music

To create a total sensory experience, you have to appeal to the auditory senses as well, so play soft music during the showing. Shoot for something closer to classical music than heavy metal and keep the volume low.

Personally, I think that the best music for a house showing is anything by Enya. It's pleasant, inoffensive, and enjoyable for most people. You may even have people asking you for the name of the CD. Vangelis is also a good choice, or you can stick with time-proven classical selections. I'd stay away from jazz, rap, rock, and elevator music.

Stepping Out When Lookers Step In

When you're selling the house by yourself, you need to be there to show your visitors around and answer any questions. But if you or the buyer has an agent who's showing the house, you and your family and animals should step out for the duration of the showing. Consider asking a neighbor whether you can spend a half hour or so at her house until your visitors leave.

Sellers often want to remain in the house during a showing because of the inconvenience of having to leave or because they're excited to show off their renovated digs, but vacating the premises makes the house appear roomier and gives prospective buyers the opportunity to freely discuss the purchase. In other words, your presence as the owner can foster a sense of discomfort, which may be a turnoff.

Chapter 21

Negotiating the Sale to Maximize Your Profit

*Y*ou followed my advice and hired an agent to sell your house. That's an excellent decision, but it's not the last decision you need to make. Your agent can find prospective buyers, show them the house, and convince them to submit an offer, but the sales price and terms are up to you. And although your agent can help guide you through the often sensitive negotiation process, you can always benefit from a few extra techniques and strategies. You need to know for yourself how to haggle with buyers in a way that gives them what they want without giving away too much of what you need.

In this chapter, I assist you in evaluating various offers as they come in and show you how to use multiple offers to your advantage. Finally, I lead you through the process of closing the deal and introduce the paperwork you need to shuffle to make everything legal.

If you do decide, against my advice, to sell the house without using an agent, check out *House Selling For Dummies,* 2nd Edition, by Ray Brown and Eric Tyson, MBA (Wiley).

 Think twice about flying solo when you put your house on the market. According to the NAR (National Association of Realtors), the average seller receives 16 percent more for the house when the seller uses a Realtor. The reason the seller gets so much less by not using an agent is that both the buyer and seller try to save the commission. When nobody comes looking at the house, the seller subtracts the commission to make the house a more attractive purchase. The buyer, who knows that the seller isn't paying a commission, also subtracts the commission when making an offer. See Chapters 4 and 19 for information on hiring an agent.

Comparing Seemingly Similar Offers

When average homeowners sell their property, they often act as auctioneers looking for the high bid, but price is only one component of an offer (or purchase agreement). In many cases, a lower offer is superior if the buyer can close quickly and doesn't demand a lot of extras, such as closing costs and repairs.

When you're flipping houses, you need to be able to evaluate offers and see beyond price to weigh all factors. In the following sections, I reveal the major factors you should consider, so that you can compare offers as you receive them. Consult with your agent for specific advice on issues that concern you.

Your first offer is usually the best offer, so don't reject it outright thinking that better offers are soon to follow. If you receive an offer soon after you put the house up for sale, you may be tempted to assume that you priced the house too low and try to sabotage the deal so you can raise your asking price. This tactic is often a costly mistake. That first offer may be the only one you get. Pigs get fat; hogs get slaughtered.

Does the bidder have financing?

A buyer doesn't have to be able to afford your house in order to bid on it. He can have a dollar in his pocket and ten dollars in his bank account, submit an offer, and tie up your house for several days of negotiations until you discover that he can't get financing. When fielding offers, don't sign a purchase agreement unless the bidder provides proof of one of the following types of financing (see Chapter 6 for general information on financing):

- ✔ **Cash:** Cash offers are tops, but you should verify that the buyer has the available cash to close the deal. Verification can be in the form of a letter from the buyer's bank or credit union or from Grandma Roland, who's putting up the money. Or, you can ask for a copy of the buyers' recent bank statements — advise the buyers to black out their account numbers, so that the information doesn't fall into the wrong hands.

- ✔ **Preapproval:** Preapproval means that a lender has already okayed the loan. This offer is the next best thing to a cash offer, but preapproval letters are only worth as much as the paper they're printed on. Ask the buyers to talk with your mortgage person (a loan officer you trust or one your agent recommends). Don't trust the word of the buyer's loan officer, because that person may not be the most reliable source of accurate information. If the buyers balk at this suggestion, tell them that buying and financing a home is important business and they wouldn't have major surgery without getting a second opinion, so they should consider your professional. More than likely, your mortgage specialist will be of a higher caliber than the one they may have just stumbled on.

✔ **Pre-qualification:** If the buyer has pre-qualification, a lender has researched the buyer's financial records and decided that the buyer is probably able to secure a loan. Pre-qualification is one rung down from preapproval.

All things being equal, a cash offer is best, but if the cash offer is more than 5 percent lower than a noncash offer, you have to weigh the benefits against the lower purchase price.

Accept offers only from serious buyers who are at least pre-qualified for a loan that's sufficient for purchasing your house. Have your mortgage specialist on call to check up on a prospective buyer's qualifications before you sign the purchase agreement. Your mortgage specialist can contact the buyer's lender and perform background checks to ensure that the buyer has sufficient financing in place.

How earnest is the bidder?

Most offers have an earnest money deposit attached to them that shows how interested the buyer is in purchasing the property. If the buyer backs out of the deal without due cause, he forfeits the earnest money deposit, and you get to keep it. Needless to say, an offer with a large earnest money deposit is less likely to fall apart at the last minute than an offer with a smaller deposit.

When you sign a purchase agreement, you take the house off the market for the duration of negotiations. Whether the buyer submits a purchase agreement with a $500 or $5,000 earnest money deposit, when you sign it, your house is off the market. Because an offer with a larger earnest money deposit is more likely to close on time, that larger deposit carries a lot of weight.

A reasonable amount to offer as an earnest money deposit is one percent of the price offered. Any less shows a weakness in the buyer's financing or interest. Any more shows that the buyer is in a stronger position to purchase the property and more interested in closing the deal.

When buyers offer a low deposit, explain that by putting down more money now, they have to come up with less money at closing. You can also consider adding an incentive for putting down a higher deposit by saying something like, "I'd be much more comfortable with a deposit of $5,000 than with the $1,000 you're offering. In fact, I'd be willing to drop the price of the house by $500 in exchange for a larger deposit." If you figure that each day you hold the property costs you $100, $500 is a small investment for insuring that the deal goes through.

I strongly recommend that you not hold the earnest money deposit yourself. Ask your agent, attorney, or title company to hold onto the cash. That way, you won't be tempted to dip into the cookie jar before the deal is done.

What else is the bidder asking for?

Buyers ask for all sorts of stuff when they submit an offer. They may ask you to remove that pool you just installed to boost the value of the house. They can ask for the sports car you have stored in your garage. They can request that you pay up to 6 percent of their closing costs, pay for a home warranty, or immediately vacate the property at closing. When evaluating an offer, take all these requests into consideration. Following are suggestions on how to handle common requests:

✔ **Possession at closing.** Buyers often want to take immediate possession of a property. When you're flipping, this situation is ideal, assuming you don't reside in the house. If you're living in the house you flip, draw up a contingency plan and try your best to accommodate this request. It may inconvenience you, but as a flipper, you want to sell your house as quickly as possible to cut your holding costs and have cash to finance your next flip.

✔ **Payment of closing costs.** Many first-time homeowners request that the seller pay a portion of the closing costs, so that they don't have to pay these costs upfront. If buyers ask for closing costs, consider offering to pay the closing costs upfront if the buyer is willing to pay a little more for the house to cover the closing costs. Many first-time buyers would rather roll the closing costs into their mortgage than pay the fees upfront.

✔ **No tax proration.** At closing, you normally get back any taxes you paid for the months that the new owner is going to live in the house. When buyers request no tax proration, they're asking you to pay their property taxes. Ask your title company to calculate the amount you would be getting back at closing. If the amount is small — only a few hundred bucks — you may want to agree to this request. (Chapter 4 has tips on finding a title company.)

In some states, homeowners pay taxes in arrears rather than in advance. In other words, the homeowner pays this year to cover last year's property taxes. In states in which taxes are paid in arrears, the seller customarily credits the buyer at closing for as much as one year of taxes. The theory is that because the seller used the property in the previous year and those taxes are being paid this year, they are the seller's responsibility. In such cases, you're better off if the buyer doesn't ask for the taxes to be prorated. Consider offering to pay the next installment due after the closing — it can save you approximately six months in taxes versus a full year's proration. But again, if the buyer won't budge on this term and is presenting a sweet offer, you may want to give in.

Beware of the red herring move. Buyers often request something they know you won't agree to in an attempt to focus your attention on that one request and give in on everything else. If the buyer requests something odd, such as that you leave the oriental rug in the living room, it should raise a purple flag. Unless giving away that oriental rug eats up your profit, giving in may be your best option.

Under no circumstances should you offer a buyer cash back at closing. Con artists often use cash back at closing deals to gyp lenders out of money. With a cash back at closing scheme, the buyer agrees to pay a little more for the house (often much more than the asking price), and the seller kicks back a portion of the extra money (or all of it) to the buyer after closing. These deals are fraudulent; if you get involved in one, you may find yourself on the wrong end of a judge's bench.

What conditions has the bidder included?

Conditional statements (weasel clauses) accompany every offer. Some are built into the offer, but the buyer can jot down additional conditions. If you're smart, you probably did the same thing when you bought the house (see Chapter 11 for details on buying a house). Following are the most common conditions buyers stipulate:

- **Financing must be approved.** Every purchase agreement has this condition, and if you're already screening out anyone who's not pre-qualified for a loan, this clause shouldn't pose a problem. (See "Does the bidder have financing?" earlier in this chapter for more information.)

- **Property must appraise at the sales price or higher.** If you've done your homework and priced your property competitively, this condition shouldn't pose a problem.

- **House must pass inspection.** You had the house inspected when you bought it, and you repaired everything, so this point is another nonissue.

- **Title must be clear.** Before you purchased the house, you researched the title and purchased title insurance, so you're safe here, too.

- **My existing home must sell first.** You don't want the sale of your house hanging in limbo because the buyers can't sell their house. If you like the offer, consider countering with an offer that keeps the house on the market but provides the buyers with ten days notice before you sell to someone else. The buyers then have ten days to match any offer you receive. If you don't like the offer, give your other offers a higher priority.

Avoiding the domino effect

Having the sale of your house dependent on the sale of another house is known as a *domino effect*. I've seen this go seven deep. Each house is dependent on another one selling. If something happens anywhere along the line, your deal is dead. My advice is to sign a 72-hour contingency that allows you to keep your house on the market. This contingency gives you two opportunities to sell the house. You can sell the house to the first buyer, or if another buyer comes along, you can sign an agreement with the second buyer contingent upon the first deal not going through. You then give the first buyer notice that he can lift his 72-hour contingency or you will act on the second offer at the 73rd hour. Top-producer agents are well trained in this method, and you should be, too.

Keep in mind that each offer stands on its own terms. The first buyer is under no obligation to match a higher offer. Price has nothing to do with the contingency.

Beware of any conditions that the buyer adds to give himself an unfair advantage or saddle you with all the financial risk. Anything that enables the buyer to easily back out of the deal with no financial loss should raise a red flag, including interest rate contingencies (offer is removed if buyer can't get a loan at a certain interest rate), buyer's attorney must review and approve the offer, and the buyer's right to back out of the deal without cause.

How soon does the bidder want to close?

As a flipper, you're well aware of holding costs. Every day you own your property costs you money, so the sooner you close, the less money you're out. When comparing offers, check the date on which the buyer wants to close. If one buyer who wants to close immediately is offering $2,000 less than another buyer who wants to close a month from now, the lower offer may be the better offer, assuming all other conditions are equal.

Mastering the Art of Counteroffers

Some offers are so low, all you can do is laugh and shrug them off, but in most cases, no offer is too low to reject outright. When you receive an offer that appears to be a little irrational, don't take it personally. If you're not ready to say either "yes" or "no," simply reply with your counteroffer.

Take-it-or-leave-it ultimatums have no place in negotiations. Defuse your emotions. Depressurize your passions. Proceed with logic and always treat buyers with respect, even if you think they're off their rockers.

The following sections explore counteroffers in greater depth and show you some techniques for turning the tables on buyers without insulting or confronting them. For information on handling counteroffers when you're the buyer, not the seller, head to Chapter 11.

Never counter yourself. For example, say that you're asking for $200,000, and you get an offer of $180,000, so you counter with $195,000, and the buyer hesitates. You begin thinking about it. Maybe you should have countered with $190,000. You have bills to pay. Baby needs new shoes. You want to call back with a new counteroffer. Don't do it. Your baby doesn't need new shoes that badly. Wait for the next counteroffer to come in before you decide on your next move.

Submitting a counteroffer

After you receive and evaluate a reasonable offer, you have two choices — you can accept the offer as is or submit a counteroffer in writing. If the buyer offers the full price and attractive terms (as I cover in the earlier section "What conditions has the bidder included?"), accept the offer immediately. Don't start to second-guess yourself or wonder whether you sold yourself short. Lady Fortune has smiled down upon you.

If the offer isn't stellar but shows some promise for negotiation, craft a counteroffer. I show you the basics in the following sections.

Coming up with a savvy counteroffer

Offering and counteroffering is like a game of chess, in which buyer and seller attempt to anticipate one another's next move. You never know what a buyer is going to request or state as a condition, so you need to tread carefully and think creatively. Following are some examples of counteroffers that have worked for me in the past:

- **Buyer offers $5,000 less and no tax proration.** Knowing that the loss of tax proration will cost you $1,000 at closing, you counter that you agree to pay the tax proration if the buyer pays the full asking price.

- **Buyer offers $10,000 less than asking price.** Knowing that your home is priced competitively with comparable homes in the area and that you're currently in a seller's market, you counter with your original asking price but provide a comparison chart showing that your house is well worth that price.

- **Buyer makes a firm offer for less than you can accept.** Return the offer with a note that says, "Sorry, but I can't accept less than ____."

- **Buyer requests that you provide a home warranty.** A home warranty typically costs around $350, so it's usually not a deal breaker. A home warranty is a reasonable request, and if it doesn't break the bank, accept it.

Putting your counteroffer in writing

If you decide to counter, write your counteroffer on the copy of the purchase agreement you received from the buyer or the buyer's agent, initial your changes, and either fax or hand-deliver your counteroffer to the buyer's agent or directly to the buyer if she's not working through an agent. If you're using an agent, have your agent present the counteroffer. Be sure to stipulate the time period in which the buyer needs to respond to your counteroffer.

Only what's written on an offer counts, so make sure that all offers and counteroffers are in writing. Don't make verbal agreements. They won't stand up in court.

Leveraging the power of multiple offers

When you receive an outstanding offer, jump on it. If the offer falls short of outstanding, call your other prospects and let them know that you've received an offer and are going to pursue it if you don't receive an offer from them by a certain deadline (one or two days). This tactic applies pressure to all interested parties, encouraging them to get off their duffs and act quickly or lose the house for good. Keep the details about the offer you received a mystery, so new bidders don't have an unfair advantage.

If additional offers arrive, you can now compare offers (I show you how to accomplish this task earlier in this chapter) and accept the best offer or counter it. Keep a copy of those other offers on hand, however, just in case what you consider to be the best offer falls through.

Thinking like an agent

Agents are master negotiators, so when you're selling a house, it pays to think like an agent or work with an agent. Skilled agents know how to break down the numbers into minimums. For example, if a buyer offers $5,000 less than the asking price at 6.5 percent interest, the seller is out $5,000 over a single transaction. For the buyer, that $5,000 represents about $30 a month or less than $1 a day! Presenting these numbers in this way to the buyer puts the offer in perspective. I've found this strategy to be highly effective in convincing buyers to up the ante when the seller won't budge.

Another strategy we use in our office is to place the buyers and sellers in separate conference rooms — we have several of them. The buyers and sellers exchange letters. They each jot down bullet points of what they like and dislike about the offer, and we eliminate their differences one by one. After everyone is agreeable, we join together in one room and sign documents.

Countering two offers constitutes fraud, so when you receive two or more offers, you can't negotiate with all your prospective buyers. You can still play them against one another, however. If you have competing offers, get word back to both buyers that you're going to be looking at their best and final offer. If you have an agent, let the agent do the talking. After both offers come in, you can then pick the best offer and start negotiating. Remember, countering on two offers is fraudulent — don't go there.

Shuffling Papers and Other Legal Stuff at Closing

After you and the buyers reach an agreement on price and terms, and assuming nothing happens to sabotage the deal, the sale proceeds to closing, where you receive your money and sign over the deed to the buyer. At this point, you have two goals — to make the closing proceed as smoothly as possible and to ensure that your back end is covered. In the following sections, I show you how to proceed with a closing from start to finish.

In real estate, everything must be in writing. Everything must be disclosed. You can't hide anything or make deals on the side.

Having the right folks represent you

Even if you sell the house yourself, you should never try to fly solo during the closing. Closings are complicated legal and financial transactions accompanied by mounds of paperwork. You need to make sure that your interests are protected at closing by hiring a closing agent and real estate attorney to represent you and ensure that all paperwork is properly completed. Your agent can attend the closing but usually advises you to have your attorney present; whether you choose to have your attorney present is up to you.

In most cases, your title company supplies the closing agent, but in some cases, the buyer's lender insists on handling the buyer's end of the closing. However the closing is handled, you should supply your attorney with copies of the paperwork to review before the closing date to avoid any nasty surprises at closing. See Chapter 4 for details on hiring a title company and a real estate attorney.

As soon as you and the buyer agree on price and terms, call your title company or real estate attorney and schedule a closing date. Closings typically occur 30 to 45 days from the day you sell the property, so you don't want to waste any time. As soon as you sell the property, you must order the title policy, the mortgage commitment. Neither the buyer nor seller need to worry about this — your real estate agent keeps the process moving forward and can recommend a title company or attorney to handle the paperwork.

Prepping for closing

To ensure that the closing proceeds as smoothly as possible, supply your closing agent with any documents she may need to put together the closing packets. Documents typically include the following:

- ✔ **Termite inspection report.** If the buyer is receiving FHA (Federal Housing Administration) financing to purchase the house (see Chapter 9 for details), immediately schedule a termite inspection and send the report to the closing agent or attorney who's handling the closing.

- ✔ **Purchase agreement and any addendums.**

- ✔ **Mortgage payoff information and any second mortgages or other liens.**

- ✔ **Buyer's financial information.**

If you use the same title company at closing that you used when you purchased the property, the title company often discounts the fee it charges for title work. Even if you're using a different title company, turn in your old policy. You can usually receive a credit for it.

Sealing the deal with paperwork

At the closing, the closing agent or attorney in charge supplies you and the buyer with separate closing packages. The buyers' package is typically much thicker than yours, because they're the ones borrowing money. Your package should include the following items:

- ✔ **Settlement Statement:** You and the buyer both receive a settlement statement that breaks down the charges and credits for the buyer and seller and shows the net amount each of you receives or must pay at closing.

- ✔ **Deed:** The deed is the document that transfers ownership of the property from you (the seller) to the buyer.

✔ **Bill of Sale:** If you included any appliances in the sale of the property, your closing package may include a bill of sale that transfers ownership of these items to the buyer.

✔ **Mortgage Payoff Statement:** If you took out a loan to purchase the property, your lender supplies you with a letter indicating the full amount due on the closing date to pay off the mortgage. After the closing is final, the lender receives full payment.

✔ **Escrow Statement:** If your monthly mortgage payments included escrow payments to cover bills, such as water and sewer, homeowner's insurance, or property taxes, some of the money held in escrow may be returned to you at closing. The escrow statement shows you how much you can expect to get back.

✔ **1099-S Report:** The federal government requires that the 1099-S be filed to report the exact sales price of the house.

✔ **Estoppel Certificate:** Some title companies require the buyer and seller to sign an Estoppel certificate that verifies they are of legal age to enter into a legally binding agreement, that the deed has no hidden liens, and that nobody's currently disputing the title.

✔ **Homestead Exemption Update:** Some properties qualify for a homestead tax exemption. At closing, you may be asked to rescind the exemption that's in place, so the buyers can claim the exemption, if they qualify for it.

A lot of times the buyers sign their closing paperwork first because they have so much more to sign. Often buyers and sellers sign together, sometimes separately, and sometimes through the mail. No way is wrong as long as it fits your circumstances.

After you and the buyer sign the required documents, the deal is done. Hand over the keys and the garage door openers to the new owner. At this point, you should also inform the buyers of the date on which utilities will be turned off. Bring the phone numbers of the various utility companies to the closing. After closing, you and the new owners can call the companies and have the utilities transferred to the new owners. Because your name is on the utility bills, you may need to verify with the utility company that you approve the transfer. Overlooking a minor detail like switching over the utilities can inconvenience the new owners and result in your receiving a huge unexpected bill down the road.

Part VI
The Part of Tens

The 5th Wave   By Rich Tennant

"You'd be surprised how much a fresh coat of polish and some new laces increases the resale value."

In this part . . .

Every dollar has ten dimes, every dime has ten pennies, and every *For Dummies* guide has a Part of Tens. This guide is no different in that respect, but it does offer a unique collection of lists focusing exclusively on flipping houses. Here you discover ten obvious signs that a house is packed with flipping potential, ten savvy ways to trim renovation costs, ten ways you can botch the job (so you know what to avoid), and ten survival tips to keep you afloat during a slow market.

Chapter 22

Ten Signs of a Great House Flipping Opportunity

In This Chapter

▶ Spotting real estate hot spots

▶ Working with homeowners who are eager to sell

▶ Discovering properties that look much worse than they are

Successful house flipping demands that you execute a series of successful steps, but the most important step is the first one — locating a property at a price low enough for you to fix it up and sell it at a profit. If you trip when taking that first step, you're doomed. In this chapter, I point out ten signs of a great house flipping opportunity to help you over that first hurdle. For more tips on finding excellent flipping candidates, check out Part III.

The Location Is an Obvious Hot Spot

In any neighborhood where housing demand exceeds supply, you have a much wider margin of error. When housing values are rising at an annual rate of 10 to 15 percent, you make money simply by buying and holding on to a property. You make even more money if you can acquire a property at a discount — a distressed property.

Observe the housing market in your area and identify the trendy areas — where people would live if they could afford to. Head to Chapter 8 for more information about targeting different neighborhoods.

Nobody's Home

In your target area, you know the sales prices of homes in various price brackets. After you identify the high-rent district, drive or walk around the neighborhood and look for the following signs of a vacant property:

- ✔ Overstuffed mailbox
- ✔ Newspapers piled on the front porch
- ✔ Weedy or overgrown lawn
- ✔ No window dressings
- ✔ No furniture inside the house

The "For Sale By Owner" Ad Is Shrinking

Sell-it-yourself homeowners often begin advertising with $50 or $100 ads. The longer the property is on the market, the less money the homeowner has available for advertising, so the ads keep getting smaller and smaller. A tiny ad is a great sign that the homeowner is getting a little desperate and is beginning to realize that the property may not be worth the original asking price. If a homeowner places a 4-inch ad, he isn't ready to bargain yet.

Keep tabs on the classified For Sale By Owner (FSBO) ads on a weekly basis and take note of any ads that seem to be shrinking. Shrinking ads are the most attractive. Head to Chapter 9 for more information about FSBO properties.

The Seller Is Highly Motivated to Be Freed from the Burden of Ownership

Part of your success as a flipper hinges on your willingness to be an ambulance chaser — to capitalize on the misfortune of others. You find your best deals when homeowners are facing foreclosure, when they're getting divorced, or when a family member dies and the property ends up in probate or goes to relatives who already have a place to live. Here are some helpful tips on finding and handling these types of deals:

- ✔ Act professionally and with integrity. A homeowner's misfortune may lead to a great deal, but what they're experiencing is real pain.

- ✔ When a property is passed down to relatives, two or more relatives may own the property together and be unable to agree on what to do with the property. In these situations, you may have more luck by negotiating separately with each owner. Chapter 9 has more information on finding probate properties.

✔ Whenever you're dealing with a divorce or probate attorney, send a letter of introduction and follow up with a face-to-face meeting explaining who you are and what you do. The relationship can cultivate future leads.

✔ Stay on top of the foreclosure notices in your target area. Remain vigilant of any signs of divorce: comments from the seller or seller's agent, only men's or only women's clothes in the closet, or any news flowing through the neighborhood grapevine. Chapter 12 delivers the full scoop on foreclosures.

The House Is Ugly Outside

To a flipper, the ugliest home on the block is the bombshell on the boardwalk. The homeowner wants to sell the property but the exterior looks so bad that it's driving away paying customers. As an investor, ugly homes should have the opposite effect on you — they should grab your attention and pull you inside. See Chapter 10 for details on signs of a potential quick flip.

The House Is Ugly Inside

The landscaping and outer shell of the house may be attractive enough to draw visitors, but if the interior is ugly, it can push prospective buyers right back out the door.

Some houses just don't show well for any of several reasons. Sometimes the owners appear to be color-blind, picking color schemes that make normal people gag. In other cases, the homeowners simply put no effort into staging the house. Whatever the reason, if the structure is sound and the floor plan works, the filth, clutter, and foul smells may be to your advantage. You can acquire the property at a discount, do some heavy-duty cleaning, properly stage the home, and make a good profit with a very small investment. (Chapter 14 shows you how to give a house a quick pick-me-up, and Chapter 20 demonstrates techniques for properly staging a home to get top dollar.)

The Décor Is Outdated

A house can be clean and properly maintained, but if the décor has fallen out of style with time, it can repel buyers as quickly as a herd of roaches.

Of course, if you're dealing in historical homes, vintage décor can be a big plus, but if the décor is old without the accompanying elegance, you can quickly redecorate and place the property right back on the market. Such houses are a perfect opportunity for a quick flip, as described in Chapter 14.

The House Exhibits Some Unique Character

Some homes have panache. Something about them just has a universal appeal. Maybe the floor plan makes the human soul feel expansive. Perhaps the landscaping creates a sense that you've returned to the Garden of Eden. Or perhaps the décor pulls everything together and creates a healthy balance. Whatever it is, you know it when you see it. Don't dismiss the value of character when looking at houses. Character sells. For more information about spotting character when touring homes, see Chapter 10.

The House Has Undeveloped Living Space

Look for properties with unused or underutilized attic space or an enclosed porch, and modify that space to make it livable. An extra bedroom or bath typically raises the value of the home the most, but home offices are also growing in popularity. If the house has an attic that's too small to use for living space and the house needs a new roof anyway, calculate the costs and benefits of adding a dormer. Chapter 18 has details on reconfiguring spaces.

The Property Backs Up to Nothing

Few homeowners like to have neighbors in their backyards. They prefer having their yards back up to a wooded area, a park, or even a cemetery. If you find a property that has all the essential qualities of a good flip, *and* the property backs up to nothing, you've struck gold. Just make sure that all the numbers work and that the zoning board doesn't have plans in the works to rezone the property for commercial or industrial use before you make your offer.

Chapter 23

Ten Renovation Cost-Cutting Strategies

In This Chapter

▶ Finding advice and planning tools on the cheap

▶ Hiring skilled and unskilled laborers for less

▶ Bargain hunting for building materials and tools

▶ Timing your projects wisely

*T*he old saying that "A penny saved is a penny earned" isn't quite accurate. It doesn't account for taxes. When you figure in taxes, a penny saved is about 1.3 cents earned, because to earn a penny after income tax, you really have to earn about a penny an a third, and when it comes to flipping houses, those penny and a thirds quickly add up.

When renovating a property, many new flippers get a little carried away. They hire top-of-the-scale contractors and insist on the highest-quality building materials from the nearest suppliers. This chapter reveals ten secrets that can slash your cash outlays and boost your bottom line. For details on drawing up a tentative budget and other planning tips for your flip, check out Chapter 13.

Getting Free Advice and Planning Tools

You don't have to hire a professional interior designer to draw up plans for remodeling a kitchen or a bath. Most home improvement stores have their own designers on staff to assist you. If you purchase the materials from the store, the store frequently throws in the design consultation for free. And who can say no to free?

You can often find additional planning tools and calculators online. Larger home improvement stores and manufacturers typically feature cost estimators, material lists, and installation instructions and tips on their Web sites. For some excellent online resources for planning your projects, check out Lowe's at www.lowes.com, Home Depot at www.homedepot.com, and Bob Vila Design Tools at www.bobvila.com/DesignTools/.

Play dumb. Ask a lot of questions. Your contractors can be excellent educators, so pick their brains for suggestions. See Chapter 4 for full details on hiring contractors.

Hiring Moonlighters

Larger construction companies often have larger overhead costs, so they have to charge more for their work. A roofing company, for example, needs to purchase and maintain its trucks, pay rent on office space, and cover payroll expenses and insurance for its workers. To earn an extra buck on the side, the employees of many of these companies *moonlight,* which means that they provide the same high-quality service on the side for a fraction of the cost.

You can often locate prospective moonlighters by visiting worksites in your neighborhood. Ask to see the boss, and if he's not around, pitch your proposal to the workers. If the boss is around, you can ask him for an estimate, so you don't blow your cover.

Hiring moonlighters is a great idea, but first, make sure they have health insurance with accident coverage. If your workers don't have proper insurance and one of them gets hurt working on your house, your savings could quickly grow into losses and complications! See Chapter 4 for details on how to check for proof of insurance and how to obtain insurance for workers who don't have their own coverage. In addition, realize that moonlighters typically moonlight in the evenings and on weekends; if you're a weekend warrior, however, this fact shouldn't pose a problem.

Hiring Students over the Summer

When school's out, college and high-school students flock to area businesses to secure summer employment, and they're often turned away simply because so many people are looking for jobs. That's where you come in. Post an ad in the local newspaper and hang a notice at area groceries stores for summer laborers. Students are eager and well-qualified to perform the following reno-vation chores:

- Mowing, weeding, trimming bushes and trees, planting flowers
- Patching and sealing driveways and walks
- De-cluttering garages, basements, and attics
- Vacuuming, window washing, and other cleaning
- Demolishing old storage sheds
- Tearing out old carpeting
- Patching and painting inside and out
- Refinishing decks

Safety is key! You can help protect your laborers' heads, eyes, and hands by requiring your helpers to use safety glasses and to follow proper precautions. Providing adult supervision at all times is important. Also, verify that your summer warriors have the proper health insurance and accident coverage. (See Chapter 4 for details about insuring your workers.) Many flippers pay their laborers cash without providing for insurance. I suggest that you put them on an official payroll, complete with W2 forms. Consult your CPA on how you should pay and consult your insurance agent for advice on coverage.

Buying Overstocked or Discontinued Building Materials

When you wander the aisles at your local hardware or building-supply store, find what you want and then ask about any overstocked or discontinued materials that are similar in appearance. Talk to the manager, who most likely wants to clear the old, overstocked items from inventory to make room for the new merchandise that's in greater demand. You can often purchase over-stocked or discontinued merchandise for a fraction of the cost.

You don't have to buy all your materials at one store. Shop and compare prices. Browse through the Sunday sales inserts in your local newspaper for bargains and discounts. If you really want to flip on the cheap, search the Internet for _recycled building materials._ Large building-supply stores donate damaged goods to nonprofit organizations, including Habitat for Humanity, who are set up to accept and to resell donated surplus materials. You can find anything and everything a rehabber needs at huge discounts.

Buying Builder's-Grade Materials

When shopping for building materials, ask the salesperson to direct you to the builder's-grade materials — the more affordable options, such as prefab cabinets and low-grade carpeting. If installed and maintained properly, these materials are perfectly suitable for most homeowners. If you're flipping on the ritzy side of town, however, you may need to buy the good stuff.

Gauge your selection of materials by the visibility and importance of the rooms. Consider using higher-quality materials for the kitchen, main bathroom, and master bedroom and a lesser quality for the other bedrooms and the second or third bathroom.

Trimming Costs with Remnants

Carpeting stores, countertop manufacturers, and other suppliers often have *remnants* in the back that may be sufficient for completing small jobs. Picky customers often return items that have tiny scratches or dents as well as materials that they cut a little too short. These gently used materials may be just what you need, and you can pick them up for pennies on a dollar. Following are some additional leads on where you can find materials at a bargain:

- **Check your local convention center.** Often, various large-scale events (such as car shows and national conferences) require convention centers to roll out the red carpet — the highest quality carpet on the market. (Don't worry — red isn't the only color they use.) The convention center uses it for a couple weeks and then sells it. You can pick up $50-a-yard carpeting for only a few bucks.

- **Visit the manufacturer and purchase in bulk.** Many investors make the trip to their local carpet mill and purchase large quantities at discount prices.

- **Consider joining an investor group.** You can hook up with other investors to buy in bulk and find additional leads to low-priced local suppliers and contractors, but be careful. Real estate con-artists set up many investor and landlord groups.

- **Ask your contractor whether he has any gently used building materials from tear-outs on other projects.** Finicky homeowners often remodel perfectly good kitchens and dump their old cabinets, countertops, and more. You may be surprised at the high quality of these materials.

Buying Time-Saving Power Tools

When you hire a contractor, you indirectly pay for the tools that make the job much easier. When you rent a tool, you have to return it. When you buy your own tools, however, you have them for as long as they work, and you can spread the cost over several flips.

If you're a do-it-yourselfer, buy the tools that make it easier for you to do a professional job. In addition to the standard hammer, pliers, wrenches, screwdrivers, tape measure, paint scraper, and paintbrush, almost every house flipper can simplify do-it-yourself jobs with the following power tools:

- **Heat gun** for stripping wallpaper and paint
- **Power washer** to clean everything from decks to siding
- **Power roller** for painting inside walls and ceilings
- **Cordless drill** with a well-stocked drill-bit case
- **Screw gun** with Phillips and flat-head screw bits
- **Circular saw** for decks and other woodworking projects
- **Reciprocating saw** for cutting anything you can't cut with a circular saw
- **Nail gun** for quick and easy single-handed nail driving
- **Vibrating sander,** or belt sander, for sanding out scratches and gouges in wood surfaces
- **Power spatula** for actually flipping the house

Charging Purchases on a Rewards-Back Credit Card

Credit card companies offer some pretty sweet deals to reward customers for using their cards, and as long as you pay the balance in full when you receive the bill, you're not socked with any high-interest charges. If your building supplier offers its own credit card, you may get a discount on all purchases. If not, shop around for other cards. Companies offer everything from cash-back deals to frequent-flyer miles, free merchandise, free groceries, 0 percent interest for a specific period of time, and other attractive benefits. Take full advantage of these perks.

Building-supply companies may offer you 10 percent off your first purchase when you open a new account. Be sure to buy a whole bunch of stuff on the day you register for the card (with the intention of paying it off as soon as the bill comes, of course, to avoid the often huge finance charges).

Scheduling Work Off-Season

Trying to find a contractor to install a central air-conditioning unit on the hottest day of the summer for a reasonable price isn't going to happen. When a contractor's work is plentiful, you pay top dollar for materials and labor.

Consider scheduling work off-season, during the dead of winter for most projects. During the off-season, larger companies have to keep their employees busy in order to pay them and finance their benefits. Use this as a bargaining chip when negotiating the cost of repairs and renovations. However, don't delay a project that needs to be done just to save a few bucks — *holding costs* (the cost of maintaining a flip) can outstrip any savings.

You reap two additional benefits by scheduling work off-season. The contractor is more likely to complete the job on schedule and generally becomes more responsive when you need her services in season.

Pooling Your Projects

Most skilled laborers charge a minimum for just showing up. You pay for their time and travel expenses no matter how small the job. To save money, pool your projects. You can draw up a list of projects for the plumber, a list for the carpenter, and another list for the electrician. Have them complete all the projects in one trip.

Better yet, if you have several houses going at one time, ask the contractor whether she'll consider giving you a discount if you guarantee that she can work on all your properties. Talk with your neighbors. If they're having the same work done on their homes, you may be able to negotiate a better price for multiple jobs.

Rent a large dumpster for all the tear-out and construction debris, so all your contractors have one place to dump rubbish from your flip. By supplying the dumpster, you can tell your contractors to remove the cost of waste removal from their estimates.

Chapter 24

Ten Common House Flipping Blunders

Many eager, ill-informed investors become overenthusiastic about the big picture and lose sight of the critical details that can make or break a deal. They pay too much for a property, underestimate the cost of repairs and renovations, fail to inspect a property or research the title, or sign contracts that they don't fully understand. In this chapter, I present ten common house flipping blunders to help you avoid costly mistakes and maximize your profits from the very start.

Falling for a Scam

Money attracts entrepreneurs, but it also attracts thieves. When you flip a house, you stand to earn tens of thousands of dollars on a single transaction, but being successful requires determination, diligence, and hard work. Don't let anyone convince you otherwise. Don't be a sucker. Be on guard for the following threats:

✔ Get-rich-quick schemes, cash-back-at-closing schemes, no-money-down deals, and anything else that sounds too good to be true

✔ Partnerships, especially those that require you to take on all the risk, supply most of the money, or do most of the work

✔ Anyone who offers to take care of everything for you

See Chapter 1 for more warnings about house flipping scams and illegal and unethical practices.

Speculating on the Housing Market

Like the stock market, the housing market has its ups and downs. In a hot market, investors often become infected with irrational exuberance — the belief that current appreciation rates are an accurate representation of future rates. They overpay for properties, expecting them to appreciate, and when the market flattens or takes a dive, they're stuck with a property that they need to sell at a price that no buyer is willing to pay. Don't bank on double-digit increases in housing values, and be prepared with plan B, as I explain in Chapter 25.

Waffling on an Obviously Good Deal

Some investors experience paralysis by analysis. They overanalyze a great deal and can actually talk themselves out of it, or they waffle until another investor shows interest, and then it's often too late.

When you see a good deal, act quickly. You don't necessarily need to buy the property right away, but by making an offer on the property, you can tie it up for several days, so you can research the title and inspect the property (I cover these tasks later in this chapter).

Backing Yourself into a Contractual Corner

Very rarely do people hand you contracts to sign that protect your rights or interests. They hand you contracts that protect their rights and interests. Before you sign a contract or purchase agreement, read it carefully and make sure that it has a weasel clause — a legal back door through which you can make a graceful exit. See Chapter 11 for a complete discussion of conditional (weasel) clauses.

Failing to Inspect the Property Before Closing on It

Don't rely on the seller claims and disclosures. The real estate community has a saying: "Buyers are liars, and sellers are worse, and sellers by owner eat their young." Have the house inspected. A city inspection is best because it provides you with an inspection team consisting of a professional plumber, an electrician, a heating and air conditioning specialist, and a builder (for structural features). In some areas, however, city inspections are unavailable or are performed only on new construction.

If you're buying a house at a foreclosure sale, obtaining a thorough home inspection before handing over the cash may not be an option, but you should inspect the home yourself as thoroughly as possible. Drive by the house, inspect the outside, and do what you can to get inside to take a look around. The less you know about a property, the higher you should set your margin to cover unexpected costs. Check out Chapter 11 for additional information about house inspections.

Assuming the Title Is Clear

Anyone can sell a property. Even people who don't own a property can sell it. Some con artists wait until the owner takes an extended vacation. They move into the house, pose as the owner, print out a fake title, and sell the house. Sometimes, they sell the house to several buyers!

A homeowner may try to sell you a house without telling you that the property has multiple liens against it. Unless you research the title and have the title company perform a title search (see Chapter 4 for details on hiring a title company), you can't be sure that the title is clear or even valid or that the person selling the house really owns it. And if you're not 100 percent certain, don't buy the property.

Underestimating the Cost of Repairs and Renovations

When a contractor tells a homeowner that a complete kitchen remodel costs about $30,000, the homeowner acts like one of those old geezers who grew up during the Great Depression, when you could buy a candy bar for a nickel. Beginning investors often experience that same sense of sticker shock when they hire contractors to perform repairs and renovations. Just make sure that you have your sticker shock before you buy a property, not after you own it — when it's too late to do anything about it. For necessary repairs and renovations, you should have an accurate estimate of all costs before you buy a property. You can jot down notes while you're inspecting a property (see Chapter 10); you can then draw up a tentative budget for your renovations (see Chapter 13).

Doing Shoddy Work to Save Money

Sellers have all sorts of tactics to cover defects in a home. They may carpet over a floor that has extensive water or termite damage, pump out a septic tank that's gone bad so the toilets keep flushing for a couple more months, or install wood paneling in the basement to hide defects in the foundation.

As an investor who wants to remain in business, you should treat these tactics as taboo. Don't sell your soul for a few thousand dollars.

Over-Improving a Property

Transforming a bungalow into the Taj Mahal may be a noble vision, but it ultimately lands you in the poorhouse. Know the housing market in your area and routinely visit open houses to remain abreast of current trends and market demands (see Chapter 13 for details). Gauge repairs and renovations to meet or slightly exceed what's currently selling in your area. Your renovated home should be more appealing than comparable homes in the area, but not *that* much more appealing.

Forgetting to Pay the Taxes

In the flurry of flipping, taxes are easy to overlook, especially property taxes. Forgetting to pay your taxes, however, can further complicate your flipping operation, and back taxes and penalties can take a big chunk out of your future profits.

Set aside a certain percentage of your profit from each flip in a separate account, and pay your taxes out of that account. This separate account reduces the temptation to spend the taxes you owe. If you fall behind on taxes, catching up can be tough. Check out Chapter 7 for additional information about taxes and tips on trimming your tax bill.

Chapter 25

Ten Strategies for Surviving a Slow Market

*L*ike the stock market, housing prices rise and fall in response to events — the growing popularity of a geographical area, factories moving in or out, inflation, layoffs, and so on. When flipping properties, you need to keep track of movements in the housing market and adjust your strategy to ride the waves. In this chapter, I reveal ten ways to adjust your strategy in a declining market. Check out Chapter 8 for details on taking the pulse of the real estate market in a particular neighborhood.

Buying Properties for Less

You make your profit when you buy a property and realize your profit when you sell. In other words, by purchasing the property at a price that ensures your future profit, you make money, but you don't really see that money until you sell and cash out. You can make the same profit in a slow market as you can in a hot market as long as you can acquire properties for less. Don't let a slow market get you down. When sales slump, buying opportunities soar. See Chapter 5 for tips on ballparking your potential profit.

Homing In on HUD/VA Homes

Housing and Urban Development (HUD) and the U.S. Department of Veterans Affairs (VA) home sales rise when the economy slows, and more initial offers fall through because the buyer's loan application is rejected. Hook up with an agent who specializes in selling HUD homes and check the listings daily. Never assume that just because a HUD or VA home is listed as sold that the deal is final. Many of these deals vaporize when the buyer can't come up with the financing. See Chapter 9 for details on shopping for HUD and VA homes.

Focusing on Foreclosures

As the economy slows, foreclosure rates gradually increase, but just as the economy begins to recover, foreclosure rates spike. The peak in foreclosure rates typically lags behind the slump in the economy by about a year, because foreclosures take between 7 and 12 months to process. When you're in a slow economy, big opportunities lie ahead. Head to Chapter 12 for the full scoop on buying properties in foreclosure.

Bedding Down in the House

As a real estate investor who's just starting out, you need to remain open to shifting your strategy to compensate for changes in the market. (Chapter 3 has information on different flipping strategies.) Perhaps you decided early on that you don't want to live in the house you're flipping, but if the market slows down, conditions may limit your choices.

One of the best ways to cut back on expenses in a slow market is to reside in the house you're flipping. Because the house provides you with a place to live, you reduce the personal expense of putting a roof over your head.

If you own two houses — a primary residence and an investment property — put both houses up for sale when you're ready to put your investment property back on the market. If your primary residence sells first, move to the investment property. Listing both houses gives you twice the opportunity to escape in a slow or difficult market.

Adding Improvements Strategically

Throughout this book, I warn you against over-improving a property, but in a slow market, you need to be particularly careful to make the house you're selling a step above comparable properties in the area. You want your house to be an A+ property, so it can out compete properties in the A, B, and C range. You don't want to go broke when flipping a house, but you may need to go a step or two beyond the basic renovations you make during a hot or steady market. So, put a little extra thought into which improvements will get you more bang for your buck. See Chapter 13 for details about planning and prioritizing your renovations. Chapter 10 also offers some tips about gauging renovations for your market.

Pricing Your Property Right

In a declining market, you can't afford the luxury of setting too high a price. If your house lingers on the market, it could be worth less with each passing day. Check the sales prices of homes that have recently sold in the area and set your price at or slightly below current prices to make your house even more attractive.

Every day your house sits on the market costs you an average of $100. By lowering your asking price by a couple thousand dollars, you may be able to save money in the long run. See Chapter 19 for more information on setting an attractive asking price.

Offering Attractive Financing

When the market's soft, the economy is usually in a slump, and people generally have less money to spend on housing. By teaming up with a loan officer, you can often help first-time home buyers secure the financing they need to make the house affordable.

Consider offering a 2-1 buydown arrangement as an incentive. A 2-1 buydown provides the buyers with a lower house payment early on that gradually rises over the first few years they own the house. For example, the buyer may pay 5 percent interest the first year, 6 percent the second year, and then 7 percent in subsequent years, assuming they can qualify for that 7 percent rate. Consult your agent or loan officer for details. See Chapter 19 for more about offering attractive financing.

Motivating Buyers' Agents

In a slow market, buyers are scarce, so when you sell, you're competing with other sellers for a limited number of buyers. You may need to sacrifice a small portion of your profit in a slowing market to move a house quickly and establish positive relationships with buyers' agents — after all, they're the people who are going to sell your house.

Don't advertise a higher sales commission on the Multiple Listing Service (MLS) or your other marketing materials, because you may turn off prospective buyers who equate their agents' enthusiasm with the fat bonus you're offering. Instead, work through your agent to communicate this boost in commission to the buyers' agents.

Leasing Your Renovated Property

You've lowered your asking price to the bargain-basement level, and you still can't sell the house. If you lower the price any more, you stand to lose your shirt. In some cases (for example, if you buy into an area where the market slumps and shows no sign of recovery), you may have no choice but to cut your losses, but that's rarely the best solution.

By leasing the property, you can often ride out a slow market for a year or two and then put the house up for sale. Real estate prices generally rise, and if you can afford to hold the property, rental income may cover your holding costs until the market recovers and you can sell the house for the price you want. For more about renting out property, check out *Property Management For Dummies* by Robert S. Griswold (Wiley).

Riding Out the Market with Your Agent

In slow markets, work more closely with your agent. A good agent keeps tabs on the market. She reads up on trends. She knows what's going on in the neighborhood. And when the market shifts, she has contingency plans already in place. (I show you how to find the best agent for your needs in Chapter 4.)

Being aware of an impending downward shift in the market enables you to adjust your strategy accordingly and beef up your marketing efforts well in advance. In a slow market, you can begin to lower your expectations and reduce your asking price before the competition has time to react. A simple adjustment is often all it takes to separate the successful flipper from the flopper.

Index

BUSINESS, CAREERS & PERSONAL FINANCE

0-7645-5307-0

0-7645-5331-3 *†

Also available:
- Accounting For Dummies †
  0-7645-5314-3
- Business Plans Kit For Dummies †
  0-7645-5365-8
- Cover Letters For Dummies
  0-7645-5224-4
- Frugal Living For Dummies
  0-7645-5403-4
- Leadership For Dummies
  0-7645-5176-0
- Managing For Dummies
  0-7645-1771-6

- Marketing For Dummies
  0-7645-5600-2
- Personal Finance For Dummies *
  0-7645-2590-5
- Project Management For Dummies
  0-7645-5283-X
- Resumes For Dummies †
  0-7645-5471-9
- Selling For Dummies
  0-7645-5363-1
- Small Business Kit For Dummies *†
  0-7645-5093-4

HOME & BUSINESS COMPUTER BASICS

0-7645-4074-2

0-7645-3758-X

Also available:
- ACT! 6 For Dummies
  0-7645-2645-6
- iLife '04 All-in-One Desk Reference
  For Dummies
  0-7645-7347-0
- iPAQ For Dummies
  0-7645-6769-1
- Mac OS X Panther Timesaving
  Techniques For Dummies
  0-7645-5812-9
- Macs For Dummies
  0-7645-5656-8

- Microsoft Money 2004 For Dummies
  0-7645-4195-1
- Office 2003 All-in-One Desk Reference
  For Dummies
  0-7645-3883-7
- Outlook 2003 For Dummies
  0-7645-3759-8
- PCs For Dummies
  0-7645-4074-2
- TiVo For Dummies
  0-7645-6923-6
- Upgrading and Fixing PCs For Dummies
  0-7645-1665-5
- Windows XP Timesaving Techniques
  For Dummies
  0-7645-3748-2

FOOD, HOME, GARDEN, HOBBIES, MUSIC & PETS

0-7645-5295-3

0-7645-5232-5

Also available:
- Bass Guitar For Dummies
  0-7645-2487-9
- Diabetes Cookbook For Dummies
  0-7645-5230-9
- Gardening For Dummies *
  0-7645-5130-2
- Guitar For Dummies
  0-7645-5106-X
- Holiday Decorating For Dummies
  0-7645-2570-0
- Home Improvement All-in-One
  For Dummies
  0-7645-5680-0

- Knitting For Dummies
  0-7645-5395-X
- Piano For Dummies
  0-7645-5105-1
- Puppies For Dummies
  0-7645-5255-4
- Scrapbooking For Dummies
  0-7645-7208-3
- Senior Dogs For Dummies
  0-7645-5818-8
- Singing For Dummies
  0-7645-2475-5
- 30-Minute Meals For Dummies
  0-7645-2589-1

INTERNET & DIGITAL MEDIA

0-7645-1664-7

0-7645-6924-4

Also available:
- 2005 Online Shopping Directory
  For Dummies
  0-7645-7495-7
- CD & DVD Recording For Dummies
  0-7645-5956-7
- eBay For Dummies
  0-7645-5654-1
- Fighting Spam For Dummies
  0-7645-5965-6
- Genealogy Online For Dummies
  0-7645-5964-8
- Google For Dummies
  0-7645-4420-9

- Home Recording For Musicians
  For Dummies
  0-7645-1634-5
- The Internet For Dummies
  0-7645-4173-0
- iPod & iTunes For Dummies
  0-7645-7772-7
- Preventing Identity Theft For Dummies
  0-7645-7336-5
- Pro Tools All-in-One Desk Reference
  For Dummies
  0-7645-5714-9
- Roxio Easy Media Creator For Dummies
  0-7645-7131-1

* Separate Canadian edition also available
† Separate U.K. edition also available

Available wherever books are sold. For more information or to order direct: U.S. customers visit www.dummies.com or call 1-877-762-2974.
U.K. customers visit www.wileyeurope.com or call 0800 243407. Canadian customers visit www.wiley.ca or call 1-800-567-4797.

SPORTS, FITNESS, PARENTING, RELIGION & SPIRITUALITY

0-7645-5146-9

0-7645-5418-2

Also available:
- Adoption For Dummies
  0-7645-5488-3
- Basketball For Dummies
  0-7645-5248-1
- The Bible For Dummies
  0-7645-5296-1
- Buddhism For Dummies
  0-7645-5359-3
- Catholicism For Dummies
  0-7645-5391-7
- Hockey For Dummies
  0-7645-5228-7
- Judaism For Dummies
  0-7645-5299-6
- Martial Arts For Dummies
  0-7645-5358-5
- Pilates For Dummies
  0-7645-5397-6
- Religion For Dummies
  0-7645-5264-3
- Teaching Kids to Read For Dummies
  0-7645-4043-2
- Weight Training For Dummies
  0-7645-5168-X
- Yoga For Dummies
  0-7645-5117-5

TRAVEL

0-7645-5438-7

0-7645-5453-0

Also available:
- Alaska For Dummies
  0-7645-1761-9
- Arizona For Dummies
  0-7645-6938-4
- Cancún and the Yucatán For Dummies
  0-7645-2437-2
- Cruise Vacations For Dummies
  0-7645-6941-4
- Europe For Dummies
  0-7645-5456-5
- Ireland For Dummies
  0-7645-5455-7
- Las Vegas For Dummies
  0-7645-5448-4
- London For Dummies
  0-7645-4277-X
- New York City For Dummies
  0-7645-6945-7
- Paris For Dummies
  0-7645-5494-8
- RV Vacations For Dummies
  0-7645-5443-3
- Walt Disney World & Orlando For Dummies
  0-7645-6943-0

GRAPHICS, DESIGN & WEB DEVELOPMENT

0-7645-4345-8

0-7645-5589-8

Also available:
- Adobe Acrobat 6 PDF For Dummies
  0-7645-3760-1
- Building a Web Site For Dummies
  0-7645-7144-3
- Dreamweaver MX 2004 For Dummies
  0-7645-4342-3
- FrontPage 2003 For Dummies
  0-7645-3882-9
- HTML 4 For Dummies
  0-7645-1995-6
- Illustrator CS For Dummies
  0-7645-4084-X
- Macromedia Flash MX 2004 For Dummies
  0-7645-4358-X
- Photoshop 7 All-in-One Desk
  Reference For Dummies
  0-7645-1667-1
- Photoshop CS Timesaving Techniques
  For Dummies
  0-7645-6782-9
- PHP 5 For Dummies
  0-7645-4166-8
- PowerPoint 2003 For Dummies
  0-7645-3908-6
- QuarkXPress 6 For Dummies
  0-7645-2593-X

NETWORKING, SECURITY, PROGRAMMING & DATABASES

0-7645-6852-3

0-7645-5784-X

Also available:
- A+ Certification For Dummies
  0-7645-4187-0
- Access 2003 All-in-One Desk
  Reference For Dummies
  0-7645-3988-4
- Beginning Programming For Dummies
  0-7645-4997-9
- C For Dummies
  0-7645-7068-4
- Firewalls For Dummies
  0-7645-4048-3
- Home Networking For Dummies
  0-7645-42796
- Network Security For Dummies
  0-7645-1679-5
- Networking For Dummies
  0-7645-1677-9
- TCP/IP For Dummies
  0-7645-1760-0
- VBA For Dummies
  0-7645-3989-2
- Wireless All-in-One Desk Reference
  For Dummies
  0-7645-7496-5
- Wireless Home Networking For Dummies
  0-7645-3910-8